THE
ABU DHABI
BAR MITZVAH

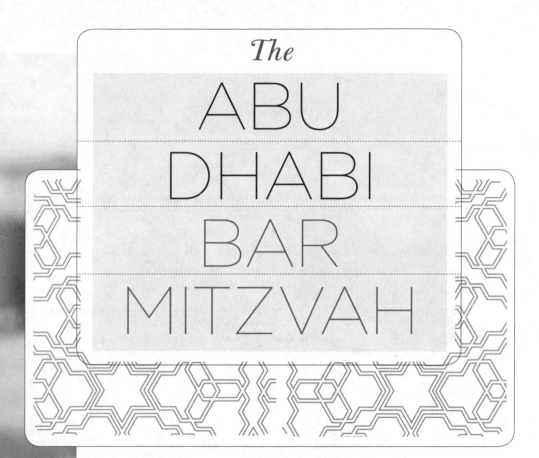

The

ABU DHABI BAR MITZVAH

FEAR AND LOVE IN THE MODERN MIDDLE EAST

ADAM VALEN LEVINSON

W. W. NORTON & COMPANY

Independent Publishers Since 1923

NEW YORK LONDON

Excerpted lyrics to "On the Road" © 2009 by Tom Hambridge
and Richard Fleming. Reprinted by permission of Tom Hambridge Tunes
and Richard Fleming Music.

For information about permission to reproduce selections from this book,
write to Permissions, W. W. Norton & Company, Inc.,
500 Fifth Avenue, New York, NY 10110

For information about special discounts for bulk purchases, please contact
W. W. Norton Special Sales at specialsales@wwnorton.com or 800-233-4830

Manufacturing by LSC Communications, Harrisonburg
Book design by Barbara Bachman
Production manager: Julia Druskin

Library of Congress Cataloging-in-Publication Data

Names: Levinson, Adam Valen, author.
Title: The Abu Dhabi bar mitzvah : fear and love in the modern
Middle East / Adam Valen Levinson.
Description: First edition. | New York : W. W. Norton & Company, 2018. |
Includes bibliographical references.
Identifiers: LCCN 2017026967 | ISBN 9780393608366 (hardcover)
Subjects: LCSH: Levinson, Adam Valen—Travel—Middle East. |
Middle East—Description and travel.
Classification: LCC DS49.7.L48 2018 | DDC 956.05/4—dc23
LC record available at https://lccn.loc.gov/2017026967

W. W. Norton & Company, Inc.
500 Fifth Avenue, New York, N.Y. 10110
www.wwnorton.com

W. W. Norton & Company Ltd.
15 Carlisle Street, London W1D 3BS

1 2 3 4 5 6 7 8 9 0

To Life

A hundred reasons clamour for your going. You go to touch on human identities, to people an empty map. You have a notion that this is the world's heart. . . . You go because you are still young and crave excitement . . . you go because you are old and need to understand something before it's too late. You go to see what will happen.

—COLIN THUBRON,
SHADOW OF THE SILK ROAD

. . . .

So have they not traveled through the earth and have hearts by which to reason and ears by which to hear? For indeed, it is not eyes that are blinded, but blinded are the hearts which are within the breasts.

—THE HOLY QURAN, 22:46

. . . .

What the fuck are you doing in Afghanistan?

—A FRIEND

CONTENTS

———

PART THREE | ANOTHER PEOPLE BEGIN

AUTHOR'S NOTE

———

Everything in between " " is verbatim. Transcriptions are taken almost exclusively from audio recordings, and occasionally from handwritten or hand-tapped notes in the moment. A very few names have been changed.

THE
ABU DHABI
BAR MITZVAH

PREAMBLE

—

I KEEP TELLING MYSELF it was worth it.

Twenty-three countries, depending on who did the counting. Most of my first-job earnings pilfered to see them—except for what I locked in an IRA because I thought I was an adult. Just before I left America, I left my heart in San Francisco and then Skyped with it. For 534 days of summer, I spent the warm weeks of the Arab Spring in and out of my apartment in Abu Dhabi.

I keep telling myself I've grown, that I've answered the questions I needed answered, and that I've learned to ask better questions. I keep telling myself to stop telling myself things.

Fresh out of college, I fled the pressures of decision making and friend-to-friend comparisons, and the bleak job market under the cover of idealism: I would explore. I would learn about the world *Nine Eleven* made us fear, and I would justify my roving lusts with stories of why we needn't fear it.

I wouldn't purely explore, though. I wouldn't follow my childhood friend Danny to Syria, as we'd decided before federal grants told us both no, just to hone our Arabic and steep in the Middle East. I'd work in the Emirates, that country where Dubai was, and oil-rich Abu Dhabi. When I made landfall in a new place (its name familiar from wartime datelines), the pictures in my head matched both fully and not at all. Simple truths came wrapped in complexities I didn't understand, and every time I thought I had learned something solid, it went soft in my sweaty palms. Impressions and new truths jabbed at each other like skittish kids on a playground, and tumbled out as jokey stories in hotel bars.

"You'll end up dead!" my friends said as I window-shopped flights to Beirut or Damascus or Kabul, laughing or shouting or shaking their heads. But I kept not ending up there. It seemed something was really wrong with our predictions.

"Go here! Don't go here!" I'd hear. And I'd listen until I really didn't want to—until the curiosity outweighed the risk, until I felt I could climb one rung higher on the ladder of forbidden nations.

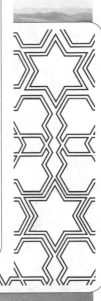
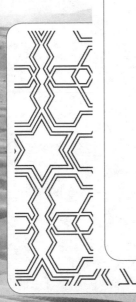

PART ONE

البار ميتزفه ابو ظبي

The

ABU DHABI
BAR MITZVAH

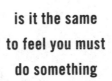

is it the same
to feel you must
do something

as to feel

you cannot
do anything
else?

—CALVIN LAX COLE,
some of its parts

WHAT IS ABOVE, MY DOG?

WE WERE MOSTLY AMERICANS on the flight out of Chicago, crossing Greenland and Sweden, passing over Lithuania and Turkey, then Iran. No one had taken advantage of Etihad Airlines' falcon policy, by which a bird of prey is permitted at merely three times the cost of an extra checked bag. Two more are welcome if you buy them a seat. With no such distractions, I watched the Chinese game show *Just Go*, and felt the world grow small: it was just as terrible as American TV, and just as glorious.

"Juice?" said the pretty attendant in a pretty hat, balancing three glasses on a tray, two of them shades of orange.

"What's the orange one?" I asked.

"It's orange," she said.

Clearly, I didn't belong. *Obviously*, one of the oranges was orange—or had even that been too hasty an assumption? I took the glass of the mystery orange, and a tentative nip. It was fitting, in a way: the root of the Arabic for *carrot*, *jazar*, is shared by the words for *island* and *peninsula*, as in "the Arabian Peninsula," or "the island of Abu Dhabi." Of course, it was total coincidence in that place where linguistic bloodlines run tangled back into ancient history, but as we headed toward *Jazirat al-'Arab*, I couldn't help but imagine our destination like a great carrot on the map.

I had never been much for going with the flow, but a certain flow had brought me here. I left high school dreaming of Russian study, and Hebrew, and Modern Greek—languages I connected to through ancestors once or twice removed, and thought sounded sexy. But in the last four years, I had hardly questioned why I spent my first week of college auditing two Arabic classes in the hope of winning a spot. Consciously, in my only moment of choice, I just thought it would be fun.

My cousins in Jerusalem thought I was mental. When I talked to Itai in his camp in the Negev at officer's school in the Israeli army, where he trained boys younger than we were to train boys younger than they were, I could hear him shaking his head over the wire. "I just don't get it. Why don't you learn Hebrew?"

"Because you speak English," I said.

In a windowless belowground classroom uptown, my elementary Arabic class met four times per week for seventy-five minutes.

Seven miles from the deadliest attack ever on American soil, the study of this language—the official tongue of the religion claimed by these attackers—carried a special emotional charge. There were native speakers of Arabic dialects unversed in the literary language, political scientists, Hebrew-speaking Jews, and total neophytes like me, and no one denied the impression that this was a language that represented a certain opposition—that it was on the other side of something. Many of us were drawn in because we were nosy, and we looked for bridges across the murky gap.

Downtown five years earlier, 9/11 had forced *Arab* and *Muslim* and *Middle Eastern* on to the airwaves—it was wartime with rhetoric to match, and the battle lines of our new enemies were painted with huge, clumsy brushstrokes. The attack had made us all forcefully self-conscious. We perceived *them*, assumed their perceptions of us, and then canceled all the flights to Beirut. But by learning the primary language of this region, some of us thought, we might be able to figure out what *them* were really thinking. Learning to spell *salaam alaykum* seemed like a good place to start.

I was hooked long before I felt the language let fall the first of its veils, revealing morphology as finely calibrated as the engine of a race car: from the words *to know* (*'alama*) we can divine, through patterns; *to teach* (to make know—*'allama*); *to learn* (to make oneself know—*ta'alama*); *to inquire* (to seek to know—*ista'alama*); *scholar* (a knower—*'aalim*); and *information* (the knowns—*ma'alumaat*)! And in the reverse, the unknown is knowable if we can recognize the root. A little familiarity can go a long way.

Of course, we often guess wrong. That word for scholar—*'aalim*—usually means "world."

"To live in Arabic is to live in a labyrinth of false turns and double meanings," Jonathan Raban wrote in *Arabia through the Looking Glass*. "No sentence means quite what it says. Every word is potentially a talisman, conjuring the ghosts of the entire family of words from which it comes." Its trademark haziness can only be cleared, as far as it will ever be cleared, by knowing as many members of that family as possible.

And yet, the language unfolds even through the missteps, and as we skitter along the web of rules and quirks, the ghosts of Raban's Arabic come quickly out into the daylight.

But there are other traps. In school, from a Moroccan teacher or a Tunisian or a Syrian, we learned Modern Standard Arabic. Known as *Fusha*, from a root that means "to be eloquent," MSA is the official language of two dozen countries and is spoken nowhere. Formal Arabic is the native tongue only of television (but only the news) and print. Everywhere else, regional dialect takes over, complete with homegrown rules of conjugation, syntax, vocabulary, and pronunciation.

As a saving grace, MSA is understood far more widely than it is used. Schoolchildren learn the formalities of case endings and the sounds of the official language, but it's like putting scaffolding on a building that's already finished. When you begin to speak with a newscaster's diction, they'll get it—the news sounds like you, after all—but with every word you say, you'll say more than you mean—and less.

Studying in our underground vacuum we practiced a kind of childlike curiosity, abstract and theoretical and not yet made to answer to the strictures of real life. Soon, it would be. Arab friends tittered when I said something in *Fusha* outside the classroom. *Say it again!*

To them, it sounds like you're speaking in Elizabethan English, my Moroccan professor told us. Then, he continued to teach us how to sound like Shakespeare.

BY GRADUATION, the bits of my identity I could put a finger on were well muddled in the labyrinth of that mild geographic focus: some Arabic language, political science courses that hinted at the region, too many visits to the falafel shop on Broadway that closed for sanitary violations.

"You love the Middle East, don't you?" someone asked me in the May drizzle at commencement. I didn't know what to say. College hadn't given me the tongue-tip arsenal of quotations to pluck off as needed, and I looked for words as we lined up behind St. Paul's Chapel.

If I'd been to more weddings, I might have looked to the chapel and seen a clue. In that same Paul's First Epistle to the Corinthians, the nuptially overworked chapter 13, he writes, "Love does not delight in evil but rejoices with the truth. It always protects, always trusts, always hopes, always perseveres." If looking for true things was love, then I loved, and I did so with the bias of a faint hope.

Seventy-seven years earlier in Washington, a bible lay open to that same page. As he would on three such occasions over the next dozen years, FDR put his hand over these words: *love*, perhaps at the first joint; *hope*, maybe at the knuckle. Under his palm, it said, "When I was a child, I talked like a child, I thought like a child, I reasoned like a child. When I became a man, I put the ways of childhood behind me." And then, the man in a morning coat and striped trousers was made president of the United States.

The only thing we have to fear is fear itself, he said then. "Nameless, unreasoning, unjustified terror, which paralyzes needed efforts to convert retreat into advance." All that in a four-page speech. While he spoke of facing fear, his hand was grounded in love.

I still loved the Middle East like a child, I could have said. I still reasoned like a child with the blackened memories of a September Tuesday in eighth grade when the headmaster told us to go home. My father was home early, too. He hugged me, and in the one extra moment we lingered I knew everything had changed. But I had no idea how, my reason clouded by fear and easy explanation. I loved the Middle East because I wanted to know something true.

First, though, it was all rebellion. Dad a musician, mom a therapist, who both cared about people and liked new things. They had studied abroad and lived abroad and allowed me to choose any path I'd seek. They never forced one. When I was even younger, they didn't give me any authority to fight; if they'd told me not to watch TV, I would have watched it uninterrupted til I died. They didn't—they didn't give me any hard limit to push against. But the world did, later on. It said, as I heard it: *don't go here.*

At the end of my first year of Arabic, Kanye's *Graduation* dropped and he said what I was thinking before every class: *nuh uh, you can't tell me nothing.*

In my bones, I felt that I was the product of 9/11. I couldn't say what that meant, but I knew that it had given me lenses to see the world, and had shaped me like a parent. I was suspicious. Before I came to New York from the leafy Philadelphia suburbs, the city scared me with its chaos and possibility. I moved to New York to lock eyes with my bogey-men, for no reason I knew but to make the world expand. America was my suburb now, and there were voices all around that told me to stay within earshot.

Yalla, into the wild. How could I live without an answer: *What if they're all wrong?*

AFTER GRADUATION, I TOOK the Language Pledge in the spirit of curiosity at a summer program in Oakland. For ten weeks before I left for Abu Dhabi, I promised to speak only in Arabic. Just before I was to leave the continent unfettered, I met a girl there who would tether a part of me to it, and we were nearly dating before we ever said words in English.

It was astonishingly easy to feel close when we accepted that we wouldn't dig for meaning in the minutiae of word choice and turns of phrase, as we would have on first dates in English. Masha and I were in just the right place to simply feel *at* each other.

Says Raban, Arabic "is perfectly constructed for saying nothing with enormous eloquence; a language of pure manners in which there are hardly any literal meanings at all and in which symbolic gesture is everything." Just as the words that follow sneezes in languages around the world are loosened from their literal meaning—the French *to your wishes!* the Pashto *patience!*—Arabic back and forths often serve the connection far more than the dictionary. Something is said and heard, and meaning is made from the interaction.

There is a single word (*na'iman!*) to greet the freshly shaved or recently showered; there is a common answer to any request (*'ala ra'si*—"on my head"). Words become gestures and the roots are forgotten. *Na'iman* comes from one of the many words for paradise, but it's silly to think paradise is invoked every time a friend trims his mustache.

With only literature and textbook grammar to go on, though, we made our own symbolic gestures out of direct translations of American slang. The trouble: word-for-word renderings of "What's up? What's cracking? Yo dawg!" sound like total nonsense. And if we were really thinking in Arabic, calling each other "dogs"—unloved and thought unclean across the Arab worlds—should have been deeply offensive.

The silliness was a welcome distraction from the truth: that we were getting no closer to learning how to say nothing, how to be eloquent in real live Arabic. We still said too much with every word. We shouted "What is above, my dog?" across the courtyard and thought it was hilarious.

Masha and I both laughed at things like that, and saw each other laughing.

It was a star-crossed beginning after a night of Iraqi food in San Francisco. I continued to eat and drink with the abandon I had practiced all through college, and by the time we got home I was vomiting and falling in love. Masha and I had sex in the way twenty-one-year-olds do, and then, as people don't say but maybe should, the Trojan War was lost, and we might have been parents.

I stumbled to the bathroom and puked. Not from fear or guilt, I don't think—just from okra. It was Fathers' Day. I took Masha to a friend who took her to get Plan B, and we began our tumultuous courtship.

It felt like we had skipped many of the wordy steps in the construction of American romances. Weeks later as I boarded the plane to the Gulf, she was signing her e-mails with love.

CARROT JUICE BECAME COCKTAILS, caviars and steak in my massage recliner between Coral and Diamond classes.

And then, by the light of a red sunset above the clouds, I caught my first glimpse of the Gulf. And we descended and the triangle of Abu Dhabi stuck out into the water like a slice of baklava. And dark came all of a sudden, eased by the moon not two hours from full, and the plane landed by the lights of the city.

FROM: ME ‹A••••••••••••••••••@••••••.COM›
SUBJECT: HELLO HELLO
MON AT 12:38 AM

YOU are like the Lewis to my Clarks.

- - - - - - - - -

FROM: MASHA ‹MASHA.••••••@••••••.COM›
RE: HELLO HELLO
TUE AT 9:14 AM

How will you brush your teeth without me?

Love
Masha

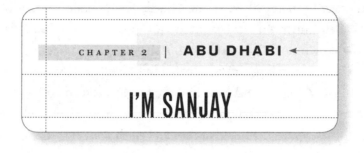

CHAPTER 2 | **ABU DHABI**

I'M SANJAY

T WAS HOT. Cresting a hundred degrees in the evening steam, the air grabbed at my legs and chest, fogged camera lenses, and matted hair. Fire shot from the walls when I tested the first outlet of my new apartment, and I wandered my new neighborhood on Electra Street while I waited for the cheery electrician. As one old fable goes, a man is promised all the land he can walk in one day. If it were an Emirati story, the man would have won about half a block in the heat, and traded it for a glass of tea.

Soon enough, two Bangladeshi men came to replace the fuse. As soon as I could turn the lights on again, I turned them off and went to sleep.

Fresh off the plane from California in 2010, I was a program coordinator for New York University Abu Dhabi. My title meant nothing, and my employer's name looked like a paradox. Two incongruent place names pushed together without so much as a hyphen, bridging every cultural and temporal and physical divide with a flash of smart branding. Purple. Everything was purple.

"I coordinate programs," I'd explain to anyone who asked, a half joke that left neither one of us more enlightened. It worked in Arabic, too. And then I would return to coordinating, or playing hooky, on the campus that claimed the essences of two cities and felt almost absolutely like neither.

I'd never been anywhere in the Middle East, outside of family visits to Jerusalem and a two-week jaunt to Morocco. I had studied the worlds that might be unlocked by Arabic, but they had never been real.

And still, I was the guide to prospective faculty on tours to the reful-gent Sheikh Zayed Grand Mosque, the world's eighth largest (besting their Omani neighbors in one of the region's favorite kinds of keeping-up-with-the-Joneses). There is room for ten thousand inside and thirty thousand in the courtyard and the nation's founding father rests nearby in a quietly locked mausoleum. It was magnificent, almost always. A blend of Mughal and Moorish styles, selected from the palate of Every-thing Available. The white marble foyer with green vines inlaid, marble flowers—this was a Quranic interpretation of paradise. The white ceil-ings and towering pillars laced with gold: milk and honey. Here, the ninety-nine names of God upon the wall that faces Mecca, with a blank spot for the name we cannot know until the end of time.

If it seemed like I knew anything, the American professors would ask, casually, "So, you're Muslim?" And I'd tell them the truth, hoping they'd laugh. Mosque tours from the unbar-mitzvahed Jewish boy.

Look, I'd say, *the largest handwoven carpet in the world (two billion stitches!) shipped in a thousand pieces from Iran. And look, the largest chandelier on planet Earth*. Immense, fruit-colored Swarovski baubles fixed to a kind of golden hat rack, dangling from one of eighty-two domes like Christmas decorations awaiting a tree. *From Germany.*

Other days, I might accompany someone like the university presi-dent's young cousin "dune bashing," off-roading in a heavy SUV on soft desert sand until I threw up, and then to an intercontinental buffet at an uncountably starred hotel with infinity pools onto the waterway at the city's edge.

Months passed quickly. I wore suits to work, partly because it made me feel like I was doing something, and partly because it made other people think so, too.

Nights vanished like college evenings in a quiet neighborhood. Inside, I often forgot which side of the globe we were on, and I remembered only by smelling curry. It came, always, from a magical restaurant called Canopy, and I cultivated an easy addiction alongside Jake, a giant poet tutoring English, and with my neighbors Dan and Jordan, a couple from New Jersey and Atlanta via Brooklyn, university employees all.

Not once did the saints of delivery judge me for my four packets of onion *kulcha* and chicken tikka masala—not the day after *raita* and *jalfrezi*, not the day after exactly the same. Some weeks, I called six times.

For five dollars, the bag arrives at the door, delivered with gentleness and warm smiles that, even before opening, remind the deliveree of where he is not. These were among the rare moments of glee I felt in the UAE. When anyone simply unplugged from Abu Dhabi, Canopy remained.

On those nights, we watched TV shows from our native land. *American Gladiators. Wipeout.* All easy-to-digest slapstick with American budgets. But they were not shows I'd known before. Abu Dhabi became this to me: memories of my country that weren't mine, and celestial Indian food.

SUNDAY MORNING AND THE START of a new work week found me taking old business cards, restaurant coupons, and pharmacy memberships out of my wallet like someone checking into prison. *You won't need these in here.*

The vacuum of my all-white apartment in our hyperclean new building rarely sparked memories of home. I had shipped over a piano keyboard whose keys I tickled the way a kid doodles in class (both because I was distracted and because I wanted to be)—but when I turned it on, a smell conjured my childhood labors in the kitchen, mixing cookie dough with an overheating beater. This time it was the scent of fizzled electronics and smoke: the keyboard adaptor was not dual voltage. Some things are not so easily transformed.

Luckily, my address on Electra Street was no joke: down the kilometer-long block of Abu Dhabi's enormous grid, on the stretch between Old Airport Road and New Airport Road (Second and Fourth Streets), there were no less than fifteen shops selling appliances, miscellaneous electronics, cables. In the shadow of sprouting skyscrapers, they sat next to one another amicably, selling exactly the same things. But without fail if they couldn't help, they'd send me one store to the left, then across the street, and on forever. An unsuccessful shopkeep would rarely let me leave without at least a spot of hope.

And there is almost always hope in the land of the miscellaneous: People who do a little of everything are quite flexible. If they don't have a cable, they'll make it out of wire and pieces; if they don't know how to fix something, they'll try.

Mumkin. In Arabic, the word *maybe* also means "possible."

I learned to haggle in the UAE even with reality's most intransigent features. Nothing was quite so certain as it was to the West—not even time. With a soft tone, you might push someone else to perceive it a little more like you do.

"I'm forty-five minutes away," the man stated. Fact. Distance. Time.

"Could you make it thirty?" I asked. A friend told me to say that— she'd been here far longer than I had.

The man came in fifteen. Everything was *mumkin.*

I felt a bit like I'd unlocked a secret of the universe, like Lucy Pevensie, who discovered a wardrobe that led to a land of lions and witches, or Arthur Dent, who learned that flying was learning to throw oneself at the ground and miss. The grammar of Arabia came one step further out of the shadows.

Time may be the first thing to grow fuzzy in that latitude where there is not much difference between the seasons. When I landed in Abu Dhabi, the announcement to turn off electronic devices came ten minutes earlier in Arabic than it did in English. There was less urgency in each minute.

When I accepted that another's logic simply wouldn't follow the rules I knew, my anger could fade toward those who had been breaking them. In my state of—call it *peninsulation*—the island took on its own logic.

INSULATION DOES MANY THINGS, especially in the blinding heat of a hot island off an equally hot peninsula. Most emerge from the tumble dry of Abu Dhabi immigration and find their matches—American with American, Indian with Indian—like paired socks. It is a melting pot where nothing ever melts. In this uniquely modern frontier town, we had all come for some piece of the riches.

After two decades of scouting, oil was struck at sea in 1958. Now the UAE claims reserves of ninety-eight billion barrels, enough at current rates to last a neat century. Almost all of it is to be tapped from the emirate of Abu Dhabi, 8 percent of the world's black gold under a footprint the size of West Virginia.

Censuses are fuzzy, but high birth rates and unprecedented immigration have multiplied the UAE population about fortyfold since independence in 1971 (the world's population has only doubled). And yet, a sense of belonging is not forthcoming in the UAE, where the jobs are, but where 85 percent of the bulging resident society are not and will never become citizens. Perhaps that's what makes it feel so free for some—a summer fling with no expectations, no commitment; for others, it is a more pointed reminder that they are subjects, fully beholden to the whims of the monarchy. Either way, the UAE has no path to citizenship for its foreign labor force, and so we reach out for the communities that remind us of home.

While we reach out laterally for comfort, the country stacks us into neatly color-coded strata. We were stratified nationally here, and stratified by the shades of our skin: Construction recruiters fill Workers City apartments fourteen to a room with men from the Indian subcontinent (a moniker all too consonant with their role as a subclass); from Southeast Asia come maids (Sri Lanka, Indonesia) and the hospitality industry's front office (Philippines); East Africans do security; Arabs from Lebanon and Egypt handle security as well, own restaurants, and mingle more fluidly, but remain a step apart. Businesses pull from each of these, but white-collar jobs are filled overwhelmingly with

Europeans and Americans, and within each business a microcosm of the social order is noticeable, as if described by lines of invisible ink.

At the top of it all, there are Emiratis, the spontaneous kings of their own land. As a nation, they are self-made; as individuals, they are largely reliant on the national trust.

When we sought connection within these castes, the structure made it so that we were even more likely to grab on to likenesses of ourselves. The university, though it would organize itself by many of the same principles, began with different premises. It piled students and most of its employees (but not the drivers or subcontracted security or lower-level staff) into what was then the tallest residential building in the city. Insofar as we knew who our floormates were, we were offered the chance to connect.

My dearest friend Iman was an NYU grad from Pakistan, half-Venezuelan and fully too kind and honest to keep her head above the flow of office drama and bureaucratic bullshit. We spent most evenings with Gila, a half-Iranian, half-Mauritian mother of two, raised in London and Paris, with more spirit for nightlife than I could ever muster. We went to Ladies' Nights with the Kenyan and Dominican contingents. We made pancakes and drained bottles of Bailey's into our coffee with Jake, the six-foot-six-inch poet from Erie, kitty-corner from me across Pennsylvania, and a travel partner to places we knew nothing about. Later, I'd escape the Emirates with Neal from Iowa, a fellow member of the tribe—that is to say, the Jewish one—which had never mattered much to me except as permission to make jokes of a certain kind.

On the university's opening day, when the inaugural class arrived from six continents, I met tree-tall Oleg from Kaliningrad, a little Russian exclave separated from the motherland by the Baltic States.

Newly isolated (by varying levels of choice) from what we knew, we formed young relationships in a young country. They hatched as in high school: some de facto friendships from sufficiently shared schedules, others more deliberate—at times, one became the other.

Jake and I ordered from Canopy and drank vodka tonics on long lunch breaks on slow days, which were many. We breezed through the side entrance and out the side exit of African and Eastern wine and spirits, never once needing the alcohol license by which non-Muslim residents are permitted the purchase of 20 percent of their monthly salary in alcohol. ("You must be of legal drinking age and a non-Muslim to visit the African + Eastern website.") We hauled the loot that clanked in black bags past the storefront with equally black windows, down Seventh Street, named Sheikh Zayed the First Street but called Khalidiya Street until it crossed the ten smooth lanes of Airport Road and became Electra. Up the elevators home. The grid of modern Islamic architecture below could not have been anywhere else we'd ever lived, but it was easy then to forget every reason we had come here.

- - - - - -

EARLY OCTOBER AND IT IS ninety-three degrees by the pool. The beaches along the Corniche are lapped with warm, salty seawater, overprotected from the counterclockwise current of the Gulf by the breakwater and the 1,050-acre Al Lulu Island that men made by scooping up the ocean floor. It looks beautiful—seven miles of untouched shoreline, some facing jet skis at the Abu Dhabi skyline from a flattering distance, some opening onto the turquoise strait. But access, since 2009, is by private boat only.

I'm almost comfortable, but I'm restless. I'm too comfortable. I notice myself growing accustomed to the last-minute grocery deliveries—a bottle of Coke, an egg, two tomatoes—that materialized from the store one elevator ride and fifteen steps away. I am ready for Mustafa to come and ask for dry cleaning, to whisk it away and return it folded and hung. Over sixteen months, I would never know where this magic was done.

The culture of the Emirates is so defined by its stratification that one draw for white Westerners is the instant shift in social standing awarded just for showing up. In the evenings, whether from a smelly taxi or a blacked-out Maserati, we guests arriving at hotels (the homes of many high-end restaurants and bottomless brunch spots, of bars and nightclubs and a large share of the things to do) are sorted immediately by the style of our costume—coveralls, jeans, suit, *kandura*—and the color of our skin. "Good evening, sir," the African doorman says to me, with something just short of a wink. He knew me well—hundreds of me had already arrived at Le Royal Meridian that night.

This is the comfort, for some: families, working mothers and fathers, emigrants from places where no amount of long hours ever earned anything close to a wink from the doorman. But I haven't earned the *sirs*— not when I show up in matted Jewfro and a T-shirt. And I know that if I'm getting it for free, just like the free cheeses at the trendy café by the conference center, someone else isn't.

Even at the very top, life could seem compartmentalized, preordained, immobile. The United Arab Emirates is one of the world's two elective monarchies; the other is Malaysia. Every five years, the Supreme Council (the rulers of each of the seven emirates) picks the president (who will also hold the offices of supreme commander of the Armed Forces, and chairman of both the Supreme Petroleum Council and the Supreme Council itself) and the vice president from among their own.

Historically, the president has always been the ruler of Abu Dhabi, the capital, and the vice president has always been the ruler of Dubai, both hereditary posts. Even for the living sheikhs I could see in the pictures along the highway, in the banks, the supermarket, behind the front desk of every hotel—there would be no movement outside those frames.

Despite all the metaphors about shifting sands, deserts are a place of supreme consistency.

BUT . . . AND YET . . . THERE WAS SOMETHING I felt close to, thrillingly, for the first time. I had not expected Lawrence's Arabia when I deplaned in this desert—but I felt like we had made it to his foyer. Here were planted the stories to follow. The four-fifths of us sweating without citizenship were exactly what made the whole national enterprise feel rootless, but looking closely, it was exactly this coalition of rainbow passports that brought the Gulf to absurd life unlike anywhere else in the world. The curries at Canopy brought me over the sea to the South.

Cabbies from the hill behind Tora Bora gave hints of their homes in the White Mountains. Endless falafel and fresh hummus by delivery whisked me over *Arabia Deserta*, across the Great Carrot, to sketches of Damascus.

The hodgepodge was a grip on the otherwise frictionless city. I loved everything that was confusing—for in that confusion there was something to look for, something to dig around. I loved the haggling that gave us "Lawrences without-a-cause" something to fight for. I loved the addresses for the 2.5 million residents in Abu Dhabi, as landmark based as my grandmother's directions. There were no street numbers and official road names were hardly used: instead of 1500 Rashid bin Sa'iid Al Maktoum Street, you'd ask for the road formerly known as Airport Road behind Domino's Pizza. This seemed the greatest hope against a fading heritage—listen to any cab driver: he not only speaks of the past, he drives you right through it. After I left, the roads were renamed and numbered, but it hasn't stuck. "The cabbies still use the old names," Gila wrote me later, "so it's useless having new addresses!"

While I lived on Electra Street, our new skyscraper Sama Tower began to develop landmark status among the taxi community. I once heard ominously that it was built atop a graveyard (unmarked as they typically are according to Islamic tradition). At fifty stories, named from Arabic for "sky" or "heaven," Sama was very briefly the tallest residential building in the city. Soon, something else sprouted higher on man-made land.

Out its back entrance to Foodlands falafel, across from the New Muslim Center and behind the New Medical Center in the infinite web of parking lots that act like side streets within the city's oversized grid, I met Ali from Daraa, a midsize city an hour south of Damascus. Sometimes I went for a sandwich and to say hi, other times I went to say hi and have a sandwich.

"Ya, Ali!"

"Adam! *Kifak* Adam?"

After months of that, I felt like we knew each other. My age exactly with black hair and a white uniform, Ali had bright eyes and a smile that could cook rotisserie. He manned the falafel and shawarma nightly, shaving chicken or lamb from the spinning poles according to customer demand: regular, or the chili-spiced meat collage called "*Mexiki*."

He greeted me with such loyalty that I thought of him like an old friend, and felt guilty when I had been too absent. Arabic makes it easy—if a young man isn't *akhi*, my brother, he is *habibi*, my dear, like every friend or foe, man, woman, and child across the Arab world. At Foodlands, our Arabic moments felt like connections, the beginning of something, his first language to my second. It wasn't the novelty of practicing a school subject on anyone who understood, like discussing pressing options with Mustafa the dry-cleaning deliverer in his fourth language. That just let me feel far away.

But a brother should know true things, and Ali and I never spoke about anything important for long.

"*Kifak? Kif ommak wabbuk?*" How are you? How's your mother? Your father? he'd ask, rolling pickled carrot and chilies into the pita.

"*Alhamdulilah*," I said, the only response possible—the "Praise God" that subsumes all states and feelings. Say more if you'd like, but the whole range of human emotion can be contained in its lilt. "*Kif a'iltak?*" How's your family?

"*Alhamdulilah*."

And I'd grin, and wish I had the words to say more, and wander off into the night two dollars lighter.

And when that wasn't enough, when I felt those connections were far too flimsy to hitch me to the real city, I pretended I was in paradise. I pulled a towel from the door handle of my drunkenly designed bathroom—a miniature shower stall alone in a large room—and spent two shawarmas-worth on a five-minute cab to the beach. It was winter where my friends lived.

It was hot, and I had found enough change on the nightstand to cover the ride. The walk was never pleasant anyway, across pedestrian intersections where eight-lane roads merged. It was safe enough at the crosswalks; cars followed all the rules because the city was built for them.

"Everything is two aspects. You know, *everything* is two sides," the driver said on the way.

I blinked.

A woman passed at the crosswalk. "Take this lady now, I say to her 'Habibi, go.' Yes?" That *habibi* is the ubiquitous corsage upon the already well-dressed Arabic language. "This is the best word. My heart is clear." But, he said, "this is the worst word, thc bad word also." *Habibi* could be used to cajole, to deceive, to misrepresent the speaker with an unclear heart.

"You're confused," he laughed.

I swore I wasn't, not enough to give up. While the oppressive heat of the summer months barred most activity but pressing elevator buttons, winter in the Gulf had space for thought. We navigated each other's accents, his turning p's into f's and losing v's among the frontal vowels, dusted with Arabic where nothing else would do. (*Kharban*, he said, to describe a bad person. The word means something like "ruined," but sounds so much more like it means it.)

He was like the Madonna of cab drivers, only one name written on the screen that beeped and spoke when we topped the speed limit: LIAQUATH. It means "light," he said.

He picked up his phone from the console. "This is a mobile, yes? This is the good thing, if you use for the good thing, this is the best thing. If you use this for bad, this is the worst thing. It's depend on you."

I nodded. The aspect was a function of our intention and our action; no object was innately good or bad. We passed new glass towers germinating along the Corniche road.

A person, though, could be just *kharban*. "Listen. I'm from Pakistan, from Peshawar. I do something bad. Listen, listen: then you not think Pakistan is bad, you only think this man is bad. Yes?"

"Yes."

"If I say this country is bad, then myself I am bad." The important thing, said Liaquath, was that we mean what we say. Then, at least the words are good.

As I moved to slide out of the car, Liaquath soliloquized at someone out the window. Habibi, he said, followed by something in Pashto.

"Was that a good habibi or bad habibi?"

"You know," he said with a wink.

THE SAND IS DREDGED UP from the Gulf floor and plopped along the Corniche beach, too fine and too pure. There is no seaweed or rocks, no driftwood along the coast. Marina Mall sits on the breakwater across a stretch of oversalted water that can't circulate, adorned with a huge Emirati flag waving from what was once the world's largest flagpole. (It is now the fourth largest; in this department, the Emirates has faltered in keeping up with the Al Sauds.)

All he needed was the genie's robes and Liaquath would have made the perfect cabbie-guru—a stock figure in his uniform.

I hailed a cab the next day, and lo—there was Liaquath, in the flesh, in the exact same of Abu Dhabi's ten thousand gray cabs.

"Wa—*huh*?!" I asked.

He didn't look at all surprised.

These accidents were the happiest magic, unplanned, like all the best things in the Emirates. Halfway down the Al Ain Truck Road to the oasis city at the Omani border, runoff from a wastewater treatment plant collects against the highway. The freshwater pool now attracts thousands of pink flamingos—just passing through like the rest of us—on their migratory circle from Russia around Azerbaijan, toward Iran. Clinging to their legs for hundreds of miles, little passengers have fallen off into the pool. There are now tiny shrimp in the heart of the desert.

BEFORE 1961 ABU DHABI didn't have a single paved road. Then: unfathomable wealth. Instantly there were resources for the rulers' aspirations and, as if selected from a catalog, cities sprang up in the Emirates from absolute nothing.

In this new nation without citizens, starting from scratch is the national pastime. For those of us lured to the Gulf, not tricked, we could be anyone we wanted.

It even gave me options.

I answered calls from India, from Senegal, from every emirate asking if I wanted something or if I had something. With language getting in the way, I wasn't ever sure of a single answer I gave until they asked, "Sanjay?"

No, I'd say. *This isn't Sanjay.*

Twice a week for my entire life in the Emirates, I answered calls for Sanjay. *This still isn't him*, I'd say. Some days, I could hardly persuade them that they had the wrong number. It wasn't a wrong number after all, just wrong timing—in a past life, those ten digits were his. He was in the finance business, it seemed, or he tended to leave our phone number somewhere bankers could find it. Sometimes, the caller never knew they had the wrong man. To this day, I retain contacts at almost every bank in Arabia.

IN THE EARLY DAYS of my employment, one conversation began like many. I was assisting the university's Procurement Department in a job that felt very Middle Eastern: I called vendors, delinquent in their side of whatever bargain, and begged them to make good. Chairs, ping-pong tables, laboratory equipment—no tracking numbers here, just tracking people.

"What is your good name?" said a man who introduced himself as Rafiq, on the other end of the line.

"Adam."

"Aarif?"

"Adam."

"*Aarif*?"

"A . . . dam."

He took a moment to process this. "Aarif."

"Yes," I said. And then we attempted to do business.

Certainty and inflexibility tend to close doors in *this part of the world*, the Westerner's term for the geographical cloud that has settled unintelligibly wide over the region. It implies the freedom we have within it—the haziness of borders, names, everything—and that the men from the subcontinent do not. In many cases, it was irrelevant who I was; by asserting less, I could learn more. I could converse in symbolic gesture. And I could find out what happened to the storage cabinets from mid-August.

And I wondered if there was anything so certain about myself that I could not deny it to strangers with a touch of accent, new clothes, better posture.

Really, I was only taking a page out of the city's book. Abu Dhabi itself expands onto landfill, surpassing the past boundaries of the island it is built upon. In the last forty years, the city has increased its surface area by a sixth—the Sheraton Corniche, once beachfront, is now almost a thousand feet from the water. It's a common practice from Battery Park City in New York to Hong Kong—Masha's hometown Boston has more than doubled in size since its founding in 1640—and every time it reflects a kind of enterprising audacity, of man asserting himself over the wild. The process is called land *reclamation*, as if this is how it once was, even though the new territory was never anything but sea or swamp. It is *reclaimed* so that we begin to forget what was old and what was new, what was "authentic" and what was an adaptation. And it works. Soon, after those decades of construction, there is no difference. I never knew what the beach would have looked like with driftwood. The old limits are erased by the ebb of the new high tide.

IN ONE OF THE BARBERSHOPS near Saloon Tarek and Saloon Wave Beach and Shahrezad Fadl Gents Saloon (subscribers to a kind of nationwide typo), the Sri Lankan barber was insistent about my sideburns.

"I'll give you *the style*."

"No, thank you. Just neatened up a bit."

"It's *the style*."

"Please, just the most normal trim."

"You don't want *the style*?"

"No. . . ." I felt guilty that I wasn't giving him a proper canvas for his talents, but I felt freer as something simple, vague. "I'm American," I said, hoping that might count as an excuse.

He shrugged like a cashier watching me buy the world's tackiest wedding ring. But he couldn't hold back. In ten minutes, I saw South Asian artistry plastered to my face. The hair on my head was chopped short against the heat, and my sideburns tapered, curving ever so daintily, into little peaks.

I never got another haircut in the country. The more my hair grew curlier and long, the more it betrayed my foreign roots.

When I put the phone down and walked the eight-lane Abu Dhabi roads, I became something more rigid. This is the up- and downside of "American," the loudest branding label in the world: pointy sideburns or no, my hair and face and clothes walked ten steps ahead of me, and always spoke first. That was the limit on what I could be; in brief moments of possible connection, there was baggage. It was too hard to start fresh because nothing was ever fresh.

I struggled with that. Emiratis did, too. On a small street behind our apartment that wound around a juice shop, I sat on the curb with Khulood, a fellow administrator at the university. I felt tighter with her than I did with any other Emirati women, if only because we'd talked the most. And it always seemed easier to talk to Emirati women than Emirati men.

We held juices named for the Burj al-Arab, the sail-shaped ultraluxury hotel in Dubai that wears a helipad like a sailor's cap. Khulood was from Dubai, and whenever she told people so, she saw hands beginning to outstretch—envy and need and a rare brush with riches. When she was abroad, she felt like she was a sounding board for ignorance, and instantly a potential patron to everyone's dreams.

"So I came up with Mirchi," Khulood said. "Mirchi is off of the coast of Yemen. It is an island."

"Um," I said. "It is?"

"No!" Her head flew back as she laughed at me, and she teased her headscarf forward. "So when people would ask *Where are you from?* I'd say, 'I'm from Mirchi.' *Oh, Mirchi, where is that?* I'm like, 'It's an island in Yemen.' And that's just how the conversation ends."

I'd *always* wanted to do that. Too curious to see reactions to what I actually was, I had never let my imagination run so wild. But how wonderful, to be blank!

"It was great from there on. No conversations, no more questions."

I EASILY BECAME SOMEONE both fixed and disconnected. I experimented with identities that were vague enough to take root in something I didn't understand. And at first it didn't bother me—it was all so American, I thought, to be this kind of self-made man.

Once, the ballet came to Abu Dhabi. Ten minutes by gray taxi down the waterfront boulevard, I went to see them at the Emirates Palace. The towering blonde freshman Oleg arranged tickets for two dozen students and staff from a Russian contact at a good price. In classic Russian fashion, the man had sold five hundred more tickets than there were seats in the Emirates Palace Auditorium. In classic Middle Eastern fashion, there was always another way in.

And as always in the Emirates, there were extra seats despite it all. Around the other side of the theater, I fell into line behind one of Their Highnesses in the black and gold overrobe as they glided across the red carpet. I babbled nonsense into my phone and stayed close. I came back out to Oleg's door, from the inside, and began to usher our group in by the handful.

"Let's go, there isn't time!"

The women at the door looked confused and upset—one Russian, one Arab under a headscarf—but they wouldn't block the way. The Russian's eyes narrowed. I started saying things in Arabic.

"Yalla, ista'ajilu!"

The women scowled at me as the students began to play along, squeezing past. "Who are they? Do you speak Russian?"

"Arabi, English, *Russki,* whichever," I said. I spoke no Russian. Oleg filed in with some others.

"*Kharasho*—" I said to him, and interrupted myself like I had more Russian words to say. In the short moments the women tried to figure out what kind of an asshole I was, more students passed through.

The confusion tactic is a beautiful one, more commonly used on the defensive than as such a brazen sortie, but desperate times had called. I turned to the Arab woman, to say a few words in a different language.

"They are very important guests of the sheikh. This isn't good," I said.

"Which sheikh?" she asked.

But then they had all gone in and found places, and I looked hurriedly at my phone and said *Oh!* and disappeared back among the gold-colored seats.

I don't know what it was about the Emirates Palace that made it feel like the perfect playground for these kinds of shenanigans. Maybe it was its name—a "seven star" luxury hotel that was not, in fact, a royal residence. (The Presidential Palace was under construction down the road.) Maybe it was the magical look of all that gold, gold, gold, and diamonds that made reality melt away, and made me feel like we could all start from scratch.

Every so often, that was where I played second trumpet in the now-dissolved UAE Philharmonic Orchestra. After a concert, we carried our instruments up from the auditorium to the central café that serves a fifteen-dollar old-fashioned and cappuccinos peppered with gold leaf (that tastes exactly like you'd expect hammered-thin soft metals to taste). Luscious leather couches facing glass cases of French patisserie. A South African trio jammed, under a six-days-a-week contract, until eleven. It was against the rules for a fourth to join in, especially brass, but I took the hotel employee's begrudging shrug as something else.

"Blame me," I said. "If anyone makes trouble, just tell them to blame me."

"I can't," he said, eying my trumpet.

"But we never talked," I said.

"Who are you?"

I looked back at the rows of *macarons* and mille-feuilles. No one who knew me was looking. "I'm Sanjay."

Onyx on piano was happy to let me play a few choruses over "Mannenberg," a South African tune I half-remembered from high school, and I took off like no one was listening. I knew the key, but I didn't know the chord changes underneath—the harmonic framework of the song, its house rules for improvisation. This is like knowing words in a language without grammar, like furnishing a house without knowing the floor plan.

I danced over the rules until a wrong note would tell me that I'd broken one, and then I'd float again. It was shallow, and I couldn't refer to the deepest roots of the piece because I didn't know them, but—it was something. It might have been the freest I ever felt in that country on the beach—and it was all forbidden.

There like anywhere, I could violate the rules by not understanding or by deliberately ignoring them. In the airport, an ad for Swiss watches said: "To break the rules, you must first master them." But you cannot master the rules of the Emirates, and we existed in a state of constant bending. The chord changes of the country, the cultural-religious-historical roots that still hold sway, are hard to find, and so I felt like we were just skimming the surface, ready to drift off into nothingness. We were, to a point. But if I loved the place—which, damn it, I was starting to if only because I was beginning to know it, and which is different from wanting to live there—then I would rejoice with the truth when I found it, and hope for the best until then.

IN TINY BURSTS, the country revealed itself. One Friday morning, I packed into a van of Americans at dawn for the Al Wathba Camel Racetrack. It was the first day of camel-racing season.

Think of all the glamour, the maquillage, the frenzied betting and crowds screaming, the graceful galloping of horse races: It's none of that. Some thousand gangly camels run dozens at a time in back-to-back races around a horseshoe track nearly five miles long. Owners shadow their entries in crammed white Land Cruisers from an internal track, paved that season for the very first time. While the driver speeds ahead in what looks from the inside like rush hour in the desert, the owner clicks a remote control that triggers the camel's whip.

Oh right—they're ridden by robots.

Little boxes in hats cling to the speeding camels just behind the hump, spinning whips on command. It's a great improvement: in the middle of the desert thirty miles east of Abu Dhabi, camel breeders emancipated child jockeys in favor of their no-frills droid replacements.

Handlers pull the camels through as the starting gate shoots up, some animals still losing their way, turning against the tide and racing back toward home. Others somehow escape the track and, foaming at the mouth from exertion, charge unsuspecting bystanders looking through camera lenses.

Still, the radio reception is *no great sheikhs*, as we punned when drunk or tired, and owners must be nearly within earshot of their camels to use their whip remotes.

Of course, I wanted to be part of the action. So did Nils, my friend and colleague, who—because the world is small and loves jokes—was Masha's former classmate at her 120-kid high school in Boston.

It took but a friendly *"Can we?"* and a hand on the door handle to be invited in to race around with an owner and his driver. Our first hosts were consistently in second-to-last place and drove in a serious, subdued silence, but after one lap, Nils and I managed to land seats in the media van.

An announcer rattled off names and standings to the radio, as frenzied as an auctioneer. Unfortunately, it seemed camels weren't christened as creatively as racehorses. Because their owners didn't tipple, I joked.

Pulling in at dawn, owners race these camels out at the racetrack, drinking coffee in their cars from paper cups filled by Iranian men wearing traditional garb and daggers. When Abu Dhabi struck oil and tailors rushed to sew deeper pockets into every *dishdash*, city dwellers found more things to buy, shinier things to polish, and bigger things to invest in. But in the immutable desert, there is only desert—men whose fathers raised and raced camels continue to raise and race camels, only now with a little more land.

We reached the end of the race, accepted CapriSun juice bags from the announcer, and settled in for another lap.

IN ARABIC, EVERY OTHER DAY is named for its order in the week, but Friday is *yom al-jumu'a*, from a root that means "gathering." No doubt it referred to gathering at the mosque—the *jaam'a*—for communal Friday prayers, but it became (or has always been) a day for many other kinds of communion.

The more I lost track of myself, the more I gravitated toward gatherings. They all pulled: anywhere it seemed like people came together, not by accident or for money but because they knew one another and they wanted to—this was what I felt I needed.

One day per week across the rough triangle of the UAE, on Friday, gathering day, veils of sterility lift. After the camels finish their galumphing rounds, one hundred miles away in Dubai a thousand South Asians are convening in a huge ring around a sandy lot to compete in *pehlwani*. They come from every emirate in the hour before sunset to watch this style of wrestling, brought to the UAE by their compatriots in the eighties. Men strip down to brightly colored briefs, a jester-like promoter bangs a drum and plays a nasal horn, and crowd favorites and newcomers take to the dirt.

At the same moment just over the Hajar Mountains in Fujairah, families are gathering at another rough arena by the sea. This one is for bull fighting, or rather, "bull butting." Here, men do not challenge bulls to the death; a fearless man with a switch persuades bulls to challenge each other to the point of dishonor. Bulls never die—they can only lose.

Emirati men in all-white robes—the Arabian *thobe*, called *dishdash* here and elsewhere in the Gulf, called *kandura* only here—pull the animals close with ropes until they lock horns. Children plop down just behind a thin fence installed only recently, others lean out of their sunroofs or lounge in folding chairs with bags of snacks. A candy man with only sweets peddles his stock.

The tidiness of UAE life is displaced here by a shock of chaos, a messy spectacle with glory for the taking and tradition older than the buildings. Fujairah is among the smaller and poorer of the seven emirates, with no huge oil reserves or financial havens—just morsels handed down from the national coffers that are filled in Abu Dhabi and largely tapped by the capital's favorite relatives in Dubai.

I couldn't be sure what laws of the land I was learning when a one-ton Brahman bull escaped the ring and charged into the parking lot pursued by a train of men in spotless white, but we all jumped and I felt a little giddy, like I'd heard my grandmother curse.

For that split second, I glimpsed the nation's roots. All the while, bored Fujairans screeched by hanging off the back of their roaring ATVs, looping up and down the Corniche road, and making people frown.

In 1922, archeologist D. G. Hogarth reported: "Social differences have always been less in Arabia than perhaps anywhere else, not only between one community and another, but between one class and another in one community." Hogarth, mentor to T. E. Lawrence, wrote that before the oil, before the apartments were filled four parts to one with foreigners. It could hardly stand in greater contrast now, with the nation's reputation for unearthly wealth and the squalid treatment of the labor class. And yet, on these Fridays on the dirt where everyone was welcome, you could see it: the community, the mixed crowds all looking in the same direction. And then the sun sets, and we retreat again to our separate villas.

ONCE EVERY YEAR, right on cue, the strata dissolve nationwide for one night. "*Eid sa'id*," we wish each other—*Happy holiday*. Diwali has passed. It's not Islamic New Year yet. It's not Hanukkah (although it sometimes is). It's not Christmas—even if the buildings all draped and merry in glittering yuletide neon suggest otherwise from every window.

On the second of December, the UAE comes alive for National Day.

My first year marked the thirty-ninth anniversary of the unification of the seven emirates, an occasion commemorated by the only tradition befitting its significance: shooting Silly String from spray cans in strangers' faces.

Thirty-nine. In people years, the last crossroad before a great transformation, a faintly depressing maturity. But the UAE celebrates its youth with unabashed pride, and its age as an accomplishment. Its fortieth would be just the same, just as messy. Up and over the Gulf of Aqaba they played with aerosol, too, in that country ripening past sixty-five: *It's like Israeli Independence Day!* I thought quietly to myself.

At the best moments, it's pandemonium. Abu Dhabi car owners en masse relieve their vehicles of their mufflers, burning rubber and backfiring on the busiest street in the city. The Corniche road, which runs from the port past the beaches and the billboard for Our Father Zayed and up to the driveway of Emirates Palace, is at a standstill (as if anyone would be anywhere else). Thousands rev engines and blare music from trucks painted red, white, green, and black, arrayed with faces of the sheikhs and overflowing with garlands and streamers. Exhaust pipes howl under pressure, letting out bursts that sound like automatic gunfire from a distance, and almost feel like it up close. Friends ride in pickups or huge flatbeds, shaking them until they almost capsize. Others dance in circles in the street. Fireworks are exploding all the time. And everyone is shooting everyone in the face.

Roaming salesmen sell cans of colored Silly String for five dirham, around a buck thirty-five, and passengers in or on top of cars fire back with a vengeance. Beware the accomplices riding shotgun and brandishing shotgun-like water guns. Some shoot string, others shoot water, many shoot a kind of bathtub foam that fills the air and sticks to clothes. It's every national resident for himself. And tonight—if you want to be—you can be a national, too.

With a can of string, I attacked a car through its open window and four men exploded from the doors. I was drowned in soap—a clear defeat, witnessed by the line of bystanders along the sidewalk who watched battles unfold as you would from a saloon porch at high noon.

On December second, soap scrubs away distinctions between

owner and renter, laborers and locals of leisure, leaving those who go home to wash in palaces as vulnerable as the crowds. Maserati drivers with open windows suffer sneak attacks, and clever infantry shoot soapy jets through sunroofs—the more you own, the more you have to get covered in string and spume.

Yet in this chaos, there is a code—a wild Middle Eastern gunslinger's rule book. I stand rattling my can streetside, armed only with the power to intimidate and get foamed in the nose. A car drives by; a Pakistani man sticks his head out of the window, holding his can. He turns his hand over and back: *Empty?* I'm empty. *Shoot you next year.*

Dawn rises again over the Corniche. The street cleaners have already washed the roads and lifted the trash from the grassy islands, as if Rumpelstiltskin had come in the night to do the impossible job. (What will we owe in the end for this magic?) The transient unity of the UAE fades again, and communities drift further apart.

Luckily, the day after was a Friday. *Yom al-jumuʿa.*

"The best day on which the sun has risen is Friday," Muhammad is quoted as saying in the hadith; "on it Adam was created, on it he was made to enter Paradise, on it he was expelled from it."

TWO WEEKS LATER, two men came to visit us bearing the unique scent of home in their scraggly beards. They both took off their baseball caps, and under them—yarmulkes.

Dressed and bearded to the nines of Hasidic custom, these two Chabad rabbis had come via Dubai from Brooklyn to light Hanukkah candles with relocated Jews on the fortieth floor of our brand new apartment building, where everyone I knew lived stacked on top of one another.

I hardly thought of myself as a Jew in this place. Jewish, sure, but I felt about my Jewishness the way you might feel about being left-handed. To those who knew me, I was a white American. To those who didn't and saw me in a suit, I lived somewhere in the spectrum of well-situated tan. But for tonight, I belonged to the Jews by dint of ancient nationality.

I didn't know who had invited the orthodox rabbis to Sama, but I sure as hell was going to go. Not out of Jewishness, and not for the religious community that wasn't mine, but because—sweet Mary and Joseph!—we were going to have a real Hanukkah shindig high above the mosques, and down sweet Manischewitz above the teetotaling deserts.

Rabbi Shuki and Rabbi Yisrael led the blessings, touching the *shamas* to five candles, now burning brightly with the green light from the minarets below. It was the fifth night of Hanukkah, nicknamed "the darkest night" for falling every year on the new moon. Although the lunisolar Hebrew calendar prevents it from ever falling on the Sabbath, the week's most holy day, the fifth night is distinctly holy. The rabbis resolved the paradox: clearly, this day must need no help to get holier.

We all reflected in the polished tile under florescent lights. All around us, we perceived Gentile expatriatism and an image of Islam in low resolution. I felt the contrast not as a mark of oppression, but one of distinction: what made us run-of-the-mill deli patrons in New York now made us bakers of homemade bagels and fasters at unpredictable seasons. We were *Jews*! And with shared distinction comes a kind of solidarity, a kind of fort-like refuge. I didn't want to build a moat—however much we welcomed one another in, I feared keeping the outside out. But with blessed juices flowing, chocolate coins clinking against the tile floor, and kids screaming at their dreidels, I slipped into the comfort of familiar things. For a moment, the impulse to *Do something!* quieted. The wandering urge slowed, and I began to feel attached.

It was a more Jewish gathering than I'd ever gone to in Pennsylvania, where we did lip service to the high holidays and moved quickly on to the wine. This was my great-grandfather's territory, where Soviet identity cards considered "Jew" a nationality; for me, it was like I had come home to a home I'd never known.

I don't always look "white" but I check it on boxes. And within the standard boxes, Jewishness conflates concepts of ethnicity (call it race) and religion, and even nationality in the straightforward sense; to the unfamiliar, "Jewish" and "Israeli" often substitute for each other (*When did your family come from Israel?*)—though none of the people who made me had ever lived there. But to tangle it all more, I had family in Israel *now*, and I felt close to them.

My identity, the part of it that defined me as *different* from the most accepted of mainstreams—male and white and connected and upwardly mobile—was a murky one. I couldn't even tell if it *was* murky, if it made me different or if it just reinforced my sameness with The-Way-Things-Are.

Jewishness was the single thing about my biography, my heritage, that I was most aware was most objectively different. And I accepted that distance most readily, I think, because it was the thing that allowed me to make some variety of joke at the expense of (us) outsiders. And in that permission to mock one minority, the "inside" gave me its blessing: to identify as "out" and to also *be* "in." (Cake: had, eaten.) And yet, to the degree that my outsider status had ever been felt—it had been felt most in memory.

In the suburbs of Philadelphia, in New York, I was not forced outside for that thing that made me different. Those memories were older: my grandfather threatened in a Pennsylvania coal mining town for being of the tribe that killed Jesus. That was what I remembered, though I'd never seen it: him running.

My difference was not in what I had chosen to be, but in what I inherited. It meant my identity, as a thing that distinguished me from others, depended on a life older than mine. And in that way, lightly, I felt very old.

AS WITH ANY JEWISH GATHERING—there were these bits of back of back and forth, of bargaining. Existential questions writ tiny, little requests standing in for something giant.

"Have you ever put on tefillin before?" Rabbi Shuki asked. I waffled—I couldn't remember what that was exactly. He explained: tefillin are boxes containing bits of scripture that very observant Jews may wear on the arm and head during morning prayers, known also as "phylacteries." It sounded like a kind of nosy dinosaur you'd meet at the pharmacy. I wasn't sold.

"Uhh, I don't think so. I was never bar mitzvahed." Sheepish, I told him how my parents had offered me the choice when I was seven or eight to go to Hebrew School and prepare for a bar mitzvah. It wasn't a big deal to them and, seeing my Jewish friends complaining and missing hours of playtime on Wednesdays and Sundays, it wasn't a big deal to me either—hell, we didn't even get an afterlife out of the whole thing. It had always just seemed like a bad investment.

"Come join us tomorrow morning—it will be your bar mitzvah."

It was all so fast. These were the guys I'd always given a berth wider than earshot on the Columbia campus or on subway platforms for fear of joining a Jewish cult or missing *The Office*. But in Abu Dhabi, I felt I could listen.

I had always defined my Judaism with terms of exclusion: I'm Jewish *but, though, not, I don't*. . . . It was easier that way, to reject the uncertain territory I had never trod, and to have an excuse ready for my inaction or ignorance. The rabbis asked me to forfeit one of my most prime excuses.

"I . . . I have to be at work tomorrow," I explained.

"We'll do it beforehand—plus, isn't that your boss?" The provost was sipping Manischewitz by the window.

Could I really change my identity as an unbar-mitzvahed Jew *that* quickly? So efficient and convenient to my work schedule? Wasn't religion supposed to be difficult?

But it wasn't really religion. For me, it was a tradition all its own, with roots in a place I recognized but didn't know. This was some descendant of a rite that someone with my nose might have performed five millennia ago—not in words, not even in faith, but in some kindred sense of conviction.

And Yisrael then, perhaps unknowingly, made the perfect appeal to the absurd. "Where else," said Yisrael, "if not in Abu Dhabi?"

Touché, rabbi.

I might have seen the lights atop the minaret wink.

The next morning, already late for work at 9:30, I ascended to the apartment the rabbis had been given for the night. Shuki answered the door, welcoming me in to an apartment strewn with tchotchkes no longer common on the Arabian Peninsula.

Yisrael handed me a skullcap. He lifted the tefillin and wrapped the leather strap of the *shel rosh* around my forehead, the *shel yad* round and round my left arm, down to my palm and several times around my middle finger. Each held a box filled with unknown words—one pressed against the head, the other wedged against the heart.

I held a page-long prayer, written in English. "God understands all languages," said Shuki.

I never mentioned that I wasn't very sure there was anyone there to do the understanding. I started reading.

Sacrilege! I imagined the whispers of the orthodox turning sour. But Yisrael and Shuki smiled at me as I read, and they were staunch defenders of the orthodoxy. Still, I feared the unknown others who would have found me an immensely unsuitable candidate for this procedure.

By the book, though, I was already *a* bar mitzvah. A Jewish boy automatically becomes a "son of the commandment," rite or no, at the moment of his thirteenth birthday. But to *be* bar mitzvahed is something else. To partake in the ceremony is to accept the responsibilities of adulthood, to make a sanctified promise to follow new rules.

I wouldn't make the promises—not by the standard rule book at least—but I could try to make good on small resolutions. Fear would no longer excuse a lack of action or the lazy comfort of simple assumptions. Like Paul: "When I became a man, I put the ways of childhood behind me." If I've become a man, I said, accepting the celebratory Mekupelet chocolates Yisrael brought from Israel, I'll try to do the same.

Looking out at decades of Islamic architecture and a cityscape adorned with mosque domes and enormous pictures of the founding sheikhs, I performed the Jewish liturgical version of a Las Vegas wedding. Boxes properly wedged, I read words I'd forgotten from a laminated card. For those who put on tefillin every day, it is a continuous affirmation of their beliefs, of their devotion. For me, one time only, I rode this *mitzvah* on the express train to manhood, eight years late by traditional custom and only an hour late for work.

—

THAT WEEKEND, DOWN THE Corniche road past the new skycrapers sprouting like okra stalks, I stood with my back to the plastic bristles of the diamond-draped Christmas tree, the most expensive ever known, and lifted my trumpet to play carols under the golden dome of the $3 billion Emirates Palace Hotel.

"Happy Hanukkah!" I shouted to the pools of English children, and the unfazed Emiratis on their way across the marble.

The principal trumpet in the United Arab Emirates Philharmonic Orchestra was half-grinning. "Shhh!"

"No one minds," I said. And it was probably true. There we were, in our own little Western bubble, with our tinkly music refracting off the Swarovski chandeliers. Many thousands of dollars each around a fourteen-dollar lightbulb (my estimate), they glittered high into the cupola, from whence echoes of "O Come All Ye Faithful" rebounded through jangly acoustics.

My eyes leaped like a baby's to all the shiny things.

This was all a pregame, featuring the children's brass band from the British School, before, in the waning hours of a lesser Jewish holiday, the now-bankrupt Philharmonic that bore the name of its officially Muslim host country played its annual Christmas concert. Past the portraits of the sheikhs, beyond the gold-plated vending machine for gold coins and bars, through the colonnade of petrified palm trees, the auditorium had seats permanently marked "Reserved" for *His Highness* and *Her Excellency* and other members of the Royal Family, but they weren't coming today. Today, the theater was open to the homesick.

This is the land of the indoor ski mountain, of the tallest building in the world, of the billionaire's name HAMAD carved so large into the flesh of a private island that it can be seen from space. This is the home of perfect winters and oil-cooled summers, of cars, and cars, and cars. This is a place where we could ask for nearly anything we could imagine—and it would be delivered, as if by magic, like a rabbi in a hat.

—

THE GATHERINGS ALWAYS DISSOLVED. I could only touch noses—an Emirati greeting—with these faint hints of community.

It felt like something to communicate in Arabic with the Egyptian security guards, but it still was what it was: superficial small talk between employees of a building and a resident.

Instead of giving me clear windows into the greater Middle East, Abu Dhabi gave me playdates with alter egos. I could cast myself as a traveling businessman, or a crawler of seedy bars, or a new man entirely. But I didn't feel like much of a man lounging in constant detachment, watching the clock tick at the top of an Excel sheet.

And then, two weeks after my bar mitzvah, Mohamed Bouazizi set himself on fire in central Tunisia, and the world began to watch itself shift.

The *Arab Spring*, I learned to call it. But it was still winter then: electricity. Bashful excitement—what were we allowed to feel?

The next month, restaurant-owner Abdou Abdel-Moneim Hamada Jaafar Khalifa self-immolated in the heart of Cairo. Now the Egyptians were talking of true things.

"Eh rayik 'an thawratna?" *What do you think about our revolution?* Ahmed the Egyptian security guard swelled behind the desk at the back entrance of Sama Tower.

"Freedom is beautiful."

"Yes!"

In those days, they were all beaming. The Egyptian contingent of our security force, almost all supporting family back home, were then quite open champions of the overthrow of Mubarak's autocracy. Supporters of the regime, dejected, made themselves less visible. Engulfed in the politics of the Arabian Peninsula, our American institution made very evident its support for nonviolent protestors, democratic ideals, and the fights of all Middle Eastern countries against their respective "The Man."

Over the next year, idealism would be complicated by reality. Now we were all jittery with hope. Everything was up for grabs again, as ministers resigned, governments disbanded. Men doused themselves in gasoline and put fire to their own skin. For the rootless, this seemed to indicate the kind of chaos from which ashes bring only rebirth.

But aside from the tenuous interpersonal links to the region's groundswell, the UAE barricaded us in an air-conditioned bubble— a piece apart from the line of dictatorial dominos that wobbled in the weeks after Tunisia. Normal carried on. More curry from Canopy. More four-dollar bottles of dark Old Monk rum imported from Uttar Pradesh.

When I felt an electrical current in my veins, I had nothing to plug myself into. *Protest* once meant, for Romans, to "assert publicly." But here, the most disenfranchised were voiceless resident laborers, not citizens. How could anyone *assert publicly* in the UAE, when those with the most reason to assert were hardly members of the public?

In untouchable Saudi Arabia no less: a Day of Rage. It looked like the region really could be reborn of flame. Everything would be shaken with such force that something completely new would take shape from whatever was left. With my feet so lightly on the surface of this place, the vast possibility of re-creation took up all the room in my head. I had never truly known the roots of this region, and now under this smoke they were even harder to see, especially from the air-conditioned pseudoclimate of the UAE.

We were inches away from the action. The proximity to that heat made the Emirates feel especially chilled. *Do something.*

Sometimes even when I didn't want shawarma, I found myself half-running to Foodlands, to talk with Ali, whose hometown of Daraa was now known worldwide as ground zero of the Syrian revolution.

"Adam! *Kifak* Adam?"

"Ali!"

It was all the same. Same pickles, same spicy sauce, same toothy grin.

"What's up. How's your mother, how's your father?"

"*Alhamdulilah.* How's *your* family?"

"*Alhamdulilah.*"

In the same breath he'd mention some dark effect of the war and then wave it away. His family huddled indoors some nights. It was unsafe to go out after eight, or seven, or six, *but it was okay*! For me, the world of that fledgling violence was covered in a sandstorm of news coverage and Ali's smile.

For a year, my anxiety was tied to the angle of the corners of his mouth above his chin. If it dropped below about sixty degrees, I'd be forced to stomach a brutal truth. Until then, caught between Chicken Little reporting and Ali's unshakable cheer, I knew that I really knew nothing.

I had come here to the Middle East to face the fears about this swath of the world that I'd absorbed in 2001. If it was all in flux now, wasn't it the perfect time? Everything about the implosion of the region told me that *now* was when I could connect to it.

IT WAS HARD TO KNOW where to start. Friends from the Arabic program in Oakland began to communicate their movements all around the region: a friend was evacuated on the last government-arranged plane out of Egypt; another learned which squares to begin avoiding in Bahrain.

Masha came to the UAE when I was itching with comfort. Before starting law school in the fall, she would work for two months in Abu Dhabi taking care of the children of high-profile professors. They had commanded a bright, young, American nanny, and she had been delivered.

Every day I was ecstatic to come home to her, and every day I felt an urge to leave the UAE like a twitch in the neck. Movement or constancy— I could reconcile that tension for short stretches by being in motion with her, by racing over to the fish market behind the docks where the old wooden dhows still go out to cast nets every dawn, or celebrating my birthday on an island the UAE's founding father turned into a free-range zoo, now home to cheetahs and gazelles and luxury resorts.

I distracted my revolutionary urges with luxury, and defended those distractions with the rationalization that getting settled was a sign of maturity. I couldn't tell which side of me was the devil's advocate anymore.

I plopped back down on Dan and Jordan's couch, eleven steps from my door to this place made holy by the presence of pure grace. Only here, and at the source behind Mariah Mall, and on *my* couch—or any-one's couch, really—could I partake in the sacrament of my one true faith. Canopy.

Again.

It was in a moment saturated in the vapors of chicken vindaloo that we made a tripartite commitment to break the cycle—me, Dan the film-maker, and Jake the poet: a Benz.

With one exciting change, I could have the freedom a car affords, all while reconnecting to my adoptive nation. Movement and stability.

An old Mercedes is to the highways of the Gulf what a rented *vélo* is to a Paris bike lane, or what an escalator is to a mall. Driving cars is more Emirati than air-conditioning, and Mercedes, especially the old ones, are the staple of a simpler era with smaller buildings and bigger aviator sunglasses. In the Arab world, models and shapes of the cars have nicknames: late nineties' C Class were *Abu Dama'a*, "Father Tears," for their big headlights; S Class were *Abu Ayun*, "Father Eyes," for a similar look. The '92 model we found on Dubizzle—the UAE's Craigslist—was called, simply, *Shabah*. "Ghost."

"It's only 2000$ and its in amazing condition," Dan wrote in an e-mail to two friends and his mother. "Fit for Sadam Hussein."

The dark gray, nearly black sedan had boxy wide hips and drove like a boat. The sunroof was broken and mirrors were missing and the locks didn't work and the radio mysteriously operated only at frequen-cies between AM and FM, but the tape deck worked, the mechanic told us, and let us keep the single greatest Michael Jackson cassette ever mixed. From then on, that was the only thing we listened to onboard, in the jammed driver's seat set permanently to slouch.

With our aviators down and arms out the windows, this was in the family of things that were clearly too good to be true. Behind the wheel of the black behemoth, I didn't quite feel like I was in my own life, just like Abu Dhabi couldn't feel like home or like the Persian Gulf doesn't feel like an ocean. I was borrowing moments from someone else's day-to-day and from my own fantasy.

The all-black leather was a debatable choice with indoor parking a luxury and summer temperatures rising to 120 degrees in the shade of nonexistent trees. But it was February. And at the helm of *Black Chicory*—one of her many nicknames, this one pulled from the coffee Dan had carried in from New Orleans—those problems rooted in "reality" seemed pleasantly far away.

IT WAS A TRICKY BALANCE—this stillness and motion thing. Detached and reattached, clinging both to autonomy and the need to connect, I darted around the cage of the island.

Masha's job quickly became more demanding than mine. When she was too busy nannying, I played tug-of-war with myself: time with her, or time outside Sama Tower. Cheap tickets popped up to Sri Lanka, and I couldn't hold out. It seemed to make sense: I didn't know where to go in the Arabaphone world now, but I needed to go somewhere. Jake and I flew away for five days—leaving behind my girlfriend who had come to the desert to be with me—and we rampaged around the island until I ran our rental car into a ditch and it was time to come home. Where else could I run?

Back in Sama with the Benz keys on the table, Masha and I planned a trip to the eastern emirate of Fujairah. That is to say, I borrowed a tent from Angela the executive assistant, and we picked a weekend. Buddy Guy has a song about a Mercedes, as if he planned our trip in blues lyrics: *Gonna keep on driving, I'll never stop / My baby's riding in the shotgun seat / Don't let no grass grow under our feet.*

A cross-country trip in the United Arab Emirates is never very difficult. From Abu Dhabi southwest to the Saudi Arabian border, it takes no longer than four hours. It is no greater distance from the city's warm insulated nook in the Persian Gulf to the eastern side of the Emirati promontory, where waters are cleared and cooled by the Arabian Sea at the top-left corner of the Indian Ocean. Roads are wide, fast, straight— I could make no more than four turns and be through the low mountains to Fujairah, supine by the sea with a snorkel and a bottle of rum. It would be so easy.

Although a '92 Benz won't be the fastest in any Emirati fleet, it was easy to go the 120 kilometer-per-hour speed limit without trouble—

conspicuous radar detectors issue instant two-hundred-dollar fines at 140—but it wasn't good enough. On the high seas of the Sheikh Zayed Highway, we chose lanes like Goldilocks with mortal stakes: In the right lane, trucks inched along out of everyone's way; in the center, traffic moved too slowly; on the left, we were prey to the white Land Cruisers racing past. A favorite local driving technique is to charge from behind, day or night, high beams flashing: *Give me passage or give me death.* A red pickup engine roared at our bumper and I wrenched the wheel to the right—no time to check the neighboring lane. A moment of suspended panic. The pickup heaved unfazed around us into the left shoulder.

After only an hour, Black Chicory was wheezing. She would reach a top speed and then jerk slower. Michael Jackson sounded seasick in the tape deck. The ship had become a tired horse—in short bursts with my coaxing she stayed speedy, but only for moments. We pulled into a highway gas station and turned off the engine. The battery died.

One jump start later, we were soon on the Dubai-Hatta Road, following signs for EASTERN REGIONS, and heading deadly straight toward the Fujairah coast. The wheezing seemed to have abated, and golden sand dunes sprung up along the roadside, red-orange from behind my sunglasses. "Whoa," Masha and I said a lot. My god, the desert is pretty.

That's about when I smashed into the back of another car.

An excuse: the Eastern Regions have a bizarre and thoughtless proclivity for speed bumps. Often unmarked, yellow paint chipped until the lump in the road is indistinguishable from faded asphalt, speed bumps can attack anywhere: just before a roundabout, in a parking lot, between two other speed bumps only tens of meters away, before a traffic light, after a traffic light, in nightmares. This one was in the middle of the highway, half a minute from a confident sign: SPEED LIMIT: 100. No warning, no more signage: just the impending figures of two SUVs parked in the road's only two lanes. The drivers were chatting, resting their tires on the hump. It takes the eyes far too long to realize they are moving *toward* something they were only just moving *with*. When mine did, they sent my brain a brief telegram: *Oh shit. STOP.*

Before I could fear, my brain was alight with optimism. It processed everything by reflex and compared what it saw with what it knew. *We have enough space and time*, it said, *and if we hit the brakes now ... wait ... why isn't the car slowing down?* No more optimism. Confusion. The car—it was still going too fast, hurtling toward a blue jeep growing larger.

I cursed the brakes for failing, and I accepted that it might have been my fault for not checking them sufficiently when we bought the car. I felt the surge of approaching danger, and its terror.

I had time to think about almost everything I had ever thought before. *It could have been the battery failing, no? It seemed like something our saintly Syrian seller had known about. It was at least partly his fault, wasn't it? Am I hungry? I'm hungry. If I die ... Jesus, my parents are going to be really upset. What day is today? At least we're in a Mercedes. How far is it from 116th Street to Sammy's Halal? We shouldn't've gotten an old Mercedes. If Masha gets hurt ... the loss. The loss. The guilt. Is she scared? I can't swerve left: a concrete divider catching sand blown across from the desert. I can't go right: people. This might actually hurt. Do things like this hurt first or only after? The car is new—to us, at least! What will Dan and Jake and Jordan say when I tell them I wrecked our car? I'm secretly proud that I can play decent ping-pong left-handed. What town are we in? Why on earth are these cars stopped in the center of the highway? Why? What luck. This really might ruin the weekend.*

IF THERE WAS A MOMENT of impact, I don't remember it. I felt the nineteen-year-old airbags flush against my face, the weave of fine burlap.

Relief. I hadn't killed my girlfriend.

On long stretches of empty highway manned only with trigger-happy radar cameras, human assistance is sometimes hard to find. But with some luck, we were totaled near the police station, and an ambulance just happened to be passing through town.

The hood had crumpled like an old soda can on the beach. Smells of burned wiring and smoking metal, pebbles of glass across the road.

The officers all wore bemused faces, and never stopped pulling me in and out of the ambulance to look for important pieces of paper in the car. Still, they were kind. The locals we had hit—unscathed, both people and truck—peeked in; I wasn't sure whether to yell at them or apologize. I just shook their hands with my unbruised arm.

But as I was hopping back out of the ambulance again, I had the space to see something I might not have had the medics coddled me. Outside the glass and smoke: I was entirely fine. A young man doesn't need any extra help to feel invincible, but, if only as the gift of German engineering, I got some. The ditch in Sri Lanka and now this—it was like danger didn't exist, like there would never be a reaction to anything I did. Invincible, but disconnected. Ghostly.

This was the southern tip of the most conservative emirate, Sharjah, dead center on the UAE triangle in a town called Madam. *Madam, I'm Adam*, I never said to anyone, to my eternal regret. The ambulance took us on an hour-long drive in the same direction we had headed ourselves, off-road for moments on rough gravel (despite their worries that we might have spinal injuries), bringing us nearer to the beaches that seemed to get farther and farther away with every kilometer we drove toward them. "*Weyn al-mustashfa?*" I heard the driver call out to our friendly Filipino EMT. *Where is the hospital?*

We passed through Madam's nearest hospital like an afterthought, in and out without a scrap of paperwork.

As the sun set, we went to find the police, and to take camping gear and granola bars from the shipwreck in the eerie auto graveyard in Madam. "How much?" an officer asked, eying the car. He shook his head when I told him. I hadn't understood: "How much does it cost *now*?"

This was the UAE. If you have something, someone wants it. If you want to buy something, someone somewhere wants to sell it. If someone somewhere is buying something, *wallah! I swear*, you should be buying it, too. These officers, guardians of the town and its ungodly speed bump, saw deals dropped in their lot every day. With a scrap shop just across the street, there were always deals to be struck.

Old officers advised rookies, a towering Sudanese sergeant scolded an underling; I took three policemen for walks around the car. A lot of *hmmm* and *uh-huh*. I came back days later for a similar hustle until representatives who spoke in Malayalam—a language my friend Iman had compared to the sounds of falling water—came from the scrap shop, made a final offer for Black Chicory's remains, and set in motion a bureaucratic nightmare that would last three months.

The deeper I got in the process to transfer the Benz title to the scrappers, the more I felt the tethers to my host country loosen. I'd like to think that no matter what, I would have challenged my mother's fears and investigated the rumors and reputations of the world outside the Great Carrot. But I could put my finger on it then, how directly the car had helped me feel both connected and free, comfortable and flexible. How it had given me a treadmill—albeit a long one—that could have run out my energy forever. I could have slaked my restlessness with small and frequent steps. But now, momentum choked, restlessness hit me with its full force.

Either I really was too weak to pull myself from luxury, or I was capable of risking *more* than everything. Not just my life, but a life I would have died to save.

I felt the discomfort of grass growing again underfoot. It was a discomfort Masha didn't feel, shotgunning along on what was all much more like a vacation to her. So long as we weren't being carted to an emergency room she was always happy where we were. I needed to push.

Under a veil, I was bugged that she wasn't more jittery. (Jealous, maybe, that she didn't live with the tug-of-war?) I knew she wanted to understand me, but I saw a tiny tear between us, in part because I knew it was wrong to pull her into my recklessness, and I knew what made me *feel alive* wasn't going to change. The other part was physics: if one thing moves and another stays, they don't end up in the same place.

IT WAS THURSDAY and we were late for the beach. They rent cars in Dubai all night long, and so we backtracked. Fujairah, said the man handing me keys, was only two hours away. I didn't tell him what I'd just done.

Masha and I made camp on the brittle coastline by the sand south of Dibba. I produced a stubby bottle of Old Monk rum. In the morning, there were warm waves at our feet and jellyfish in the sea.

FROM: MASHA ‹MASHA.••••••@•••••.COM›
RE: (NO SUBJECT)
SAT AT 5:48 AM

*I want to know you better, I want to get inside your head
and see the way you think so i can understand what your
silence means, what your faces mean, what everything
about you means.*

THE WESTERN PERCEPTION OF ISLAM DEPARTMENT

———

WHEN MASHA WENT BACK to the United States, the icy tower felt colder. I leaped at every chance to get out. This time, it was my job that gave me a little fix. It was a confuddling job whenever I tried to explain it to friends back home, but I could say something clear this week: I was the twenty-two-year-old "trip leader" to Kuwait for twenty university students. My job was to shuttle everyone along, and to keep things safe.

"Woo! Spring break Kuwait!" I joked. That time last year, I'd been permanently drunk on my own spring break in Nicaragua. Now, I was "in charge."

With eight thousand dollars wrapped in a paper envelope and tucked away in my backpack, I packed onto a bus for the Dubai Airport. Terminal 2 is detached from the main concourse, where mostly budget flights leave daily for the home countries of those who have escaped their home countries. Kuwait isn't one of those places. We were on a kind of educational trip up and over the revolutions in Bahrain where students had been forbidden to go, to find things like cultural insight.

We launched out of Dubai and left The World Islands behind. In less time than it took to drive from Abu Dhabi to Dubai, we were descending over a stretch of barren, oil-caked desert—a sandbox sprouting spiny TV antennae from last century.

FOLLOWING THE USUAL gravitational forces of tourism in most major Gulf cities, our first destination was the Grand Mosque. Our tour guide was a short man with a long beard in thick black-rimmed glasses who spoke bits and larger bits of a million languages and answered his phone with, "I hope it's not my wife!" He knew just how to make us laugh.

He handed me his card: "Khalil. GRAND MOSQUE: western perception of islam dept."

I blinked. I read it again.

Gulf countries appear, for the most part, to include young and successful parvenus who don't seem to need your help or give half a damn what you think, but it isn't so. In Kuwait especially, where George Bush the First finds his framed place among family photos, allies are more precious than gold, and blood runs thicker than oil.

Perceptions are monitored and framed in a manner made possible by Kuwait's particular circumstances: small population, strong governmental oversight, little economic disparity among citizens, a high percentage of foreign workers, money. Religiosity runs high, too, especially here at the mosque—coupled, apparently, with a deep interest in my home.

In the late 1980s as the Grand Mosque construction was completed, Kuwait played the role of principal financier for the first-ever construction of a mosque in New York. The Kuwaiti emir laid the cornerstone of that glass and granite place I knew on 96th Street as the home of the Islamic Cultural Center.

Khalil guided our group into the subdued prayer hall, floored in blue carpet with room for ten thousand men. There is space for about a thousand women in an adjoining hall. Khalil pointed to the dome 141 feet high, marked with the ninety-nine names for God. His phone rang.

"I hope it's not my wife!"

At the end of Khalil's tour, I turned over the back of a tissue box to find a list of "Projects of the Grand Mosque." Number one, in Arabic: "Fatwa phone service, direct dial '149.'" Number one, in English: "Providing a fatwa (consultation) service." A fatwa is literally an "opinion"; more specifically, it is a decision made on a point of law by a mufti, a legal expert who interprets Sharia law.

It was important that we Anglophones knew the fatwa process was a consultation, even if we weren't involved. It was important that we understood how Islam functioned, and not just what the buildings looked like. Khalil's office is now the Western Perception of Islam Center. On wp-islam.com, their mission is very clear: "The WPIC primary goal is to emerge as a renowned and reputable center, recognized in the West as a trusted source of information."

Recognized in the West.

The approval of the "others" was paramount. *They* cared about *our* opinion? This was high school again: life and death dramas begat by *what to wear.* Another's gaze is a powerful thing . . . I see you conscious of me, and I grow more self-conscious. Talking, I make and break and remake eye contact—don't we all?—because most other people's eyes are deep enough to lose yourself in, if you're willing.

It was nice to know the Grand Mufti of Kuwait was thinking about me, too. It was nice to see the proof in brick and mortar—or reinforced marble and concrete with teakwood doors. It was comforting to realize my Winter Semiformal date was as worried about what she was wearing as I was, and that our mutual fear of rejection took root in a much deeper similarity.

As Americans, we've enjoyed the comfort of confidence on a global scale, since the Marshall Plan maybe, or since Benjamin Franklin went to France and found that "every body presented me their ladies." We're loved everywhere we care about, or we're hated by the reprobates of the world. We've thrived by responding to our every rejection with rage or silence. We are never unknown, and we have no need for nuance, and we'll never say "sorry" on the playground.

We're not afraid of making fun of anyone—or, something even more deadly as a grade school tactic: pretending they don't exist.

But if I was leaving behind childish things, dismissal wasn't a legitimate coping mechanism anymore. The whole point of coming here was to find an alternative to the way I saw this other place—an alternative to easy dismissal or intentional ignorance, so often those face-saving masks for fear.

I was no longer just looking. It was as if I had been watching the world sleep and it opened its eyes to catch me. There was no ignoring this simple thing anymore: when I looked into new eyes, those eyes were looking back, too.

Something was collapsing. My whole life I had liked believing that the easiest way to find truth was to be entirely trusting, and so I was unskeptical. I couldn't sustain that anymore: We were all deciding how to perform. None of my interactions could be fully trusted anymore.

That's growing up, or so they say. "Trusting" is a nice euphemism for naive, which is a nice euphemism for stupid.

One more young person's transition: even my methods for seeking certainty were suspect.

The traditional authorities I looked to were on trial, too, and there was no one left to turn to but the road. All this was disorienting, and unavoidable. As my understanding of new people slipped, I became blurrier in my own head. Who was I really if I didn't know who I was to other people? I could only bounce myself against these blank Others, hoping to identify myself by discovering the way they saw me.

I could understand why a Muslim's perception of the Western perception of Muslims could be so important. I felt how deeply I wanted to understand their perception of me. As the West Indian French psychoanalyst Frantz Fanon wrote in *Black Skin, White Masks*: "I appealed to the Other so that his liberating gaze, gliding over my body suddenly smoothed of rough edges, would give me back the lightness of being I thought I had lost, and taking me out of the world put me back in the world."

At the Western Perception of Islam Center, I looked at Khalil looking at me looking at Kuwait looking at Westerners looking at Islam, and then I imagined how Islam saw the West and America and Jewishness and whiteness and Judaism—and then all that came back to filter into my gaze toward Islam, and Khalil would see all that in my eyes, and I would see all *that* in his.

I would dive as far as I could toward truth, and then I would hold it in my head and trust Khalil to see through me. And then, the final trick: If I knew what he knew, I had control again—as if I were both actor and playwright. I could build something stable from that vantage.

Khalil's business card was like an invitation to playact together.

KUWAIT WAS SUPERFICIAL, and Kuwait was mysterious. Kuwaitis said, *Four days only?!* Back in Abu Dhabi they gasped, *Four whole days?!*

The difference, it seemed, was whether you wanted to take the place at face value—intercontinental buffets and liquorless bars—or whether you wanted to study the faces you saw. Theatergoer or theater critic.

It was an unexpected place, and for four days I flitted about, ignorant of what was there for its own sake, and what was there to please the visitors. We stopped at the modern art museum, and the headquarters of the Kuwaiti Oil Company. We took the day-tripper's ferry to Failaka Island forty-minutes offshore, swarming with jet skis and pockmarked by Iraqi refuse from the First Gulf War. Behind a chain-link fence: a graveyard of hellish, rusty Russian trucks and tanks and howitzers. There are Greek ruins, too, but they were off-limits; there were active digs but no one digging, and I never knew if the gates were locked with apathy or overprotection. We passed bullet holes and angry graffiti on the road by the Baskin-Robbins.

Kuwait's Eiffel Tower is not the National Museum (designed by a Frenchman), but a functional landmark (designed by a Dane). Every year (or decade, as necessary), *Lonely Planet* and *Explorer* choose images for their guidebooks' covers, seeking ones that are both representative and alluring: Pakistan boasts majestic, snow-topped mountains; Saudi Arabia fronts the angular domes of Medina's Quba Mosque. Kuwait's good side, in the eyes of both publishers, is the two giant balls of the thirty-two-year-old Kuwait Towers. Both balls are filled with water; the tallest, which reaches 187 meters at the top, also has a restaurant. That's where we ate on our first night, savoring the most *authentic* and traditional Gulfi fare: the intercontinental buffet.

When we seek authentic, we seek something of single origins, as if

anything symbolic of ours will ever have one lineage after hundreds of millennia as a species. But what makes the Khalij *Khaliji*, the Gulf "Gulfi," is that particular adoption of damn near everything, of all lineages, with histories old and young and who-the-hell-cares.

We ascended to Ofok Restaurant. The name is Arabic for "horizons," and is pronounced just like you stubbed your toe really, really hard.

In the evening south of Kuwait City, we drove to the home of astronomer Adel Hassan Al-Saadoun, known as the Al-Fintas Astronomical Observatory, also known as Aladdin House. The manor is half Arabian archways and gardens, half American southwest stone facade, half Ukrainian bud domes, and every inch a collector's fantasyland. He said that he conceived of the design in his dreams.

Every wall drips with *things*, wrapping around the house and spilling onto the floor. Walls of model cars, cologne bottles, paintings, antique Coke bottles, pictures of the Bushes. One room has a miniature, operational model coal factory; next door among audio trinkets is an original Edison gold-mounted wax cylinder from 1904. The song: "Where Did Robinson Crusoe Go with Friday on Saturday Night?"

It was Friday night—the first weekend night here, the Middle East's Saturday—and I tried to think of quips about our easy survival on Kuwait's desert island. I got nowhere, maybe because I had already short-circuited from silliness: I wandered here as the tour guide to places I'd never been, as the recipient of questions I asked myself, choosing a route for two dozen young people when I had no idea where I wanted to be.

I also had no idea what the students thought of it all. They might have assumed, being good students, that I had led them here with a clear purpose. They might have whirred around Kuwait City and felt *This is Kuwait!* and been happy.

But my questions weren't answered here, and the need for movement was swelling again. With my head elsewhere, it took great attention to my attention to keep the group on track.

Later, I would leave the eight thousand dollars in my bag at an outdoor Egyptian restaurant in a central square. The Egyptians were holding it for me when I got back, and we took grinning photos together. I might have learned something about responsibility or consequences or something, but I didn't. I just wanted to get moving.

The astronomer was an insatiable traveler, too. He looked at stars and at human progress and sought something else always, some other border to cross. Every year, he says, he tries to travel to a new country. I asked him about this year's target. "North Korea," he said. "Two weeks."

GO FOR IT!
DON'T DO IT! JUMP!

———

M Y JOB BEGAN TO ask less and less of me, and in the spaces it left, I had nothing but time to reflect, reflect, reflect. I had been in the Emirates for eight months now, watching my itch to escape manifest in spastic jaunts, and seeing the way those trips showed what didn't work far more than what would. Like the astronomer, I asked for newness for the sake of newness.

I remembered a paper fixed above my grandmother's computer when I was a boy, something she'd transcribed from a dream. It said:

DO SOMETHING. DO SOMETHING! DO SOMETHING!

I can still picture the way it was taped, and the color of her computer desk. At ninety-seven, she still feels it. *DO SOMETHING!* But what?

As a college grad entering the world, I sneaked things-I-still-remembered-from-school into conversations. My absolute favorite cocktail tidbit went like this: the prehistoric Lapita people had a habit of setting out into the empty ocean, looking for new islands to settle. If they found one, great. If not, they harnessed the eternally westward tradewinds and sailed home.

Home, outward, home, outward, home. It was the second-born and their younger siblings who explored; eldest sons got the homestead, and were content to rule their tropical tracts. It had always resonated: I was a second son of a second son of a second son of a second son. Maybe we'd always been itchy.

Four months earlier, my first trip away from the hub was to Oman. It was a blank place to me, and a rare one in this part of the world where countries' reputations generally precede them. When I was downing Canopy or seven beers deep at PJ O'Reilly's Irish Pub in Le Royal Méridien hotel, I thought often about Oman. I didn't feel empty-handed when I'd come home. What was it I'd loved so much?

TO THE SOUND OF the afternoon call to prayer, we set off in our rented Nissan toward Oman. Just like the Lapita: off the island eastward.

For Gaar, Rachel and me, Oman had all the draws of a good road trip: it was reachable by car, and everyone said it was fantastic. (If everyone had said it was an unrepentant hellhole, I'd've been equally committed.)

Gaar was my only "program coordinator" co-hiree, brought to do administrative anythings, and Rachel was more like a teaching assistant in the army of fresh alums who substituted for the lack of upperclassmen in the month-old university. Rachel was an NYU grad from a Philadelphia mainline suburb down the street from my Quaker school. Gaar was her classmate, and a trained figure skater from a town of about three thousand in Wisconsin. For all of us, Abu Dhabi had replaced New York as "home."

Our car of three sped away from the eyes of city-center radars, toward the oasis city of Al Ain, where we aimed to cross the border. At the edge of the greenery, I found myself having trouble finding the biggest thing I'd ever looked for—we knew it was there, the three million people doing three million things—but according to the road signs, the entire country was missing.

Gaar asked a shop owner in Arabic where we could find Oman, and I listened as he gave us directions that were clear, and invited us to the dead-end from which we'd just retreated. I tried to clarify.

And in that moment, he said something that I'd heard so many times before gently and in surprise, this time curt and with disdain: "Do you speak Arabic?"

I had never had a relationship that was purely based on Arabic. Masha and I made our initial sorties in its three-letter roots, but we had our East Coast biographies to soften the blows. Even Arabs I'd met and known only through Arabic had understood that it was a foreign language for me, taking my words at more (or less) than face value, and giving me more credit than I pronounced. But here I was assumed to be an Arabophone. The jab echoed the caustic "Do you speak English?" that you might hear after failing again and again to listen to instructions. The assumption: *of course you do, fluently, but you're too dumb to listen*. In his assumptions, the shopkeeper was—in a way so rare and re-encouraging—a total shit.

We were lost within seconds. An alternative route to the border appeared: a sand-blown carriageway known only as "Truck Road." As darkness fell, we hurried toward Oman both with and against the stampede of enormous semis carrying livestock and god-knows-what, slowing only for camel crossings as farmers returned from the plains. Squinting through the headlights and the froth of sand blotting them out, Gaar might have convinced me we were in a Wisconsin blizzard.

And then we were there, waiting outside the UAE exit controls for the green light to drive our insured rental car into the Omani mountains.

And they said no.

We had one form, but we lacked another, something signed from the rental company in support of our trip. Turn around, they said. Go home.

On the fringes of the Emirati cellphone network, we got the airport Thrifty Car Rental on the line, promising to send faxes as we ate "Chili Cheese"-flavored Philippine-made snacks called Boy Bawang and blasted Ke$ha from the car stereo for all the traveling truckers.

The fax machines were silent. We waited in one of the crossing's trillion identically nondescript offices, manned by an administrator and an officer in a white shirt puffing lazily on a cigarette.

"Is he Indian?" The administrator asked about our Thrifty contact.

"Yes."

"That's the problem."

We laughed to belong. As the adage has it, *When the Syrian guards the Emirati border while the Egyptian watches, the nice Jewish boy and girl and the gay man don't pick fights.*

So we called again, pleading for an e-mail. And our office mates couldn't access their own accounts. In their prevailing apathy, they acquiesced to trade seats and allowed me the guard's chair at the border crossing office to sign into my e-mail. And voilà. Print.

The white-shirted official took a look. "But this is just insurance."

"Yes?" A pause. Again, the faint odor of apathy.

"Okay. We'll wave you through."

And as my brain did dizzy somersaults and tied itself in knots, I mouthed to the team: *It's the same form.* They had seen this an hour ago.

A list of insurance options, with just one ticked off, bedazzled with Thrifty letterhead—it couldn't be enough.

It wasn't. We waited and waited to be waved on to the next checkpoint, but no one ever came. And when I went looking for our mercifully impatient officer, he had lost himself among the sameness of the place. The supervisor came.

"Go back to Abu Dhabi. Hard copy."

Our time on the road kept slipping away, but I kept trying to think. *In a place where the systems don't make sense, the solutions don't have to make sense either.*

I wandered into other offices, speaking Arabic but looking as American and haggard as a wet flag. I signed on to sleeping computers with abandon, foraging for the letters Thrifty assured me they'd sent twice. Nothing worked, and we were on our own.

But in the shadows by the offices, one blue-shirted Omani looked listless. He was delighted to speak in not-English and committed to our hunt for a working Internet and printer. When we got back into my e-mail, the promised attachment had been there all along, scanned through twice.

"In the name of God, most Gracious, most merciful," it said at the top in plain bold typeface, as all documents do in Islamically influenced bureaucracies. The *Basmala*, as it's called, is ubiquitous in spoken and written contexts. And the Arabic root from which both grace and mercy come, means "pity, compassion, human understanding."

Two separate e-mails delayed in the ether, one Omani's compassion and a dash of pity, and more than two hours later, I marched toward Oman, insofar as a man can march in the backseat of a Nissan Altima, jaw clenched and ready for anything.

THIS BORDER IS NOT one-dimensional like the fine fountain pen line between the United States and Canada—the vague area between the Emirati backdoor and the entrance to Oman could be drawn faithfully with a crayon on a globe. The countries only finalized their border demarcation in 2008, after a decade of discussion. After ten minutes of driving through no-man's-land, we were in every man's land.

Fiftyish men puffed fiftyish *shishas*, drank tea, and watched us move stiffly in the way only outsiders can at a roadside café a half hour into the country. A huge projector blasted Spanish soccer to the going-out crowd of northwestern Oman. The coffee tasted dark and sweet, not like the light brew served too often in the Emirates, and the mint tea smelled like Morocco and older recipes. I went to ask for more coals for the shisha.

"You speak Arabic?" the owner asked me.

"*Ya'atamad 'al yom,*" I said. It was my go-to joke when I had no intention of hiding my foreignness: *depends on the day*.

A minute later, he was introducing me to his favorite customers—a group of five Omani men—and we three Americans were welcomed into their circle.

We talked about soccer, about Oman, and about finding a wife for the café owner in Washington. Then we drew them our fledgling travel plans on a napkin, to Muscat and Nizwa and onward. I mentioned the difficulties of making reservations anywhere without phones or Internet.

"Ahmed, go get a SIM from the car."

My useless Emirati phone was taken from me, popped open, and charged with more credit than I'd ever use. And after sitting for hours, Malik paid for everything we'd touched during the entire night.

"No, no," said a friend from across the table as we protested and squirmed at the niceness. "He's the boss."

WE NEVER MADE IT to Muscat, where we'd planned to stay the night. We slept in Malik's guesthouse. As it turned out, he also had morning plans to head to Nizwa and we would follow him. You do not say no to these offers. You do not say, well, it sounds nice, but it just seems a little more convenient to wake up one hour closer to the next stop in the book of my to-do list, checked out from the National Library of Missing the Pointism. Like a smoke detector in a bakery, the alarm that may sound in your head as you ask yourself, *What's in it for the other guy?* is completely obsolete—here, open doors are the default. It's not fire, it's cookies.

I often heard my traveling office mates say, *Omanis are the nicest!* It swirled around expat roadtrippers like a given truth.

Malik was also Big Man On Campus in the costal town of Saham. Every neighbor, every kid on the beach, every guy in the streets or stooping it was a friend. He greeted the harbor security guard like an old buddy, and we drove through the gate toward the fishing ships.

"*Asmak Wahid, Asmak Ithnayn,*" I read the names. Fish One, Fish Two. "Not very imaginative." Malik laughed. Then he told me his family owned some of those boats.

The next day at seven, an elderly Indian cook brought us hot, fresh roti and bottomless cups of sweet tea with milk. We set off for Nizwa, Gaar and Rachel following with our rental, Malik and I blasting Arabic jams in his hulking Lexus SUV.

The mountains of the Omani interior are like blurry photographs— up close, towering piles of dirt and earthen rubble, but from afar, sharp and rugged like camels' toenails.

We pulled over frequently onto the shoulder. Malik would say something fast and confident over the phone and some acquaintance would skitter over the concrete divider and across the lanes of the highway to deposit jugs of water, or a shisha, or a cooler full of meat into the trunk. We gathered food and people until we parked and piled into two packed four-by-fours to head into a wadi, a valley—this one a rocky riverbed lined with high mountain walls and crystal-clear swimming pools. And still the tea flowed into glasses, poured from the passenger's seat even as we rumbled through the valley. Oh, how on-the-nose the metaphors were: no matter how rocky the road or how cramped the backseat (four gangly grown men), hospitality prevails.

We swam and jumped off rocks as a whole goat simmered in a pot, engulfed in the flame of dry kindling. We basked in the chilled mountain runoff under blistering sunshine. And then we ate: some things I'd never imagined before—goat's liver, kidneys, lungs and brain—and some things I'd forgotten about since eighth grade, like Mountain Dew, the inbred cousin of decent soda and Gatorade.

"Will the brain make you stronger if you eat it?"

"Only if it was a smart goat," Malik's friend Doctor Ali answered. "If it was a smart goat, it wouldn't have gotten slaughtered."

So we sat in precious shade, eating dumb goat brain and daring one another to eat more. Doctor Ali mongered the eyeballs. At first, I thought my squeamishness was the product of my nurture, but no: everyone else thought eyeballs were gross, too.

That evening we drove nine thousand feet up into Jebel Akhdar, the Green Mountain aptly named for its coat of well-watered shrubbery. We made camp tentless in ten-dollar blankets as night fell and pushed the heat of the desert afternoon far, far below. It was freezing. I had forgotten pants.

As the day progressed, the Arabic I had once understood was lost entirely to the rapid-fire Omani dialect. For long moments I contented myself to clutch at familiar-sounding words. In longer moments, the friends spoke English while Malik did not, and we Americans sometimes slipped back into the easy pattern of our own language with un-Omani manners. In the dark as I was chatting with Doctor Ali, I realized Malik wasn't with us. He had drifted toward the cars, away from everyone. I thought of the highway deliveries, how he appeared as the image of good friend confidence, and now I had pushed him away with the way that I spoke. That change required a whole new meeting—before, I was the foreigner, but English made him the stranger at his own campfire.

I felt guilty when I tried to sleep, and freezing cold.

Halfway through the night, I had the bright idea to spoon the fire, embers still glowing and giving off much more heat and hope than my thin, too-short blanket. With my head on a rock, I was comfy and cozy and warm. I stayed asleep as our ten hosts woke for the predawn prayer, while the embers alit and fire burned holes through my blanket.

I awoke smelling faintly like smoked meats.

But in the high-altitude daze of the morning, nothing seemed to matter—I was being taken care of. Blankets weren't meant to last, tea was delivered to me at the ashen fire pit, and we switchbacked back down to Nizwa. It was true what the road trippers said about Omanis. In a time of mistrust, I was glad when certain stereotypes could withstand their first challenge.

This had not been the playacting I would see in Kuwait. I would have dueled to defend the honor of this experience as a transparent and true one. We weren't just performing here, I was sure of it.

I wanted the freedom to act as anyone at all, but I was getting exhausted from all that time on stage. Always being *on*. Comforted by Malik and his crew at a moment I felt I had no masks on, I found new energy, a trust in simple connections that didn't get tangled up in back-and-forth assumptions and deductions about the Other.

We parted ways at the bottom of the mountain.

– – – – – –

SOMEWHERE AROUND THE TWENTIETH YEAR of the Islamic calendar, Jabir ibn-Zayd was born in a village near Nizwa. If we were noticing contemporary cultural trends in the place that would be demarcated "Oman," this was when they may have begun.

Jabir moved up the waterway to Basra, in present-day Iraq, and began to gather stories about Muhammad, and his sayings, from followers who had been close to him. These are the kinds of accounts that make up the collections of hadith, the "traditions." After the Quran, the hadith are the primary manuals for every element of Islamic life, from marriage to mortgages, from fighting to peacemaking to the best day to travel. ("The Prophet . . . liked to set out on a journey on Thursdays," says one of the hadith. That might have explained our Wednesday night trouble at the border.)

Scholars taught their understandings, dissonant interpretations begat sects, and sectarianism did what it always does. Jabir became the first imam for the persecuted school of thought that would later be known as Ibadi. (Almost nothing is known about Abdullah ibn Ibad, the namesake of Ibadism.) It remains the only Islamic school of thought, known as a *madhhab*, that is neither Sunni nor Shia.

I looked up *madhhab*, which comes from the simple verb "to go," in the green dictionary every Arabic student keeps like a dog-eared bible. It has a rich entry. It begins: "Going, leave, departure; way out, escape (from); manner followed, adopted procedure or policy, road entered upon . . ."

Five imams later, early Ibadis returned to Oman; they escaped the discrimination of the caliphate to the far corner of the Arabian Peninsula, into the craggy Hajar Mountains. Smaller proselytizing groups had gone from Basra to North Africa and the Yemeni hinterland, but only in Oman did they continue to thrive.

Now, roughly three-quarters of the modern Omani population is Ibadi, as is a large proportion of Zanzibar, once within the coastal trading empire of eighteenth- and nineteenth-century Oman. Smaller Ibadi communities still exist in the Mzab Valley of Algeria and the Nafusa Mountains in Libya, and on a Tunisian island called Djerba.

Extraneous to the frequent discussions of Sunni-Shia difference, and because they number less than three million worldwide, Ibadis are simply less familiar to the world. I asked the Internet about them.

On the forum of an online school for Sunni Islamic study, one poster asked, "What to Do about My Ibadi Roommates," wondering if he could live with Ibadis (he says they have great morals and know Arabic, which he'd like to learn). The sheikh answered: "It is recommended you choose Sunni housemates."

Of course, that wasn't some grand dictum of *Sunnism*, but it sure didn't seem like it would have been the response from the Ibadi *madhhab*. In 1931, during the period when European powers salivated for new territory and Oman had effectively become a British Protectorate (after a thirty-eight-minute war), W. H. Ingrams wrote: "If one looks for a parallel sect in Christianity, I should consider the Baptists or other Puritans to be nearest them, though my experience of both, having lived for a year in a country of Baptists and Methodists, and for eight in a country of Ibathis, would lead me to choose the Ibathis as being the most tolerant people in the matter of religion I have known."

Perhaps he had eaten goat with Malik's grandfather in the wadi near Nizwa: "Ibathis consider others mistaken, as who does not, but they mix freely with all, and eat with even an infidel like myself."

For me, Ibadi tradition was something whispered in the background, and I knew it only through what I saw—the campsite on the Green Mountain, and guys like Malik.

GUARDED BY EMPTY TOLLBOOTHS not yet in commission, the smooth highway back to Muscat runs high along the coast. Prisoner to the deranged Lady Gaga-On-Repeat singalong my tripmates had organized for themselves in the front, I suggested a turnoff at the signs for Hawiyat Najm Park, a giant sinkhole in the middle of a quiet local garden. It takes its name from the supposed means of its creation: "The Fall of a Star." It is more than seventy feet from the sinkhole's rim to the endlessly deep sapphire water below, and it made sense to me to try and jump off the edge.

I peered down at it over my toes. If I could clear a six-foot ledge, I might make it. Later, I watched Rachel's video from below.

Gaar says quietly, "Emergency is 9-9-9-9."

"We don't have a phone," says Rachel.

"I really think you're going to fall, tumble down. Tumble," Gaar shouts to me. *Hawiya*—"fall"—can also mean "tumble."

I stand for a few minutes looking down, hands on my knees, frozen. I am afraid of everything. I did not trust that I was on solid ground until my toes were hanging off the edge of a cliff. Now they were, and I was undeniably attached to something solid—it was so much harder to give that up. But that was the point, wasn't it? To see what I could let go of and still survive? I looked down twelve of my heights and made symbols of bigger things out of every potential action and inaction.

"You're thinking about it too much," Gaar says.

Hawiya can also mean "identity."

I felt like I was playing host to fraternal twins, one overthinking, and the other belligerent: Do SOMETHING. DO SOMETHING! DO SOMETHING! But one could silence the other at times. As Sam Hamilton's second son says in Steinbeck's *East of Eden*: "Sometimes a man wants to be stupid if it lets him do a thing his cleverness forbids."

Gaar counts from ten, and I push off from the ground, rolling slightly in the air. Behind the camera, Rachel gives a tiny squeal.

I felt a weight lifted, but as I swam back to shore I felt it still. I had wanted to be in the air, and I had wanted to come down, but mostly I wanted to face that microscopic moment where a decision is made, where the impulse to *do* overcomes all those who say, *Do not*.

There is a muscle somewhere between your ears that gives the final authorization for your legs to swing out of bed in the morning, for your torso to plunge into cold water, for your finger to confirm an in-app purchase. There is friction on that threshold, and it can be sanded smooth with time. But I rubbed my arms and floated and knew I was still afraid. *Fear itself.*

I climbed back up the stairs. *If I could do it twice*, I thought . . . *well, then I'd have done it twice.* There were women in headscarves watching me from the park now, with a little boy sitting on the stone wall of the sinkhole. Two Omani men below were shouting confusing encouragement.

"Go for it! Don't do it! Jump!" they said.

This was the moment that would marinate and crop up at moments on my couch and at the Emirates Palace and Le Royal Méridien between when I ordered my Guinnesses and when they were delivered. The thing that fueled me was the limit that fear defined, between off-limits and not. I was nothing if I didn't confront that limit, and push it to see if it would give way to something else.

At that moment, though, it was all prove-you-wrong showmanship. "Don't jump! Do it!" the Omanis yelled.

"*Lestu dijaaj,*" I called. It might have meant "I'm not a chicken" in formal, Quranic Arabic, but the idiom was meaningless out of English. The onlookers looked puzzled. It was insulting to their powers of observation, denying something that should have been obvious by my patent lack of feathers and wattle.

The rocks were burning my feet, and I licked my hands to wipe them, to buy time. Gaar counted again from ten, and the loudest man made the sound of a buzzer. I didn't jump. Everything was quiet. And somewhere, the threshold was crossed. On the way down, air escaped my lungs like a low, excited whistle.

It was enough to feel the tingling in my feet to know I was still alive.

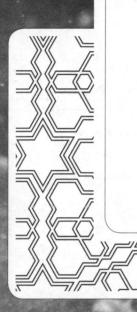

PART TWO

NX844B1G

Then she said
to me,
"By god, you
have no excuse
for your wild life;
I don't think
you'll ever
change."

—IMRU' AL-QAIS,
"Let us stop
and weep" in
Al-Muallaqat,
sixth century

*The other thing that bothers me about these trips you
want to take is that while you think that I don't take risks,
I am afraid that you take risks just for the sake of proving
to yourself you can. That scares me cause it doesnt seem
like there is any limit to the things you would do to prove
that you are fearless.*

SHE LOVES ME
BUT I DO NOT LOVE HER

———

B Y APRIL, THE COMMUNAL thrill that came with the first uprisings had lapsed into a quiet uncertainty. With nothing to latch on to, the international minglers at this short-lived middle school dance of ideas went back to their usual places along the wall. It was harder to squint now and see the Gulf afresh, to straddle that edge of paradise and purgatory. Isolation returned, and I was more aware of it.

The news shrieked of Syria, and I had vacation days. It was time to see what was really happening. My childhood friend Danny was studying Arabic in Damascus. "It could get dangerous in damascus in the next couple weeks . . . so its really your call," he wrote. "That said I'll probably be here and itd be awesome if you came." That was enough encouragement for the thing I already wanted to be stupid enough to do.

FROM: DAD ‹G••••••@SWARTHMORE.EDU›
SUBJECT: WHEN DO YOU LEAVE?
THU AT 6:02 AM / 5:02 PM

Not going to Syria, right?

- - - - - - - - -

FROM: ME ‹A•••••••••••••••••@•••••.COM›
RE: WHEN DO YOU LEAVE?
THU AT 6:07 AM

Yeah i prob wont go there

- - - - - - - - -

FROM: DAD ‹G••••••@SWARTHMORE.EDU›
RE: RE: WHEN DO YOU LEAVE?
THU AT 6:10 AM

PLease take out the "prob."

- - - - - -

ON TUESDAY, THE UNITED STATES began to evacuate "nonessential" staff from its embassy in Damascus and told all other Americans to leave. On Wednesday, I bought a $175 Air Arabia ticket out of Sharjah, the conservative emirate two-ish hours to the north. The flight was to Beirut—I didn't want the flight to get canceled, and fares were good, and I could take the easy taxis from there up and down the hill to Syria.

A week later, I spoke to my parents from the 3 A.M. bus leaving Abu Dhabi for the Sharjah airport. "Do you hear the birds?" they asked. It was springtime in the Pennsylvania suburbs. In the Gulf summer, the only natural sounds were traffic and elevators dinging. "Do you hear the air-conditioning?" I said.

It was two days before Mother's Day, and as a small gift I did not tell my mother where I was going. To my parents, I was traveling only to chic, seaside Beirut. Beirut was not so distantly the poster child for sectarian civil war, but then came intermittent wars with Israel, brief ones, and the last of those had ended five years before. For the sake of their blood pressure and sleep, it was the last time I told them I'd bought a ticket anywhere.

FROM: DAD ‹G●●●●●●●@SWARTHMORE.EDU›
RE: RE: WHEN DO YOU LEAVE?
THURS AT 6:59 AM

> *Would you please email to confirm that you're not going to Syria?*

IT WAS MORNING WHEN I landed in Beirut, the town many have named the "Paris of the Middle East"—a comparison I find fitting not because of the friendly *merci*s or the presence of crêpes and Hermès bags, but because it is a city that survived war and hardly faded in the Middle East as an image of romance and posh class. Slate streets are the city's bones and sandy-colored buildings its Parisian skin, marked with the scars of bullet holes and half-collapsed edifices. *And* twenty-million-dollar condos looking out on the Mediterranean. And the army.

Down the street by the synagogue-in-repairs, a soldier questioned me for taking pictures.

"*Hea kaniisa, sah?*" *It's a church, right?* I asked.

A little raise of the eyebrow and a smile. "*Hua kaniis yehudi.*" *It's a Jewish synagogue.*

Old and new, and old and ruined and new, and destroyed and old and refurbished, and new and under construction. Beirut's one face is like a cubist painting, recognizable patterns (outdoor cafés, the waterfront boulevard, shelled and charred hotels) elicit memories of larger spaces (Paris, Santa Monica, the smoke and gunfire in Bahraini squares). I leapfrogged in and out of the millennia, walking from the shops of the new souk (Dolce & Gabbana, Massimo Dutti, Quiksilver) to the ruins of Roman baths.

I felt very small as I passed the ancient tubs, symbols of how titanically vast the Empire stretched, of how far some travelers must have come. And when they came, it must have meant something just to make landfall.

My traveling was more me-centric than it ever had been: a stream of consciousness road trip around Lebanon in a rented Ibiza hatchback. I didn't know what I was trying to see (north first), I wasn't sure exactly how long I would stay, and no one called either of my two phones. They combined to tell nothing but the time, and even that was twelve minutes apart.

At a café, a waiter affirmed the beauty of the north. Then: "You are alone?"

"Mhmm."

"But if you go alone . . . you're not happy."

Danny might have joined, but he was stuck in Syria for fear of getting stranded if he left. Alone, with total freedom again, I was slipped of my moorings. I kept driving to quell my fidgets with novelty.

I sped up the coastal highway to Jeita, famous for its capacious grottos, one of twenty-eight finalists for the "New Seven Wonders of the World." I drove up through the ruins of Byblos, named Jbeil in Lebanon, where school tour groups swarmed a castle occupied by Ottomans and Greeks and the Crusaders and the French that looks out onto Roman ruins and a rich, blue Mediterranean cove. I spun around in circles at a roundabout in traffic-plagued Tripoli, then the road turned east and upward and didn't come down until the end of the road six-thousand feet higher in a crop of cedars, where snow and ice blocked any further passage.

THE ROAD THAT CONTINUED EAST would have come down into Baalbek, a majority Shia city where even more Romans left ruins. After all my racing, I was only two hours away from Beirut, and I retraced the drive counterclockwise from the small country's 12 to 3.

I was sick of the traffic and of looking at maps, and I was leaning further and further toward driving to a beach in the south, sticking my head in the sand, and hiring the first shared taxi out of the country in the morning.

It was either that or find another route to Baalbek, if only because the road had stopped me before. I pulled into a gas station in the Furn al-Shebak neighborhood.

In Beirut, they balked at the mention of Baalbek. "They'll put your car on blocks," said a camouflaged young soldier in the Lebanese Air Force at the opposite pump. This was what he offered instead of directions, joking with the manager at the station. "They'll leave him with nothing but the steering wheel!"

Again and again, I heard this from both Sunnis and Christians in Lebanon (whose population is divided in nearly even thirds) about this other part of Lebanon: *Don't go to Baalbek. You'll get robbed at gunpoint by Shias.*

The cadet, who looked about my age, told me not to go east to Baalbek, but not to go south either. Stay here. Go south tomorrow, he told me, and I'll go with you: fish for lunch, jet skis, the beach. His name was Marwan, and he was from the south.

But if I didn't go *somewhere*, I was midafternoon stuck with fuck all to do. I couldn't quite get that across in Arabic.

"Do you know people in Lebanon?" Marwan and the pump manager asked. *No.* "What are you trying to see?" *Nothing. Anything, something different.* "Where are you staying?" *Nowhere.* They looked at me as if I were a talking goat. I truly had no good reasons to do anything at all— no sights to see, no people to meet, and an unfaltering confidence that my rental insurance would cover robberies.

"Meet me outside Melek al-Tawwous at 8:30," Marwan repeated, putting his number in my phone. With the air force in charge, I could take the passenger seat and throw my baggage in the back.

And still: the empty time in between. I pushed the soldier once more for directions to Baalbek, and promised I'd only go half as far, only to

Zahle, as if I were talking to my parents. "Okay," he said. "Go right. And then straight all the way."

And so I drove straight, yelling names of upcoming towns out the window for the endorsements of lolling shopkeepers. Soon, billboards on the road sprang up with the faces of Shia clerics and I drove until I knew I was in Baalbek, and I turned off the radio and smelled horses.

I BOUGHT A SIX-DOLLAR KEFFIYEH from a grizzled trader outside the two millennia-old Temple of Jupiter. He lit a cigarette and brought me into his shop for coffee. "I drink forty cups a day," he said. "And five packs of these." He tapped the cigarettes. "It's good for the stomach." A woman turned away from the dubbed Turkish drama on TV to wrap the scarf around my head.

From eight thousand miles away my parents asked me not to leave Beirut, and my government had warned me not to go there at all; now it was compatriots and next door neighbors who misdrew the off-limits boundary.

Fine. So the place wasn't as bad as people said it was. But Life Going On did not mean people were sound and happy. It was a generalization to call the place *safe* after an afternoon and evening, and I wasn't traipsing around shouting insults at the clerics. Still, aside from the ATM that swallowed my debit card, Baalbek was unthreatening. No instant catastrophe, no cars nicked.

I was never really afraid of this town in the first place. The local whispers were old-school sectarianism or ignorance, and there were scads of well-informed people who could have told me so and saved me the trip. I set out to prove that the world wasn't as scary as we imagined it, but discovering just that, I was bored and restless. *Do I want war or paradise?*

I was hungry to get at something that really felt risky, that would count as real engagement. *One last gulp of paradise on the Mediterranean coast*, I thought, *and then I'd go get my goose bumps in Syria.*

—

I PICKED UP MARWAN outside the breakfast place just as we planned. "Let me drive," he said.

The day started so right. We shortcut through side streets and raced onto the highway, stopping to pick up two pirated CDs of Lebanese pop from a shack by the road. By the end of the day we'd listen to the good one about forty times and the bad one sixty-five. We learned little about each other: he fixed planes for the air force, I wandered around countries. "You have a good heart," Marwan would say to me, because I seemed willing to travel alone or with new friends. I tried to live up to his assessments by trusting in his plans for fun *à la libanaise.*

We had unbelievable hummus and fava beans and Pepsi in his town—Ghazieh—and he ran into his house to change out of his army uniform. "When I come back I will be a real person." He came back in a sleeveless muscle shirt with his hair gelled. We were going to the beach. "Do you have any cologne?" he asked. *Tolerance*, I told myself.

We stopped by the water in Saiida for tea and *argileh*—as the Levant called the tobacco-vaping water pipe because that's what the Persians called the coconuts (nargile) that might have made the first bases; or shisha, as the Egyptians called it because that's what the Turks called the glass bases they all have now; or hookah, as my parents knew it, because that's what they were calling it in India when the Brits came and exported words to English like spices to the kitchen. Marwan was delighted that I smoked *argileh*, too. And while I'd never bought or bummed cigarettes in my life, in the Middle East I let water-cooled tobacco smoke into my code of health conduct without even a dieter's bad conscience.

Marwan paid, as he had for lunch. It was cheap, but it sent a message: He might have been riding my car, but I was the guest. "Money comes and goes," he said. "Friends are the most important."

In the baffling traffic on the small streets around Lebanese International University, we circled for ages to pick up Marwan's girlfriend who was not his girlfriend. He got quieter and quieter. I brainstormed an idea for a screenplay based entirely around Lebanese traffic patterns.

"She loves me but I do not love her," he said. A girl in a tight white headscarf got into the car. She would never talk to me.

Finally we were there, in the town with three sides to the sea. Broad beaches swept along the Mediterranean—warm sand, cold water, and nearly deserted in the summer preseason. It was the American dream: a private beach. Still Marwan circled. Around the same roundabout, past the same ocean.

"What are you looking for?" I asked Marwan when my trust faltered. No answer.

Marwan fell silent when he had no plan and no answers. Even though I couldn't have been happier with the sun and sea as we found it, he wouldn't believe me. There was no *argileh*, no umbrellas by the water, no crowds.

My fists clenched, unclenched, grasping at time lost forever. I was unsettled when I was alone, and now I was trapped by their presence: Where could I tell anyone to go?

I was torn by the need to preserve the new friendship—I still believed in my marrow that he was *a good dude*, as honest as people are made—and to open the pressure valve and roar until he understood I needed nothing but nothing and wanted only to relax, *relax*, RELAX!

When we were years older in spirit, we stopped in a beach parking lot. Only I moved.

"We'll wait in the car," Marwan said. I blinked. "We have some things to talk about," he said, trying to tell me it was okay. But I couldn't bear to have them sit like chauffeurs while I baked on the sand—I knew they didn't understand that a person could sit on an empty beach for hours, and I felt far more alone than if I were by myself.

I opened my book and promptly fell asleep. They stood holding each other far, far away, in a blur of headscarf and hair gel. And when I woke up some number of minutes or hours later, the car, with my everything in it—keys, passport, shoes, phones—was gone. A flash of terror.

And then I saw the car parked slightly farther away than I had remembered it with the couple in the front seat. Marwan waved through the windshield.

The terror faded, but the vulnerability stuck.

Marwan deposited his *habiba* back at the university and we stared at the remaining hours of the day. "I don't care what it is we do, just tell me why we're doing it," I said. He asked over and over where I wanted to go. "I've never been here *ever*," I said.

We doubled back and stopped at a beach covered with trash. Plastic bottles and cartons stuck out of the sand, and receding waves uncovered buried car tires by the waterfront. But it was beautiful, and we ran into the water together to repair Lebanese–American relations. I opened a book. "What do you want to do?" he said.

We played *palettes*, the same simple beach tennis as Israel's beloved *matkot*, but I kept thinking that everything he said and did was for my benefit, to force what he imagined was my *fun* into existence. He looked distressed, and I was distressed for having made him feel that way.

"Let's go to the border," I said, to no response. "Let's go to the end of Lebanon."

That would be cool, I thought—the contested border with Israel, no more than a few dozen kilometers away. Because we were already anxious, we should go somewhere where our anxiety would fit the vibe. The border wouldn't require a peaceful state of mind.

He was afraid and confused—*It's just a border*. He was also convinced that it was at least a four-hour drive. "I'll drive," I said.

We passed white United Nations tanks. A gunman leaned out of the manhole, yawning. A soldier waved us through a checkpoint. Before the border town Naqoura, the asphalt stopped and became white rocks as big as grapefruits, packed into a smooth, wavy surface. A guard signed *halt* at a more serious checkpoint. He ordered me out of the car and asked for our papers. Only Lebanese were allowed farther; all foreigners needed a permit from the authorities up north. If it wasn't for Marwan and his army ID, I could have found myself in serious trouble: a lone male, foreign and with among the most Jewish of last names, headed for contested territory.

A little shiver: I was glad to have hit the as-far-as-you-can-go border. "So with just that permit, you can keep driving?"

The burly commanding officer handed me back my passport. "With a permit you can drive to China."

—

MARWAN SLID INTO the driver's seat with a look of infinite relief. It was curious what he found risky: at a mountaintop church, he was adamant we shouldn't go in, or try the door. It was closed, he promised. (It wasn't.) But on the way down he cracked beers open with his seat belt and took swigs between shouts out the window at friends who seemed to live everywhere. I took sunset pictures through the wires and old buildings.

And then minutes after dark, he steered us toward a hotel. Defeated from the day's silent and not-so-silent quarreling, I let us drive toward a place a friend on the street had mentioned, away from the city, away from the lights, away from anything.

The Mina Beach Hotel was run down, colossal, and pink. Every window was dark, and the facade scowled at would-be guests like a deserted prison. Dirty was no problem, and scary can be fun, but a price five times what I had paid for a bed in the city—that felt wrong. Marwan had picked up a 100,000 lira note (seventy dollars) I'd left in the console and told me to wait. "*Don't* pay him," I said.

He got out. I found short refuge in the moment before he returned.

"Come on, get your stuff."

My insides collapsed, but I was still too baffled and dispirited to yell. He had taken money from me and donated it to a soulless hellhole that, we would discover soon, was home to the world's thirstiest mosquitoes. He lived mere kilometers away. We had long since grown painfully tired of each other's company—*Why do you want to do this?*—and still we jiggled the room's door handle open. The beds were bare but for one thin sheet, a strange and unnecessary "kitchen" flaunted its one metal countertop and a fridge fringed by mildew and rust, and the ceiling dripped gently onto the floor.

Strangers were good, I told myself. Hospitality, curiosity, and kindness of heart—that's what I'd find in the Middle East. *Not* assholes, no—who undermined my every effort. But the conflict was irrepressible now: the trust I knew I'd find was made to face the doubt I knew I felt.

And then a drop hit me from the ceiling and I burst. No more silent seething: riding the waves of a year's anxiety, I erupted with the litany of every bad feeling I'd had all day, in a deluge of English when my Arabic burst under the pressure, with rapid-fire sentences I knew he couldn't understand fully but that I still needed to speak.

"I know," Marwan said to everything—to why he spent all the money I had left, to why he was content to sleep in the Lebanese Bates Motel. He was sitting slumped on the blanketless bed. "I thought you needed the rest."

I drifted outside to the balcony, staring at nothing, lending my flesh to the night's first mosquitoes. The sea was black, and I turned back inside. If only I could stop asking *why*, I'd escape with nothing but the memory of a weird day.

"I'm sorry," I said.

"You know, if any Lebanese yelled like that . . . I'd kick you." He paused. "But you're my friend, and I hate to see my friends unhappy."

I was the asshole. For whatever reason, he had used my money because he thought deep down that that was what I wanted. He drove in circles until he found answers that worked for everyone. This was a man pure of heart and magnanimous in his intentions—I was the one who didn't understand. He didn't understand how to relax doing nothing on a beach, and I couldn't convince myself that time spent getting to know someone good and different was dearer than anything else.

Or . . . was it all manipulation? A bored American to hang out with (how exotic!), who had a car and an open wallet. I wasn't the asshole, maybe. No: I was. I really wasn't. I definitely was.

For a moment, we both seemed at ease with each other's foreign existence. I wandered into the open room next door to take a shower, bags of chips and tobacco strewn on the floor and countertops by those who had escaped in the morning. When I came back, Marwan was dressed and gelled.

"We need to go," he said. "Right now."

The police had seen him in the car with me, and they wanted to see me in the station for taking pictures (of the sunset) in town. The police chief had called Marwan personally.

Marwan told me to take all of my things.

I thought back to my questioning by the Beirut synagogue. He stared straight ahead at the empty dark road; I hid memory cards in pockets. I pictured movie chases, throwing the car in reverse, spitting up gravel and gunning it out of town. I planned how I'd flee as he led me into the station.

But that was never his intention. "Go to Beirut, go to Syria," he said, pulling up short of what might have been a police station. And with that, he hopped out of the car forever.

No police had ever called, I realized. It was a melancholy relief: Marwan had found himself trapped with nothing left to give, or—and this struck me only years later—with someone too dense to see how much sex he wanted to have. I'd dismissed that thought before I'd ever had it. It still rings untrue, because Lebanese hair gel and friendship are not American hair gel and friendship. For so many reasons, though, a boy or girl never wants to believe a new friend's attention is for just one thing.

With a clever but decidedly diplomatic move he took his leave. It was the first thing he did that I ever understood.

I sat in the passenger seat for a few minutes, blocking one lane onto a bridge. And then I slid over to the steering wheel and headed back slowly to surrender to the insects at the Mina Beach Hotel. I mummi-fied every inch of my head and body in the six-dollar keffiyeh and the hotel blanket I swore I wouldn't touch. By 4 A.M. the mosquitoes had me beaten and broken in the room haunted by Marwan's disappoint-ment, and I left for Beirut to sleep in the car by the bus station.

In the morning I returned the hatchback to Graziella at National Car Rental, and hailed a taxi for Damascus.

CHAPTER 6 | **SYRIA**

MA FI SHI

T HE CLOSEST I CAME to gunfire was just after I crossed the border into Syria. If it came, I thought it would come from the cities,
from the police, from around the crowds, and not on the road that cut
up from Beirut through the mountains and back down again toward
Damascus.

I passed through each country's checkpoint without issue, accepted
into Syria without knowing my destination, with nothing but a visa
and my tempered American smiles. It had only been months since the
beginning of the uprising that would be deemed a civil war the following summer. Leaving Lebanon at Masna'a, we barreled toward the first
Syrian town, Haloua, whose name means "sweet."

I sat in the back of the taxi. Just me and the driver's fat friend in the
passenger seat. They gained interest in me with the altitude, but lost it
quickly when I told them that I wasn't at all Lebanese. We entered into
Syria and the fat friend lent me his phone, or rather *rented* it, fidget-
ing angrily when I had spent too long trying to make out my friend's
directions to a meeting point. Tension mounted as he demanded eight
thousand lira, almost six dollars, for a five-minute call. The scruffy
driver took his friend's side.

I didn't even have that much left—with my ATM card gone and a
hundred grand lost to the mosquito inn, I'd spent nearly my last lira

before the taxi left Beirut. I couldn't give more than five thousand, I said, groping for a liter-and-a-half bottle of water that was on the floor. My mouth was dry. Someone grumbled. Outside there was no one, nothing but empty green and brown hillside one thousand meters above the Mediterranean. And then: a low *thunk*—something shot fast through the air—and I tensed as it struck me square in the forehead. A moment of shock . . . broken by the fat friend's laughter. I was laughing with him: the blue plastic bottle cap rolled on the seat.

The air pressure was lower—that was all. We were nearly in Damascus. And the driver kept driving, smiling, on the threshold of the town whose name means "sweet."

Just outside the city there is a parking lot where out-of-Beirut cabs meet the into-Damacus cabs. The new driver lifted my bags into the car.

"You're not afraid?" he asked. (Everyone asked.)

"Should I be?"

He dropped me by the Saudi Arabia Embassy, at the bottom of the street by the fried chicken shop. I waited for Danny with the affable cabbie who had charged me seven times the going fare. Good thing it was all so cheap. "*Alhamdulilah,*" the driver said, *Praise to God*. He wiped his face with a soiled sleeve, answering the questions I didn't have to ask about the state of things. "*Ma fi shi,*" *there is nothing*.

He believed it, and he may have been right to. But it was certainly wrong: There *was* something. Just not today, not there.

THIS WAS WHERE THE WORLD was looking. In Syria, during the week of May 8, 2011, there were murders. There were protests against the police state and those who suckled upon it, and there was gunfire to keep criticism at bay. In Damascus and Aleppo, *Sham* and *Halab*, the ancient city centers and modern downtowns were as quiet as they'd ever been—empty of their tourists, but carrying on with life at its most usual.

Damascus was gorgeous. Wide roads led into the city, where posh residential neighborhoods oozed with cafés and fresh-squeezed fruit smoothies for a dollar. My first sight was Jabal Qasioun, a mountain one thousand meters high and many miles wide that looms as the city's inescapable backdrop; towns climb impossibly up the steep sides. It is said this is where Cain killed Abel.

In town, the streets are tight and welcoming. People passed with little glances and questions in their faces.

Danny had been living in Damascus for nine months studying Arabic. He played soccer with other international students, and still did with the ones who hadn't left. Except for momentary sulks he had always had the most easygoing disposition I knew.

We walked toward the old city with five smoothies between us, into the Umayyad Mosque by the door meant for believers. Before its 1,300 years as a mosque, the site was first a temple, then a church. I copied the exact movements of the veiled women who took off their shoes and stepped over the threshold.

Inside, the mosque stretches a city block underneath wooden arches; the four arcaded walls around the immense white marble courtyard are themselves in and of the city: visible through the archways past the *qibla* wall are the dim stone alleys of souks around the mosque, colorful neon advertising *things*. According to one of the best-respected collections of hadith, this is where Jesus will return just before the end of days "wearing two garments lightly dyed with saffron."

Crowds still pushed through the huge Al-Hamidiya souk, but we could pass through without shoving much or getting shoved. "That's different," Danny said. "That's really weird."

It was far, far quieter than it had ever been, everyone said. All of the foreigners were gone, many evacuated without wanting to leave. Still, even with reports of clashes in the suburbs, Damascus couldn't have seemed farther away from everything. A few older guys threw dice onto a backgammon board; tables of Syrians hung out with us by the mosque at an outdoor café pulling on *argileh*. "You're not scared?" a woman asked, smiling, sitting with her husband and her two sons.

They say Damascus is the oldest continuously inhabited city in the world, and there is indeed proof it makes the very short list (competitors are all nearby: Byblos in Lebanon, Aleppo to the north, Jericho in the West Bank). For perhaps as many as ten millennia, through the Aramaean and Assyrian and Babylonian and Roman rules, Damascus has hosted tourists. Now, there were travel warnings from the U.S. Department of State, and travelers took them seriously. *Demonstrations can take place anytime and anywhere*, said the last alert. It went on:

> Syrian efforts to attribute the current civil unrest to external influences may lead to an increase in anti-foreigner sentiment. Detained U.S. citizens may find themselves subject to allegations of incitement or espionage.

We hopped into a *service*, a shared taxi with eighty-cent seats for fourteen passengers, and waited for it to fill up. I noticed how exponentially more impatient I was than the driver, content to wait, smoke, wait.

In Maaloula, children still learn Aramaic as their first language. It is home to a convent carved from nature—a tree grows inside a cave, where doors shaped in the stone walls lead to separate shrines. All of Maaloula is like this in the shadow of high cliffs: the convent deep and tucked up high, only the outskirts spilling out toward the plains.

This old town in the Anti-Lebanon mountains is also famous for its wine. For four dollars at the convenience store at the foot of the convent, we took our pick from the local juice, bottled in whatever-was-on-hand. It's as if the ground is so holy the wine comes out sacramental—sweet and brand new, with enough sediment to guess whose house it came from. And brown bag or no, open container laws are far less strict than in San Francisco.

We took a repurposed vodka bottle and sat outside the Blue Café in the very center of town. Empty. The owner described everything on her menu, looking relieved but a little weary. She would have to run to the restaurant next door to borrow ingredients. "It's been one month since there were tourists at the Blue Café," she said.

So we kept ordering—every time she offered something else, we wanted to make her happy. Antonia had moved back from Miami to open the restaurant less than a half-year earlier, just to watch the tourist industry collapse. "One month ago, you couldn't find parking." Except for one van and a car or two, the whole town square was empty. Her place was a good one. She taught us words in Aramaic. I downed lentil soup like biblical comfort food.

I suggested that maybe things would get better now—it seemed calm. "Yes," she said. "Now that they know it was terrorists killing people—spies from Lebanon and from Jordan and from Israel and from Egypt."

"Um," I nodded. Part of me thought it was heartening to know Israel had moved up to the status of Other Scheming Arab Country in the eyes of some Syrians. But she believed beyond a doubt the state-run news: that the deaths of protesters (killed by army soldiers) and of army soldiers (killed by other army soldiers) were casualties of terrorist attacks, and not of her own government. Her Christian pocket in the Syrian population was nervous about any potential advances by the Sunni Muslim majority. They put their collective faith in Bashar al-Assad's Alawi government, fellow minorities and defenders of the current state of affairs. Antonia had swallowed every morsel the news fed to her.

But Danny knew better than to take this entire interaction literally. These words weren't a confession of Antonia's true feelings, at least not necessarily. Why on earth would she have trusted me as a confessor? I could have been an American spy, or a government goon, or a boy with a big mouth.

If I didn't know how to filter what I heard, what was I ever going to learn that was solid? Performers to other performers, that's all we were. I was devouring the place with my eyes, but my ears were netting nothing of substance, and my mouth was dry.

We poured the last drops of wine from the lees of the vodka bottle. And then we had to leave, the last tourists in Maaloula for a long while.

WE WEREN'T LOOKING to vulture tour the protests, but what else was *real* here? Maybe if we moved around enough, we'd absorb something worth absorbing. Danny wanted to go to Aleppo—it was still quiet there, and all the foreigners who had been seemed to like it, and I was glad to keep moving.

The windows of the train cars were fractured with ripples of broken glass, but the ten-of-seven A.M. was still busy with travelers heading north out of Damascus. The man next to me took turns thumbing through a wooden *misbaha* of prayer beads and napping; the older woman across the aisle looked out the window for all six hours. *Looks like violence*, Eeyore might have said as a foreign correspondent. The next afternoon there would be clashes, as there had been for the past two months of bloody Fridays. That's why we left for Aleppo on a Thursday, the week's last ticket out of town.

As the train neared the station at Homs, the city stared back with the empty eyes of black and deserted windows, overgrown gray-green grass, and isolation—a military operation known as the "Seige of Homs" began one week earlier on May 6. The tracks passed through a tunnel in a tiny hill, on top of which sat a big Syrian tank camouflaged in brown and green. Another tank idled on a patch of grass under a bridge. The entire crew was sprawled out on the turf, leaning against the treads, watching the train go by.

Opposite the station platform, a small cluster of men milled about on the street. In the distance, I saw a soldier patrolling with a long rifle slung from his shoulder, gesturing to passersby. Two men boarded our car. No one got off.

And that's where the train turned around, pulling backward out of Homs toward everything we had come from. Danny told me that two days earlier a train had been sent three hours from here back to Damascus. The other riders gave away nothing in their faces. Maybe they did this every day: hopped on the train and hoped it would make it to Aleppo. Maybe the train itself was the destination, a vacation from the daily grind—four American dollars for a first-class ticket to wherever-you-got-on.

Still, their quiet was a comfort, and I waited for the train to switch tracks, or to make a wide looping doubleback. The train never changed course. Hours later, we cruised into the outskirts of Aleppo. I was very, very confused and it was raining. But there we were, in ancient *Halab*, looking for a place to sleep.

—

AS THE ONLY NON-SYRIANS with suitcases in the entire city, we were looking for a deal. For a firm ten dollars there was the Jawahir Hotel, cozy and fine—tea and Internet and black humor about the demonstrations—but I felt the need to haggle, if only to feel a kind of momentary traction. I was pulling Danny along now. He was apathetic in the extreme about our bedding for the night, but we headed for the new, utterly empty four-star hotel in the heart of the old city.

We entered the gleaming lobby of the Carlton Citadel Hotel and approached the desk. The receptionist flicked her eyes at the door, firing a nearly inaudible *"Mahmoud!"* at the bellhop. Mahmoud scrambled to compromise jogging and elegance.

After ninety minutes of diplomatic discussions with two receptionists and the general manager, and three tours around the hotel, they offered their third best room for the price of the very cheapest. (It would have broken their hearts to forfeit the whirlpool bathtub of the Ambassador Suite.) And the cost of one night, we suggested, should be enough for two. The receptionist whispered this to her colleague, flushed and totally incredulous. Still, she would never say "impossible."

The Carlton is housed in what was once the National Hospital, a stone mansion built by the Ottomans centuries ago. In three years, an underground bomb would destroy the hotel. Now, the room service was impeccable.

I was vulturing the spoils of an abandoned palace.

We were only miles from the roaring crowds that would be heard worldwide on the next day's news. The old city swept out around the Citadel, which perches on a hill that long ago held all of Aleppo inside its stone walls. The thick souks below would be burned and bombed within the year, but now the shops still marketed comfort: the famous olive and bay leaf soap, *hamaam*, where skin is scrubbed soft; cafés for endless tea and shisha, as always. With a forkful of room service spaghetti Bolognese, I admonished myself for calling coziness counterfeit and for trusting only danger as *real*. I had no defense yet for those who would say, *You hid from the protests—you didn't* really *go to Syria!* It was late. I consulted an iPhone Arabic dictionary and called down to the front desk: *two pillows, please—room 111.*

I CAME BACK DOWN to the patio outside the hotel, where I'd finished breakfast and forgotten a jacket and where a man in a dark suit and purple tie sat at the table under an umbrella, very quietly smoking a cigarette. He had thick silver hair, smoothed back to the nape. Like everyone in eyeshot he worked at the hotel, and I replied appreciatively to his concerns about my stay; the newly promoted director of food and beverages looked very tired. "Sleep well?" he asked.

Turkish coffee came and we chatted in the shade until it seemed the right time to leave.

"Room one-one-one, yes?"

I nodded. I knew there weren't many guests to keep track of. "I'm Adam," I said.

His eyes might have twinkled, the corners of his mouth tapering into little peaks: "I know."

There is a person for every fact to be known in Syria, or there is someone who tries to know it. They are gathered under the umbrella of the *Mukhabarat*, the Intellegencia, that offers monthly compensation and little rewards for constant reporting on the neighborhood, especially on *al-ajaanib*, us foreigners.

It's hard to look like you're staying out of trouble when there are so many good ways to seem suspicious. Wandering up and over the windy walls that surround the old city, I found myself inexplicably inside a police compound. I slunk out through the main entrance, past an officer in a plastic chair caressing the magazine of his old wooden Kalashnikov.

In the park named Public Park in the west of downtown Aleppo, a man watched Danny and me walk. There were no qualms about staring here, and no one ever averted their eyes when I stared back at them. Heads swiveled after us. A camera unsheathed was like a streetlamp for gnats.

We labeled suspect spies with clock face directions: *mukhabarat—five o'clock, twelve o'clock.*

"Check your six-thirty," Danny said.

There's almost nothing to ever be afraid of: if they flicked their hand and waved us over, we'd go; if they asked to see documents, we'd show a copy of a passport. The panic was in the uncertainty.

In a wrinkled blue shirt, a gangly man with dark eyes lurked on the bridge over the inches-deep Quweiq River. We crossed and he followed behind. We turned right and he turned his head, deadly serious, one hand shoved deep in his pocket. We sat down on a park bench (*nine o'clock, one-thirty*) and he picked one to sit on at a distance, staring at the backs of our heads. Every time I looked he was staring, unblinking. Anxiety boiled. *Say something! Do something! Or stop!*

Maybe he did have the power to arrest us. Maybe, in this country where American diplomacy would have a hard time springing us from jail, he'd be able to make me disappear. But I could make myself deaf to all that. I told myself that anything was worth it just to know where the limits were.

The standstill was too infuriating. So I made up a little game: Danny and I would stand and walk in opposite directions, then turn around, and hand off a scrap of paper with nonsense codes scribbled on it. Like bad spies, we'd stick our hands into each other's pockets without eye contact.

A different man made two passes back and forth in front of us. A third sat on a bench at two o'clock, flicking through prayer beads, slowly taking drags. He might not have been police. He might have been the only one.

At ten paces, Danny and I hit our marks, spun, passed each other. We made the exchange—a torn scrap of city map with the message *NX844b1G* in blue pen—and wheeled toward the exit. At our six o'clock, Blue Shirt followed far behind. We stood on the street looking for a taxi to make a quick escape.

It was all storm chasing. How close could I get to danger?

Blue Shirt moved nearer, sneaking into the leafy shadows by the bus stand.

If I didn't get arrested and tortured as a foreign spy, I might find some calm in that relief . . . ten meters . . . and if I did, well, then at least I'd know where a real boundary was.

Finally, he motioned: *Come.* His eyes shifted for the first time, no longer blank but not commanding either like the others had been. Imploring, maybe.

He was almost completely hidden in the darkest corner of the street, leaning out from behind the bus stand posters. He motioned again as if maybe I hadn't seen. But here police had no need to hide, plainclothes or otherwise, and Blue Shirt was acting far too bashful. He flicked his hand again, *Come here!* and touched his hand to his chest. A button unbuttoned.

Of course.

I had to understand the face I was wearing, the fear, the expectant energy. To anyone looking me in the eye, my love of the Middle East may have looked like lust, and it might have been.

He watched as we scurried into a cab: this wasn't one of the million *mukhabarat*—this was just a man in a park trying to have sex with another man in a park. As for the others—*five o'clock, twelve o'clock, six-thirty*—we wouldn't give them the time to tell.

I was an alcoholic who chugged a magnum of wine only to discover that it was grape juice. But my heart was racing, and that took the blood from my head, and I spent a brief moment at peace with my addiction that was far easier to feed than to fight.

THURSDAY NIGHT FROM the ramparts of the Citadel, we had watched lightning strike at the fringes of this city, shooting between clouds, lunging at steeples and minarets and smokestacks. The Citadel hill in the center of the old city has seen rulers rise and fall for millennia: Ottomans ousted Mongols and Mamluks who expelled Crusaders who deposed Muslim invaders who booted Byzantines who sacked Romans who bagged the Greeks who, at the sword of Alexander the Great, wrested Aleppo from whoever was there before and who likely did the same to those who came before them, all the way back to Abraham, who is said to have milked sheep on that very hill. (The city's Arabic name, *Halab*, has roots older than the language, but *halab* also has another meaning in Arabic: "to milk.")

But as with sheep, sometimes it is easier to go up than to come back down. Friday afternoon, cries came from within the empire, shouting for new and better leadership from among their own. Now that Aleppo was more than just one hill, and the country much more than one city, these were not cries an army could answer.

Demonstrations were christened anew every week: "Homeland Protector" for the national army, "Friday of Freedom" to honor Syrian Kurds, "Great Friday" when Good Friday wasn't good enough. Twenty-five miles west or forty miles south, it was the Friday of Silks. This week, the government had for the first time promised not to shoot protestors—something they'd *never done before anyway and who told you that*.

In Syria, protests began late in the day by the new model: typically near one-thirty, after the congregational Friday prayer. Until Assad had passed a law three weeks earlier, lifting forty-eight years of emergency rule in a calculated nod to his opposition, prayer time was the only occasion when more than five Syrians were legally allowed to congregate without a government supervisor. We bought fresh juice from Yahiya and Ghazi at a stand near the Armenian quarter at one o'clock. Like alarm bells, the skies opened up: zero to wrath-of-God-hailstones and torrential rains in an instant. The overflow of men praying outside a nearby mosque ran for cover, or ran into the rain, or anywhere. For twenty minutes this was the chaos in Aleppo. Afterward, there was only news.

By late afternoon, Al Jazeera began to report the day's first casualties. Cellphone videos showed chanting and organized protest in the streets of Hama, Homs, Qamishli far in the east and the Damascus suburbs. Anchors narrated the information they had, barely polishing eyewitness accounts and Tweets and YouTube clips.

We watched from our room in the Carlton with windows on the silent Citadel. On *Syria News,* under the "LIVE" banner, videos cycled through looping clips of major cities to prove that life was the same as it ever was, denying the protests and the dead and injured until the next day's paper could blame terrorist activity. The Syrian state coverage was intriguing, provocative, artful. The art, of course, is deception: in Idleb, where protests were getting started, a few affable bakers were tossing pitas from the oven. In Homs, people looked like they might be gathering, but only very, very far away, down an empty street. "Live" from Aleppo, it was pouring rain. I pulled the curtains back just to make sure: sunshine and more sunshine.

Every city had passersby eager to crowd around the camera to tell it what it wanted to hear. Every Friday the interviews were the same, the faces hardly different: "Praise God, everything is fine. Nothing is happening." Cut to a flock of tiny six-year-olds, spearheaded by the largest girl among them, vigorously declaring, "There is no better country!"

The success was undeniable: cab drivers, young men in the street or on TV, Antonia in the café in Maaloula—they all said the same thing: "*Ma fi shi.*" *There is nothing.* They sat and soaked up *Syria News*, perhaps because their TVs didn't get other channels, or because they didn't trust other channels, or because the news on other channels was too unsettling to believe.

Meanwhile, their fellow citizens took to the streets. These were people who knew the meaning of freedom because they were willing to die for it, not storm chasers who flirted with danger to test their own limits.

DANNY TOOK THE TRAIN back down to Damascus, and I was left alone for a last day in Aleppo.

The narrow streets of the old city smell like soap or raw meat or wet stone—every hundred meters shops shift in their inventory: spice markets, then tailors, then piles and piles of green and brown soaps. Shop owners dispatch their young kids to relay or fetch or give directions, but only when approached. For that composure, Aleppo is different from a tourist-heavy old city like Fez or Jerusalem, where outdoor displays breathe and squeeze in from the walls of narrow streets. Aleppo is always dim in the channels between old buildings, just wide enough for a pickup to honk its way past, just the same every day of the week. In this oldest of Old Cities, a dozen odd shops sell the same selection of keffiyehs, the same shoe inventory, the same pots and pans. There is always the question: *How does anyone get by?*

Early morning at the Hammam Al-Nahassin, downhill from the Citadel toward the Great Mosque, a few guys sat around not really waiting for customers. At twelve dollars, it was an expensive bathhouse by Syrian standards, but this was The Place for tourists and locals alike, with its own proud directive arrow at the end of the street. Down through the unassuming door to the vaulted wooden chamber hidden from the world, I spent the day washing and steaming and lounging and getting scrubbed to the bone, commanding shisha or coffee or kebabs, reclining on pillows set up in separate boxes along the wall. What I saw departed not at all from a long-baked fantasy of the Orient, and I slipped into it the way you would a bath that neither chills nor burns. The *hamaam* men replaced my wet robes with drying robes, and soon with lounging robes and a cloth tied around my head. And with that, they served tea.

Within a short hour's commute, cities were tallying the damage of the Friday of Silks. In every Saturday paper, the government would report how many were killed by militant groups, which terrorists confessed to attacking civilians, how the weather was still hot in Damascus. Even in the airport there was no news, and no place past the taxi stand to spend Syrian money.

The purple-trimmed Qatar airbus taxied onto the runway. My iPod shuffled to "Trav'lin' Light." The man to my left was enormous in all directions, and we crossed our arms tightly and took turns uncrossing them because there wasn't space for both. In accordance with an unspoken charter, silently keeping time and heeding the other's discomfort, we crossed, uncrossed; crossed, uncrossed.

*So I've been thinking a lot about your whole everything
is risky, how can you possibly draw a line idea. OK well
today, in the library, i was reaching to plug in my computer and my chair tilted over to the left and I came very
very close to hitting my head on the chair next to me.
I could have died! I mean, probably not . . . but if the
library isnt safe then WHAT IS?*

*I think if you want to live an average, nice, kind of but
not terribly meaningful life then there are definitely lines
that define what dangers are necessary to live that kind
of life and that's why people will cross the street every
day but won't go to Afghanistan. You want a different
kind of life. I respect that in you and in lots of ways wish
I were more like that, but you know I'm a fearful person.
I'm working on it.*

*yours,
Masha*

CHAPTER 7 | **AFGHANISTAN**

WALL SAVE BUTTS

———

I sometimes felt—almost as though they were doing it to reassure themselves of their own freedom. My perplexity, of course, undoubtedly came from my unfamiliarity with American customs.

—TAKEO DOI, *The Anatomy of Dependence*

BACK IN ABU DHABI, it went like this in my head: *they said I'd die, or worse, and I didn't, and better.*

Neurons twitched with all new possibilities: *Where* else *was open now?* Maybe the places authorities had warned against were *exactly* the places I needed to go. I had a lingering invitation from Iman to visit her in Pakistan that I'd always thought was bonkers. Now I could tell her yes. It was summer and she was bored and delighted.

This was the clever trick of 9/11—or of America's reply, as I heard it, when I was supposed to be forming my own identity: It made me think the outside's inhospitality was what made my home welcome. But if anything: they always felt *more* hospitable, not less.

Where *else*? Now I read names on the map like the names of old friends.

ONE MORNING I STOPPED BY the Afghan Embassy with a two-page form and a few photos of myself. At 2 P.M., my visa was ready with a free travel brochure.

GETTING INTO AFGHANISTAN would be easy—flights leave daily from Dubai and Sharjah before dawn. Getting out would be easy, too, I was sure, on a quick flight from Kabul to Islamabad. But simply *being* in Afghanistan, or in Pakistan, was something I couldn't quite imagine. It was uncharted territory for me, for a lot of tourists, and I had no conception of what walking would feel like, what the streets would look like, what people's eyes would feel like when they landed on me.

Luckily, the style of the plurality in the Emirates is *shalwar kameez* ("pants shirt"), the chameleon skin of both Pakistan and Afghanistan. Next to the mosque just behind my high-rise was a string of a dozen tailor shops run by Pashtuns from northern Pakistan, mostly near Peshawar or Waziristan. These guys knew Pakistan. They had opinions about Afghanistan. "Don't go," they would say sometimes about both places. "Go," they'd say at other times.

It was Thursday, eight days before my flight to Kabul, and Muhammed Amir took my measurements to stitch a white shalwar kameez with a low, Afghan-style collar. He spoke only Pashto and Urdu. His cousin Khan Zaman spoke a fair amount of English. Their cousin Mumtaaz owned the shop. We spoke in Arabic.

"First, you should learn Pashto," Mumtaaz said. "Ten days, you come to the shop, every day little, little." I had eight, and that seemed enough for a fair try. Every afternoon until I left I sat with them for three or four hours in their shop, learning disconnected words in Pashto, translated to me through whatever language was convenient. *Serlatsum*

Afghanistan-la, "I am visiting Afghanistan." I swapped English words in return—*thread, needle, scissors*—and endured the tepid Mountain Dew they poured for me so graciously.

In the Abu Dhabi evening, shop people hang out in shops. Friends and random passersby came to sit—some knew the cousins, some didn't. Some wanted tea and Mountain Dew, some didn't. Some have a reason to be in the shop—others didn't at all. No one ever looked at the small TV in the corner droning the news from Pakistan. Almost everyone old enough to grow a beard had one. At times when a customer or serious-looking man entered, Mumtaaz warned me with his eyes to keep silent. Having an American in the shop might rub some people the wrong way, he explained later. He made a cuckoo hand gesture. "Their minds are rotten," he said.

It took three days for Muhammed Amir to finish my costume, and on the fourth I sat among them, greeting customers with "*Tsanga yei, chai ski?*" ("How are you? Drink tea?") and silently nodding and pretending to understand when the bigger beards walked in. When the call to prayer, the *azan*, rang out from the nearby mosque's speakers, the men gently stood and left.

Sometimes I wondered why I was putting all this effort into Pashto, spoken mainly in the south of Afghanistan, when Dari (Afghan Persian) is much more widely spoken, especially in the central areas I was hoping to visit. Persian overlaps some with Arabic, but everything in Pashto was new. And this was the Pakistani dialect, sprinkled with bits of Urdu and English, not Afghan Pashto. On the other hand, it is the native language of most Taliban fighters, and I wondered how many minutes I'd buy if I asked them "Drink tea?" in their mother tongue.

But I wasn't really sitting with the tailors to learn the language. After eight days, I wouldn't remember many words anyway, but I would remember body language: how to wear the shalwar correctly, to shake everyone's hand when entering a room, to listen for the azan and know when it was time to go.

One evening, a bomb blast killed scores in the north of Pakistan, and the men turned to the corner television. The tailors listened and looked away; Mumtaaz shook his head in unsurprised disappointment. A man leaned into the shop to ask about relatives back home.

This was the sound of the "-Stans," as I knew them from reputation. These hot zones in the American theater of conflict were familiar to me in ways Kuwait and Oman had never been, and I saw their populations through that geopolitical filter. They saw me, too, the *American*. It was as if I had been sleepwalking in their neighborhood for ten years. And I went as if it were morning, to ask what I had been up to, and to understand how my reputation had formed. If I could find human connections there, I thought, maybe each side could have a bro or two freed in some way from hardened preconceptions.

Before I could deal with all that symbolic baggage, though: *packing*. Stuffing bags was never really about what I wanted to bring, it was about what I wanted to know I had with me—and there was nothing physical that could have made me more *ready*. But the simple act of returning to the tailors, sitting with them and taking notes, was enough to feel like preparation. I wasn't just waiting to board a plane, nails bitten to the bone; I was doing something—it didn't really matter what—and with Mountain Dew and handshakes I strengthened my resolve.

Serlatsum Afghanistan-la.

I bought my tickets into Kabul, and on to Islamabad. I was so excited that I forgot to buy a ticket home.

THE DISPATCHER AT THE TAXI STAND was confused; I was a paradox. "But . . . you're wearing Pakistani clothes!" And yet, I had the Urdu skills of a wooden chair. At the airport, my looks earned me little but . . . was it discrimination? The metal detector guard merely grunted and poked. I thanked him in Arabic that certainly had no traces of a South Asian accent . . . American maybe . . . maybe French. Eyes widened.

I wanted to dissolve preconceptions for the good that I thought might come out of it, but a simpler mantra still burned under my tongue at all times: *Stereotype this!* Wearing my shalwar and Pashtun *chappal* sandals in Abu Dhabi, to Pakistanis I was at first fellow Pashtun but soon an idiosyncratic Western tourist; to Arabs I was a laborer who

walked conspicuously like an American; sitting in the airport terminal, I was at first look a resource to Afghans searching with questions
in Pashto for their gate—but soon just a Lebanese, for that was what I
told them.

It was the first time I'd lied to anyone about my nationality. A touch
of fear, maybe, but mostly it was my coy kind of research. I had so little
idea how anyone would respond to so many parts of me—it would have
been bad science to test every variable all at once.

To me, Afghanistan was half war zone, half news imagery, half
quotes and impressions, observations and assertions disconnected from
their footnotes. The other half was blank. When I landed in Kabul in
Afghan shalwar and Pashtun *chappal*, I joined the files of other men in
the same clothes, in similar sandals, with comparable skin tone—I
wanted to be blank, too.

SHARP BROWN MOUNTAINS and splashes of greenery flowed toward
the capital as the plane landed. A small group in Western clothes with
boxes of gear mixed with the passengers in hats, vests, colors boister-
ously disembarking. Military planes roosted along the runway; a pair
of helicopters kicked up dust. Idle budget airliners lined up like parents' cars on a suburban street.

On the bus that shuttled us from the terminal to the exit through
metal and cement barriers frosted with barbed wire, the driver served
me tea. Another driver collected me from the parking lot to bring me to
my room in the Gandamack Lodge, secure behind two sets of towering cement walls and barbed wire, two metal gates, a guard house, and
security with AK-47s. (We stopped only to collect American dollars
and afghanis from the high-end, Western brand-stocked supermarket
Spinney's, also manned with armed guards.) It was a sunny and warm
June afternoon inside the hotel garden where a table of Americans were
ordering brunch, birds whistling to one another. From here, Afghanistan was very pretty.

The manager and the guests told me that they never felt unsafe walking in Kabul during the daytime, that the streets were lined with police

and well-meaning youth, infinitely more intrigued by Westerners than wont to harm them. Still, I left the compound in Afghan clothes, saying little to the officers casually manning the ubiquitous checkpoints around the city. One pair, a young policeman in uniform with Asian features and his scruffy backup in a wrinkled red plaid shirt and jeans, took special interest in me, "the Lebanese." Red Plaid Shirt was cleaning his rifle, laughing: "You look Afghan!" From afar, maybe—but from up close, I always felt like they knew otherwise.

"Can you show me how to put that together?" I said, sticking my chin at the dismantled gun the plainclothes officer (was he even a policeman?) was inspecting. He smiled a big, friendly smile. I wondered why those words came out of my mouth.

I sat in the guard's chair by the gate, in the little covered shed hardly wider than my shoulders, listening to instructions as he began to jam the pieces of the AK back together. He blew dust out of one cavity with the rifle balanced on his knee—I had wooden walls on three sides with him as my fourth. Red Plaid Shirt was looking down, visibly occupied with cleaning, but I saw something else: the barrel was pointed straight at me. My mind knew that the gun couldn't function—the magazine was in his hand, half of the machinery was on a chair—but it wasn't enough. On reflex, I squeezed myself against the wall of the tiny shed. *What if?* I grappled with a thousand questions at once: why they would want to shoot me, why this was such a good place to do it, how could they have known I'd ask them about the rifle, how I was going to be late to meet friends of friends for brunch at Le Bistro, how the gun looked really old, how I holyfuckingshit really didn't want to be sitting there right then.

I stood and stepped to the side as he clicked the magazine into place. We shook hands and they waved me through the gate. I'd taken a wrong turn anyway—this was the driveway to Hamid Karzai's palace, not the road to Le Bistro.

THIS WAS THE KIND of ignorance I let flourish.

If I had to preach the Gospel of Visible Places to a stranger, I wanted to have answers not just to my own fears, but to his. Even if he believed my stories, he'd always say, *you could only do that because you have* this *or you are* this *or you know* this. He'd say: *I wouldn't know where I was going.* The flash of confidence I felt retreating from the Karzai driveway was like having a good comeback up my sleeve. *Neither did I.*

And there is another bonus to that ignorance. Unburdened by guidebooks and online reviews and knowledge, everything was a little discovery. The thrill of novelty comes easy for the ill-informed.

AFTER FRIDAY BRUNCH at Le Bistro, I went to the park. Fridays on the Shar-e Now green in the heart of Kabul, men watch animals fight. Fighting animals are status symbols and prized possessions, with tiny fighting quail fetching up to several thousand dollars—many years' salary for most Afghans. There is money to win, sure, but real winners glean honor from their birds' bloody beaks. Today, near the intersection of Chicken Street and Garden Street, two or three hundred men circled around battling birds.

I joined the onlooker's ring, conspicuously taller than most by a head, younger by half, and beardless by all. "There's no other friend?" the man next to me asked in pidgin Arabic. It was strange to be alone. And I told him that I was Lebanese, still unsure what it would mean to come clean.

Two handlers stood in the center fanning identical caged birds to make them angrier. "Why are they doing that?" I asked.

"Wind," he said. "After that, it's good."

They lifted the cages, suspense building, and stood back to monitor the carnage. The gray, duck-shaped birds stared at each other. They hopped. There is a need for patience in the Afghan original sport of *kawk* (partridge) fighting—not to be confused with cockfighting, which is also popular around Afghanistan, along with bullfighting, quail fighting, dogfighting, and egg fighting, where I try to crack your hard-boiled egg with my hard-boiled egg. In Shar-e Now park, handlers circle around their birds like boxing referees. One bird grabbed the other by his nape, and then they returned to hopping.

On another side of the city, families picnic and chill in the Bagh-e Babur gardens, designed by the Mughal empire. Lush and vast, the eleven hectares abound with midmillenium architecture, beggar children, and shisha. To walk through the city is to see its many axes of conflict: bomb-blasted ruins and five-star hotels, ragged penury and cautious opulence, dynastic history and political instability. Cradled by the hills of Kabul, the park looks out on minarets in town, on the houses that climb up over one another, on the remnants of the ancient wall that used to defend the city from everything.

At night, Westerners take hired cars to a small list of restaurants and bars. The Gandamack Lodge was one of them, with cans of Tuborg for six bucks and doubles of French Pastis for ten. For expats working in development or contracting, boredom blended with comfort—the work-driven still had their Happy Hour.

Everywhere the procedure is the same: knock and a door is opened in a heavy metal slab. One or two guards search bags and pat you down. The next door buzzes and opens with a click, and you exit the city into a Lebanese or Italian or French restaurant that could be anywhere at all.

This was the life for one segment of the population in Kabul, many of whom lived and worked comfortably without ever leaving the capital. But without novelty, others say, it's not enough.

SATURDAY, TRAFFIC WAS LIGHT on the road from Kabul to the town of Bamiyan, nestled deep in a high valley lined with sandstone cliffs 150 miles to the northwest. But for all the paving efforts that have made it among the smoothest in the country, this route from the Afghan capital through the ten thousand-foot-high Shibar Pass is less than perfect. One week earlier, the head of Bamiyan's provincial council Jawad Zahhak had been targeted and dragged from his convoy by the Taliban. Four days ago, they told me in the car, he was beheaded. Hussein pointed: "Right . . . wait—*there*."

I had found a low-resolution flier for an Afghan tour company online and guessed an e-mail address from a mush of pixels. Success came in the confirmation of a car that would deliver me from outside the dead-bolted orange gates of my hotel in Kabul to their lodge in Bamiyan. At 6 A.M., I was late. The hubcap-less white sedan drew a stark contrast to the polished and armored SUVs that take Westerners to get mango milkshakes. And there were four men inside. Open the mind's floodgates: *this seems infinitely more kidnappy.*

In the backseat were Hussein, alternatively smoking, chain-chewing gum and napping, and Qasim, texting and telling me truths about the country. The driver in black spoke no English. The man next to him never liked me. I wedged in between Qasim and Hussein, wearing shalwar kameez like everyone else, disguised and protected from the sun with a scarf that cost 90 afghanis, about a buck-eighty. Outside of the massive tanks, this was the safest way to travel, and certainly the most discreet—three fellow passengers made me three-quarters less suspect. For seven hours, I was ashamed for ever having feared them.

Danger, however invisible, was outside. I was numb to the tension in the car until, half an hour past Kabul, Qasim warned me of the anxieties building in the front seat: we had entered Taliban territory. The eyes and ears of the public, then, were also to be feared: "If they don't support, so how the Taliban stay?" Hussein explained. Lifting a camera or cellphone could be enough to arouse suspicion, or to have the car stopped, or worse. It would be more than four hours before Qasim told me it was safe to take pictures again.

On the roads south and west out of Kabul, there were Taliban checkpoints within fifteen minutes. Foreigners, if any, could be seized and killed, perhaps held for ransom if their governments were known to respond to that sort of thing.

The northern route was considered much safer—no beard patrols, violence chiefly of the targeted sort, and the occasional convoy of heavy coalition trucks, armored to the gills. Still, because the lifeblood of the Taliban is social support, entering their territory meant traversing towns whose majorities were its champions.

Somewhere deep down, I was constantly scanning for as-yet unnamed feelings of impetuous regret—*What hadn't I done that I could have? What limits are here that shouldn't be?* Always, when kept away from a place by bureacracy or happenstance, I reacted doubly hard and opposite in desire. But now, as much as I scanned, I found no need to push west to Kandahar, or south toward Jalalabad. Like a rumble strip along the shoulder of a highway, these borders around Kabul said: here is an *edge*. This was a line between possible and impossible, and I could actually see it. I was content to go north and only north.

Where legendary explorers had sought to populate empty maps, to sketch coastline where there had been only waves at the edge of the earth, new adventurers are worth their weight only in detail, or in checked facts. For myself, I erased the bit of bad-reputation coastline that had been painted thick around all of Afghanistan, and penciled in a margin around two country roads.

HUSSEIN WOKE UP from another nap against the door as the road became dirt. "Eighty percent is related to Taliban." I wondered how anyone could distinguish. "His style, his face . . ." Hussein trailed off. "Just see and watch."

"Per house, one Taliban," said Qasim with detached unhappiness. These were the armed militants, the rest—almost everyone in the towns that hosted them—were spies and donors, suppliers of food, shelter, money and the dearest commodity: information. Informants reported anything unusual by cellphone to men stationed farther down the road; to be discovered a foreigner, despite the increased peacekeeping presence, was exceedingly dangerous. But we had to have breakfast somewhere.

The man who never liked me twisted around in the front seat. "So," he said, "do you want to have tea?" I nodded. "I won't say anything."

I would wrap the small scarf tightly around my neck and wear the northerner's hat. I would imitate every act and gesture of my companions, removing my sandals next to theirs, wringing water from my hands just like Qasim had done. If asked anything, I would shove bread in my mouth and wait for deliverance.

We sat in the Afghan way, on carpets on the floor in a dark room with no chairs. I made no eye contact with the young man who brought kebabs on long, pointed metal skewers and laid them on the plastic mat that ran along the floor. I nodded for tea, and again for sugar. "They think you're Tajik," Qasim whispered.

Hussein picked up two pomegranate drinks for the road, and we left alive and full. (The backseat felt like a tighter squeeze.)

To Bamiyan and back, every cellphone, every gaze that lingered or seemed to catch mine was suspicious. In the car I alternated playing a twisted game in my head—*Taliban, not Taliban*—and chiding myself for profiling what might have been the caring, pacifist father of six. Squatting atop a tall pile of dirt, a beardless kid leaned on a Kalashnikov, fiddling with a cellphone in his other hand.

Silence was my weapon, a flowing shalwar kameez my shining armor. My camera in its bulky bag was the mark of my treason, and I shoved it down between my legs, covering the strap that read "Canon" with the hat that made me look like I was from Tajikistan. Hussein handed me a sickly sweet carton of the pomegranate juice while I picked kebab from my teeth. Qasim sent a few texts. I had no reason to be afraid. The dirt once again became pavement.

BAMIYAN'S NAME COMES FROM the Sanskrit *varmayana*, "colored." The road approaches through vivid red hills that evoke my parents' old Camry. In town, assorted shades of farmland are well tended. Far away in the distance are the brown and gold sandstone cliffs, marked by stark niches in the shape of a Russian nesting doll, the memory of their giant former tenants, the famous Buddhas of Bamiyan.

Long before Islam and its arrival in the region, Bamiyan was a stop along the Silk Road at the heart of a thriving Buddhist empire. Two short millennia later in the 1960s and 1970s, it was a popular resting place on the hippie trail—the overland route to Kathmandu—where thousands of wayfaring flower children could smoke local weed and hash at the feet of the Buddhas in their man-made nooks: female Shamama, "Queen Mother," and male Salsal, "light shines through the universe," which was then the largest standing Buddha in the world at 180 feet tall.

Across the valley floor rises the Koh-e-Baba mountain range, always black and capped with white snow at 16,000 feet high; one peak known as Koh-e-Allah, "Mountain of God," has snow drifts that spell out "Allah" in Persian script and never-melting ice. In the Bamiyan bazaar 8,200 feet above sea level, it is fifteen degrees cooler than in Kabul.

A rocky hilltop is always in plain sight from anywhere in town, bristling with the ruins of an ancient citadel where all of Bamiyan once lived: this is Shahr-e Gholghola, "City of Screams." In the thirteenth century, Genghis Khan massacred everyone in the city because he was really, really pissed off that he hadn't conquered them quickly enough. From the top of the citadel the whole valley unfolds, not narrow and angled like a canyon, but round like the basin of an empty lake, like a pie crust rising in all directions.

A quiet man heaved open a heavy metal gate and the driver deposited me with Gul, the owner of the new lodge. (His name is pronounced "ghoul" in contradiction to everything he is: angelic, ruddy-cheeked and serenely smiley, as if his face couldn't crinkle because the mountains all around were doing it for him.) As soon as we'd made our kind of international medium-small talk and he'd shown me where I was going to sleep, I disobeyed his instructions and went out for an evening stroll. Bamiyan is incredibly safe, he'd always say—but there was an uncertainty now where there hadn't been. I was their first customer since the spring, and he wasn't sure how the town responded to new faces.

THE SUN WAS SETTING over Bamiyan's residential alleyways and children were playing in the shadows. One girl in all black but for a pink headscarf, the clear leader of the pack at about nine years old, had her hands at a friend's throat. The friend was grinning in an azure dress. The other looked deadly serious. A dozen children of various sizes and degrees of disarray ran screaming in circles, slowing only to inspect me. "No Dari," I would say, *I understand nothing.* I motioned to my camera, *May I?* Some backed away, and the leader tsked loudly with a stare of pure ice, never once lifting her fingers from their neckline clamp.

I put my hands around my own neck: "No violence!" They laughed, understanding my sign language. "If you don't stop, I'm going to take a picture." I aimed at the girls—I could feel the other children jittering with excitement. Perhaps the boys had never seen *her* vulnerable before, hands still frozen in their chokehold. *TCH-CHK*. Squeals of delight as they heard the shutter click. The girls broke instantly to crowd around the back end of the camera, looking where I was looking, enthralled by the tiny screen's ability to suck in the world. *That* is *them!* I could feel the smaller ones thinking. *Ha!*

But I had reached the limit of my offensive—I could push no harder without being a monster, and I agreed to lay down my arms in return for amnesty. "Okay. You take pictures of me."

I handed over my Canon Rebel XT, a model older than some of the kids, and instigated a ferocious game—part rugby, part manhunt—with the camera as an instrument of unspeakable power. They pointed and fired upon each other shouting *bikrum! bikrum!*—ninety-seven shots, half of them completely blackened by underexposure. A small girl backed me up against the rock and mud wall and took my picture. I was not so dangerous now—if I had ever been.

It seemed so fitting: women play a remarkably powerful social and political role in Bamiyan Province, whose Hazara ethnic majority was ruthlessly persecuted by the Taliban. Already outcast as Shia Muslims with physical features passed down from Turks, Tajiks and Mongolians (including Genghis Khan), Hazaras shun the burqa and send their daughters to school—nearly 80 percent of eligible girls in Bamiyan—a world apart from the 10 percent of many southern Afghan provinces. In 2005, Dr. Habiba Surabi became the country's first female governor.

I didn't know this when I watched this little band explode with energy, or when I saw a little boy in a mussed dinner jacket wrestle with the girls twice his size. *Bikrum!* Faster and faster. *Bikrum!* (It finally got through to me: "Picture!") It was their turf, for now.

A large red van pulled into the alley. It carried two men, Pashtun engineers working to build a training center for midwives down near the bazaar. Hoping only to keep the peace, they returned me my Canon and opened their compound's iron gate, turquoise and shaped like the twin tablets of the Ten Commandments. I thought maybe the rules had changed, and I snapped some pictures as boys ran through my field of view like gleeful soldiers; Dinner Jacket beamed in straight lines, a boy with few teeth giggled in dizzying circles. Soon they were all chasing me as a pack, pulling at the camera strap in unison. I kept clicking, back-pedaling quickly—but without knowing it, I had already crossed a line.

I saw that one boy had picked up a rock, and then they all had. All with stones as big as their hands. I couldn't glean from their faces whether anger or playfulness had changed their minds, or politics or boredom. I was scared. Then, fleetingly, I relished my reason for being so among all the scenarios imagined and possible in Afghanistan. Then I was scared again.

I was still facing the children when the engineers' voices rang out behind me, delivering discipline in Dari. Rocks fell to the ground.

"You will come have tea?"

IN A SMALL ROOM there was a mattress for every wall, laid along the floor with floral sheets neatly tucked in. A single lightbulb hung from the ceiling, but the room was well lit with the last threads of sunlight weaving in through the bars on the window. I saw all fourteen of their eyes on me. Most gazed out from above friendly noses and a smile, some wore the blankest of stares—blank not with incomprehension but with openness to my whimsical appearance on their lonely residential backstreet in central Afghanistan. Naeem, one of the engineers, sat on my right side.

"They are here for you," he said in English.

These men, born in Afghanistan, had lived much of their lives as refugees in Pakistan and now lived together in a small commune to do construction work on a midwife training center in peaceful Bami-yan. Naeem was tall and handsome, clean shaven but for a light goatee, with the kind of face that could place him anywhere. I hadn't noticed an accent after a handful of words of introduction and suspected, in a flash of conspiracy, that he was another undercover American hiding in

Afghan clothes. I tried to think of a hand sign only Americans would know, a secret Westerners' salute, but craftiness came out as candor: "So, where are you from?"

"Kabul," he said.

I didn't pretend to be Lebanese anymore. Apart from Gul, these were the first Afghans in Afghanistan I told I was American.

I didn't look like their stock photo of "English"—their usual bracket for all native-English speakers. Naaem described this character, one who would arouse the wrong kind of curiosity on the road from the capital: "Big, big body . . . big and fat . . . and white. Blue eyes or green eyes—red faces." Anything but a superfecta of these qualities and a refusal to dress locally was enough for safe passage to Bamiyan.

And if they ever thought I was CIA, they never let on. My reasons for coming, just to come, did not have the sound of masked secrets.

Naeem translated for many but spoke for most, and someone turned off the television for us to question one another rather than listen to mostly dispiriting news through static in Urdu. "Tonight you will be with us," he told me in the way an oracle relates a prophecy. Hospitality is never in question in the Bamiyan Valley. If there is a guest, there is a meal, there is a bed, there is every frill the hosts have denied themselves. "We will bring you something special that you'll like it," Naeem said. "Wine, or something like this?"

I never asked if they had access to alcohol, or if they would even drink it, but I certainly didn't want to find out by sending them on a dangerous Grey Goose chase to find liquor for *the American*. The offer implied no possession, it merely evinced the willingness to give. I never once questioned that willingness—I knew they would have chased geese for me all night just to say *welcome*.

We became simpler people. The man with an angular face and ebullient blue eyes, who had met me outside, who had saved me from a pack of excited children with stones in their hands, spoke in a quiet voice. "Take tea?" His name was Osama Latif. (The guys smirked, "Pay attention to the 'Latif!' ")

I fumbled with the phrase my Pashtun tailor friends had taught me in Abu Dhabi for just such an occasion: "*Kataso skay, bya malahum raorey.*" *If you are drinking tea, then bring some for me also.*

For an hour we talked about each other. I looked for information with clumsy questions. ("Is there any cultural difference between Afghan and Pakistani Pashtuns?" Answer: "No.") They took a very different approach, prizing my character from the looks on my face, the way I sat, the way I moved. They found information in the way I reported the opinions of my compatriots, with my tone, perhaps, as the only gauge of my consent: "What do American people think about the Taliban?"

However much silence there had been, there was more. Men shifted on the mattresses and leaned in from the walls. I didn't know where they stood. I summoned every ounce of diplomatic vagueness and gratuitous jargon that had pulled me through college political science papers. "The Taliban supports a way of doing something that allows for methods that are inhumane . . ." I said haltingly. No one spoke. As Pashtuns, Naeem and company were the country's majority but the valley's minority—two-thirds of Bamiyan province is Hazara; a thousandth is Pashtun. And as Pashtuns, these men fell into the ethnic group the Taliban claimed to represent. But these men were no supporters of the Taliban. Like much of Bamiyan's current population, they had fled abroad during the height of the Taliban rule in the 1990s and returned to Afghanistan after Karzai (a Pashtun who had been living in exile in Pakistan) took over at the end of 2001; others had never left the country, but had come north toward the greater safety of the Bamiyan Valley. All of those displaced were nationally Afghan, some Dari speaking, some Pashto speaking, many ostracized by other coteries of local society. Mokhtar, Gul's employee and my best source of information, was born in Tehran and had the accent to show for it. ("And we have better style," he said.) Refugees who were born or lived in Iran spoke Dari (almost identical to Iranian Persian); their skin is lighter, their features more Caucasian. The Pashto speakers (who also speak Dari) lived in refuge in Pakistan's North-West Frontier Province, now known as Khyber Pakhtunkhwa.

Their livelihood depended on the protection of this ethnically distinct, socially advanced province from militant onslaught. I ventured an observation before an opinion: "Afghans that are Persian think it's the Pashtun—they're afraid."

Naeem was nodding. "Persian people think Pashtuns are the Taliban. Here I'm Pashtun and I'm scared of Taliban." This was the constant paradox of their lives: every vestige of Pashtun culture—clothes, facial hair, language, skin color, the nationality of their passport—these separated them from their Western contracting colleagues. So what they could change they did within reason, but beardless and Pashtun, they became typical subjects for Taliban interrogation.

"That is not Pashtun," said Osama Latif, denouncing extremists. In his mind, he belonged to an ethnic group defined not only by common language; his group was founded on ethics, too. As we might condemn with the word *un-American*, Osama Latif repudiated the Taliban for their rejection of basic ethics. *To be Afghan is a privilege that can be rescinded.*

Identities had to have some moral backing because they had no clear face: Afghanistan's quarter-million square miles have seen dynasties come and go and become other things—there is no one look to the populations indigenous to this land. I saw Mongolian boys and American men, Spanish women and Irish kids with red hair and green eyes and freckles. Whatever I'd pictured as Persian or Pashtun or Parsi or Tajik or Mongolian or Uzbek, all of this can be Afghan.

Osama Latif mocked the militants' real common trait: "Same cap and hat, now we're Taliban!" We deny their ethnicity, and we can deny their nationality—they have only their hats. By this process, the men in this room had ostracized terrorists to the brink of humanity.

Of course, in doing so they tended to overstate the role of foreigners. Taliban volunteers may be Chechen or Arab or Pakistani, but Osama Latif and the others were making a different point: they are not us, so they must not be truly Afghan.

"When he goes on vacation, he goes to Pakistan," Osama Latif said. If you're a Talib, he meant, your heart isn't in Afghanistan—not where mine is.

In Afghanistan, blame fell often on "Pakistan." In Lahore, two

men would tell me the terrorists were coming from India. In northern India, I'm sure, they will say extremists come from the south. In the south, they undoubtedly come from Sri Lanka. And if Sri Lanka ever faces another terrorist threat, blame may rebound northward, or they may well accuse evil creatures that rise from the sea to tyrannize the innocent and go bump in the night.

And so banished from the world of sense and reason, the Taliban were relegated to the one scrap of territory they had left: the domain barbed not by wire but by ridicule. Naeem asked me what I would do if the Taliban caught me, but spoke before I could try to answer seriously: "You fuck the Talib that's killing you!" The Taliban were now the butts of jokes. (As it turned out, butt humor is ageless in Afghanistan. Every so often, Naeem would tease Khial Meer, the Khandahari man opposite me who wore a look of unflappable calm all evening. "In Khandahar, you sleep with your back against the wall," Naeem joked with a big grin. "You know what they say over there? 'Allah save everything. But wall save butts.'")

I asked to video them recounting jokes in Pashto, and though first enthusiastic, they turned fearful. They reckoned that if I were ever in danger, if the American government were to be looking for me, they would find records of these particular men . . . joking. (Earlier, Naeem had excitedly run in with knives when I asked if we could pose for a picture with them pretending to kidnap me. The others convinced us it was a bad idea.) It didn't worry me that they had implied the possibility of my abduction (when I landed in Afghanistan, I'd already imagined worst-case scenarios and ignored them) but it was striking how powerfully they felt a joking attitude and a straight face might be perceived differently by outsiders.

In this room, though, it felt like there was no performance. I didn't censor myself as some kind of experiment, or for safety or popularity, and I trusted deeply that they weren't performing either.

That night we ate thick beans and yellow rice with the warm Afghan bread that is baked flat, punctured with hundreds of holes with two roles: keeping the bread flat and serving as a kind of baker's signature. A much older man with a gray beard down to his breastbone joined us on the floor. "The leader," Naeem stated proudly. The man finished eating and turned up the volume on the news; tanks rolled around somewhere in the north, no reports of violence from the south. Naeem wiped his fingers on the bread. "You're Muslim?" he asked.

"Jewish."

"What?"

"I'm Jewish."

I saw no grain of malice in his eyes, only that I had steered him into uncharted waters—exploring the close kinship of our traditions. "We did chapter one," I said. "Christianity is chapter two. The Quran is chapter three—it's all the same story." It wasn't the most eloquent exegesis of Abrahamic scripture, but it felt like a start. "Honestly, I don't really believe any of it," I shrugged happily.

This was a faux pas in the traveler's Rulebook for Devout Places. I found that differences in religion were tolerated (and understood) far more readily than a *lack* of faith. If I didn't subscribe to a higher power, how could I be trusted to live by any code of ethics? Who were we mutually afraid of?

I mentioned Adam and Abraham, *Ibrahim*, and won brief nods from the room. The man from Khandahar agreed with every word and told me so in Arabic. We hadn't gotten terribly far in our conversation, but we had opened the forum—and with that, the call to prayer sounded and the men dispersed to perform their ablutions.

EVERY DAY in the central Afghan summer, wild wind and rain rage for a brief moment, usually around 2 P.M. Making a dash from the shelter of the Buddha shells, Mokhtar and I leaped over the irrigation ditches with jacket collars pulled over our heads, scampering through the fields.

Little caves have always freckled the cliffs, once housing hermits seeking calm and stillness, or enlightenment, or a better view. Now, they were known to house those displaced by violence farther south. At the height of Shamama's navel, one family peeked out from the refuge of one of these holes, reforging a millennium-old lifestyle.

In 2001, only two years after he had promised to protect them, Taliban leader Mullah Mohammed Omar forced townspeople to drill charges of dynamite into the Buddhas. With the help of antitank mines and rockets, the icons that had stood since the sixth century were reduced to rubble.

But when they demolished the Buddhas, they unwittingly uncovered a series of fifty hidden caves and temples carved into the rock behind them. A dozen of these are decorated with oil paintings from as far back as the fifth century, many hundreds of years before Europeans ever painted with oil. In their crusade to eradicate idolatry, the Taliban helped discover the oldest oil paintings in the world.

The alleyways gave way to little absurdities like this. In an underground shed below the Rah-e Abrisham lodge, Gul neatly stacked ski gear donated from Italy. In the spring, the town had hosted the First Afghan Ski Challenge, coordinated by the Swiss and Afghan members of the new Bamiyan Ski Club. Iconoclasm discovering icons; racism succeeded by ski races. Eight-year-olds with rocks more dangerous than the land mines in the hills.

The Taliban government was ousted eight months after destroying the Buddhas; they now have no control in Bamiyan. And still, the absent niches in the cliffs are the loudest things in the valley.

It was a place that was impossible to pigeonhole, and every time I began to construct the shortcuts I use to simplify spaces and consolidate people, Afghanistan said *no*. When contradictions were still possible, my mind was open, and delighted in absurdity, and took everything in.

FIFTEEN MINUTES BY TAXI due west is Dara-e Azhdahar, "Dragon Valley," a land that is home to an indestructible legend. Past a small town pinched between sharp cliffs that look like petrified theater curtains, the road turns to face a massive stone hill with a smooth spine. This is a once-great dragon defeated by Ali, the fourth Islamic caliph, the defining patriarch of Shia Islam. A fissure wide enough to fall into snakes along the backbone and marks the strip of flesh that Ali cut from the dragon to save a young girl from sacrifice. The dragon weeps to this day: a gurgling opening at the end of the crevice spits clear, salty water in noisy, paroxysmal spurts.

I let my eyes run over the grasses as we rode the dirt road out of town. And then, camera down by my knees: I was locked in the tractor beam of a girl's gaze. Tiny, with a shaved head and bright eyes electric blue under black eye shadow, tightly wrapped in a red dress. She was about two or three and she held on to her mother's finger and stared at me. For years now, I have called her to mind.

Another fifty miles pass by beautifully through barren, sandy bluffs and lush farmland with sheep out to pasture, all with ice-capped mountains in the near distance. Paying very close attention to faded signs along the dust and mud road, ignoring them, and then relying on his instinct, our driver took a right turn through the grasses.

And when my expectations finally hit zero, an enormous lake appeared a thousand feet below. This is the driveway to Band-e Amir, Afghanistan's first and only national park, home to six sapphire-blue lakes magically sprung from the alpine desert. Entry costs fifty afghanis, one dollar, for a life-changing tableau.

Towering cliffs form the walls of each lake, stunningly reddish brown and gray and changing colors with the sunlight. Each is separated from the next by a natural dam of bright white calcareous travertine that spills over its edges like an infinity pool. The lake's overflow cascades down the calcium-rich rock in sparkling waterfalls toward the next lake. These dams are the park's namesake—Band-e Amir, named for Ali, is "King's Dam."

The other lakes are called Band-e Haibat, "Grandiose Dam," Gholaman (slaves), Qambar (Ali's personal slave), Zulfiqar (Ali's sword), Pudina (wild mint) and Panir (cheese).

The view farther along the entrance is enough to make your eyes explode—a second lake actively sloshes into the desert, accented with bright white rock and thick verdure that follow no natural pattern, all flanked by mountains that will spoil the surprises of any Martian mission. In the winter, all of this is spectacular snow and ice.

Restaurants in the area offer bread and thick local butter that tastes almost like cheese, with black or green tea and jars of blood-red jam. In the nearby town of Qarghaneh Tu, we picked up lunch: tender chunks of lamb on the bone, wrapped in a container of fresh Afghan bread, and packed with salt and spices to sprinkle on liberally by the lake.

From the end of the road at the Grandiose Dam, Mokhtar, the driver, and I clomped in sandals down the short trail that hugs the cliff face and drops down to the ice-cold lake. But no Afghan weekend get-away is complete without a swim. In its perfection, the park offers shallow and warmer crystal clear pools with sandy white bottoms, each a secluded beach, surrounded by geometric rock formations, trickling streams, and near mosquito-less greenery. We swam, we ate lamb until we needed to lie down, I covered my face with a scarf, and the fish nibbled politely at my feet.

Across the water, a shrine venerating Ali offers shelter when the afternoon gale whips dust and rain across the water on the heels of Afghanistan's 2 P.M. black clouds. The clouds pass, and picnicking families return to the flotilla of colorful paddleboats and kayaks that the park rents out for a small, negotiable fee.

THE DEPARTURE HALL of the Kabul International Airport had three gates, all without numbers. All three open onto the same hallway, to be followed past the signs marked EXIT/BAGGAGE CLAIM (this is also the arrival hall). There are no TV screens, no lists of departure times, no announcements; the scheduled boarding, check-in, and flight times come and go like summer rains. An hour or two late, the flight is announced in Dari. Maybe English, too. Plainclothes guards search bags and give blasé farewell pat downs onboard the small prop plane while passengers squeeze by into creaky seats. Pat, pat. And off we go, over Tora Bora and the scruff that looks like Arizona, above the hills where we had thought Osama might be, and was.

CHAPTER 8 | PAKISTAN ◄

COOL WIND

———

HAD PLANNED TO RIDE over the river (a narrow offshoot of the Indus) and through the woods north of Islamabad to my friend's grandmother's house in Abbottabad, Pakistan. The wolf would've been Osama bin Laden—and he was already dead.

I landed in the Islamabad airport, only two hours away by local taxi. But word in the garrison town on the Karakorum Highway, and now on news channels across the world, was that "they" were watching out for foreigners. That day, Pakistan had arrested five CIA informants who contributed to the raid in Abbottabad. In recent weeks, camouflaged military lurking in the grass around the compound had undertaken to confiscate and smash cellphones of the curious. Iman told me that even in shalwar kameez and dirty sandals, I was an American danger to myself and to everyone I came in contact with. Grandma called her daughter, Iman's Aunt S., who called Iman, who texted me with extreme embarrassment: I couldn't come for lunch—I was on my own.

I thought I'd go to Abbottabad anyway. How often are we given the opportunity to gloat at the death site of humanity's worst offenders? If I could see the tiered private retirement home where Osama spent his final years with porn and videos of himself . . . maybe the world Nine Eleven had shaped for me would dissolve. If I faced the fear of getting to this place and saw that there was nothing left but cricket pitches, maybe

the restlessness would be gone. My constant hope: that I could report back to my twelve-year-old self that the world had not been reshaped that day, and he would abstain, for the very first time, from saying "Prove it."

But . . . I'd upset what personal connections I had here if I disobeyed Grandma. I could put the family in danger, too, just to find selfish relief. It was like having Masha in a car with uncertain brakes that I hurtled down a desert road just to keep myself in motion. Plus, to visit would be to perpetuate the legend, to submit to a terrorist's posthumous power, to gawk at cordoned-off property like the encased relics of saints. I convinced myself so, and took the bus away to Lahore.

Instantly: waves of regret. So much talk about this place and I wasn't going because I told myself I shouldn't. And because I had been disinvited to lunch. The regrets gathered their reasons: the deed was *done* up there; there was no reason to think there would be any real trouble in this Boca of the North-West Frontier Province; the Pakistani government wouldn't want much with me, and the regular folk didn't even believe Osama had been killed—at least not in Pakistan. And there couldn't be any trouble I wouldn't get out of with an American passport and my one well-practiced phrase in Urdu, *"Yeh kittana hota heh?"* ("How much does that cost?").

I had forgone *doing something* for the choice *not* to do it. I followed a stubborn will to ignore the figure some Pakistanis called OBL and aggravated an even more stubborn one to *do more, more, more!*

LAHORE WAS blisteringly hot.

In all white, I adopted the look of the bluer collar while two men escorted me across the city. Iman had mobilized social networks and family ties for me: the men worked for her friend's friend's father, the president of the oldest and largest university in Pakistan. I e-mailed Masha from the president's guest house. "Got into this city with 20 cents—still havent spent it."

You can't get far without hearing, *"Lahore nahin dekha tou kuch nahin dekha"* ("If you haven't seen Lahore, you haven't yet seen the world"). The city is peppered with gardens and architecture left by the Mughal empire and parallel kingdoms. The Shalimar gardens are green even in the June broil, and families picnic and sit by the fountains. A couple of couples nap in piles.

I drifted through it in the comfort of the air-conditioned Camry. The driver was in traditional shalwar, the president's assistant was in slacks and a shirt. They were the consummate tour guides when they spoke to me, and to each other they bantered in Punjabi. A member of the Indo Arian family to which Hindi and Urdu belong, Punjabi appeared to be a language, at least before dark, that must always be spoken very, very loudly in someone's ear.

They whisked me into the Badshahi Mosque, cousin of the Taj Mahal, with its walled courtyard for a hundred thousand people. Across the scalding stones the guide pointed out a very special relic in a small room: "The Underwear of the Prophet Muhammad," the label said. "No pictures," said the president's man. Back to the car, in and out of a fried chicken joint, and back to eat in the Camry because it was the coldest place in town.

We asked out the window for a lanky boy to bring us mango milkshakes in tall glass mugs. Ambrosia against the 110-degree heat, made of mangoes from the interior of Sindh Province, with a blender powered by a generator, and ice cut from chunks delivered by a truck that dripped steadily onto the pavement. The boy knocked on the window carrying three more glasses. "More?"

With such treatment, lounging in the passenger seat of an imported car, sipping the sweetened juice of the sweetest fruit, I noticed the cocktail many tourists must certainly perceive in the Asian subcontinent: utterly deferent service and automatic, maybe involuntary hospitality. I had no idea who we really were to one another.

And then we drove thirty minutes from the city to the Wagah border with India, where every evening at 5:30 the two countries profess their friendship for each other, and for the world to watch. Indian and Pakistani border guards in peacock hats goose-step and high kick and make exceedingly silly faces at one another and lower their flags as the sun goes down. They come back to do it again the next day, just as they have done every evening since 1959.

"I like India," the president's man said. I ballooned with good feeling. "Just Hindus: no, no." Popped. "Suicide bombings—money, planning: India background," the man said. "All India."

The driver pitched in: "India and Israel." There were murmurs from the back in Punjabi, but I could recognize *shush* in a thousand dialects. The man in slacks leaned forward to pat me on the shoulder. "Israel, no, no."

And there it was: a critique hidden, a feeling suppressed. There was no joy in having this instant without masks on because I knew we were just about to put them on again, more firmly attached.

But Iman was one of the most open books I'd ever met. I flew away to find her in Karachi.

"Jewish population of Jinna Airport = 1," I texted.

I FELT BETTER when Iman's guard opened the door. Aurangzeb held an old shotgun, and smiled so lightly it seemed he might disappear. The upper middle class is well staffed and well guarded in Pakistan, even if Aurangzeb's shotgun wasn't loaded. Income inequality makes this possible and necessary.

In one corner, the Afro Pakistani maids from the interior of Sindh Province speak Sindhi to one another. Downstairs, the driver jokes with a guard in Pashto. A Punjabi Christian comes in two hours each week to help clean. Iman's family are known as Delhi Wallas because they moved from Delhi after the India Pakistan partition, and speak Urdu, brother of Hindi, natively.

The diversity in Iman's house wasn't an accident. Her dad said that he thinks it keeps things in balance. (Apart from the Christian cleaner-cum-chatterbox, though, he doesn't trust Punjabis.)

Every once in a while, old ethnic conflicts flare and the caste system is made manifest: no amount of washing will get the cook to share a mug with the trash collector. Maybe that was part of the balancing act— little outbursts kept the pressure at bay.

I floated apart from all of this, a white man entirely outside of caste, and everyone offered me mango juice in all kinds of mugs. It let me be a wild card of sorts. My tailors in Abu Dhabi had given me the right suits to wear: I sat cross-legged happily on the floor and picked at fried *pakoras* with my hands—like a native, Iman's uncle said. The maid Amina said I was just like them: I was always barefoot.

It was so much easier to mirror their hands and clothes and eyes than it would have been to decide how to use my own. What did I *really* care what kind of utensils we used for fried foods? (And how much easier to click into a new home, when we could not find ways to judge one another for the way we used a fork or chopsticks?) If it was the normal thing to do, and it would've freed me from judgment for a moment longer, I would've gnawed cans open with my front teeth.

Parsi, Hindu, Sikh, and Christian are all within striking distance in Karachi.

Twenty minutes away from Iman's, around the Jail Road roundabout and through the city's infamous traffic are the gates to Saint Patrick's Cathedral. A man with a dark, happy face guarded the impressive grounds with his sleepy dog. Diego Rodriguez welcomed us inside, to admire the stately staircases of a white marble monument, and said the rest was off-limits. The church was closed except for Sunday mass because of two recent attacks. "It is sad," said Diego.

The city was bursting with disaster- and desperation-driven immigration, from rural poverty toward urban possibility. In the town of more than twenty million, one of the world's ten largest, attacks were frequent. It was too dangerous to walk on the street—one of the reasons Iman's family had a driver. Robbery murders at stoplights were frequent. Most families were one or two degrees of separation away from a kidnapping. Still, notable attack sites carry special weight.

As we parked and approached another, the site of a double suicide bombing that claimed dozens of casualties in 2010, I felt naked on the Karachi city streets. I tightened and swelled against the dangers I imagined. If they were coming, they would come instantly and without warning.

Iman, a born-and-raised Karachiite, seemed nervous. "Don't tell my dad we went here."

The monumental Sufic mausoleum of Abdullah Shah Ghazi looks out over Sea View Beach from its hilltop on Firdousi Street. Crowned by two solid green flags, the exterior is entirely navy-blue tile and patterns of thick, white zigzags. All day and night, crowds leave their shoes beyond the defunct metal detector and climb to the shrine to pray to the ninth-century mystic saint, under whose aegis, many believe, tropical disasters have spared Karachi for more than a millennium.

At night, Iman's father and I drank Gordon's gin and tonic with no ice. The next night, we danced. Iman's family dressed me in elegant shalwar for a prewedding party with whisky on draft. Black Label in highball glasses with ice cubes almost too big for them, and orange dresses swirling in the generator's breeze—that was the picture I took from Karachi nights.

I DIDN'T COME TO PAKISTAN to drink, though. Sure, the tang of twelve-year-old scotch was one more arrow against simple stereotypes of a teetotaling Islamic Republic, but that was no more a discovery than it was to have BLTs with my Israeli cousins.

Four days earlier, I had tried to tell myself I could ignore *him*, but I was feeding myself lies. Maybe I could have learned to believe them with years of therapy or meditation or medication. I could have put regret aside and left the past behind like an unrequited high school crush, or an unwise war. There was a far deeper obsession here than my usual addiction to saying *no* to *noes*. The target was more focused, and the treatment seemed clear.

Hours before the return flight I'd just booked, I e-mailed in sick to work in Abu Dhabi. I wasn't going to stick out the way they'd thought, the Karachi family told the Abbottabad family. After all, I was barefoot and eating *pakoras* with my hands.

I followed Iman's aunt who I knew only as Aunt S. onto a night flight to Peshawar and into a car through the blackness to Abbottabad. *Sometimes a man wants to be stupid . . .*

To the west was the notorious Swat Valley, once dubbed by Queen Elizabeth the "Switzerland" of the former empire, but now primarily in the hands of the Taliban. But Abbottabad was still a destination for vacationers from Lahore bouncing up from the Potohar Plateau to escape twenty degrees of summer heat.

According to Grandma, my presence was no longer impermissibly dangerous; with the right clothes, in the right company, I was invisible. I could blend in with the young laborers returning from Karachi, or the day-trippers, or with the out-of-towners from Lahore and Islamabad who posed for pictures in front of Osama's house in the wake of his death.

Still, camouflaged Pakistani military lurked in tall grass on all sides of the house, hands clutching rifles, eyes scouring the intentions from our faces. Grandmother's friend, Osama's onetime neighbor, spun by in the morning to take us to the site. I asked if I could take a picture quickly from the car. "No." He was firm. "Someone is watching."

There it was: white, boxy, suburban. The compound looked smaller than on TV. I didn't speak to a single Abbottabadite who believed Osama had actually been there: "We would have known," said everyone. "We are nosy people," said Aunt S.

It was true, in this town that had grown immensely in recent decades, that old families remain connected and infinitely knowledgeable about local comings and goings. But there was a paradox: Grandmother pointed to the fourteen-foot walls. These are typical of large families that have moved in from Waziristan, not a sign of reclusiveness or hidden secrets. Abbottabad locals feel more tribal kinship with Waziris, she said, than they do with city folk and vacationers pushing in from the capital—for this, the little birds on the grapevine might have left these closet Saudis alone. Secrets *can* live in Abbottabad.

For Pakistani or American, believer or skeptic, this empty house was the site of a brief and powerful global focus, an instant memorial to the day when America won a war against a symbol.

And there I was, staring at it.

———

THE GRASS WAS GREEN on the short drive home and we took tea in Grandma's brick house and I melted into the cool couches and asked questions to my younger self.

He was unimpressed. September 11 had never been my impulse for travel, it had only been its ad campaign, an excuse, fears of the other substituting cheaply for real fears of myself. It was me on all sides.

As a good American, I set out to defend my freedom against the threat of the ultimate constraint: death. By imagining that some Others could bring death to my doorstep, I flew to challenge them on their own turf, to see whether the existential dangers were truly there. I faced my own doubts by giving them faces that weren't mine.

And like this, I made each person play devil's advocate to a stereotypical devil. Every little girl and old man stood in comparison to a deadly archetype—if the girl was sweet, she was also *not prejudiced*; if the man was a kind host, he was also *not a murderer*. I took the humanity out of the world I wanted to prove was human.

When over and over and over and over again the devils were defeated, I was unmoored. I flirted with the deadly just to steady myself against the dizziness of freedom.

It had taken so much energy to keep that charade alive. Try it—try pushing against your own hand as hard as you can. If I saw that I was really fighting me, I could stop pushing long enough to actually *decide* on a direction. I'd have to actually choose between *go/don't go* without resorting to the infinite simplification where the only paths are life and death, and where something else always has a hand in rolling the dice. *Decisions*. I'd have to pit abstract absolutes ("All good!" "All bad!") against each other and come to land somewhere on *terra firm enough*.

IN THE AFTERNOON, Aunt S. took me on a drive for the real reason people came to Abbottabad beyond local claims to the world's best pine nuts—to have lunch of freshly slaughtered chicken nine thousand feet up in the foothills of the Himalaya—and to make metaphors out of topography. As we climbed off a branch of the Karakoram Highway and looked down on the city, Osama's compound was hardly visible.

We climbed five thousand feet past the apiaries to a hill station called Thandiani to pick a chicken, have it killed, and drink Sprite. Like Aunt S. and her family, they spoke Hindko up here, a Punjabi dialect named for its relation to India, *Hind*, as a distinction from the Pashto all around. Thandiani means "cool wind" in Hindko—and the descent felt all the hotter for it.

*I have been trying to help you be you by accepting that
you would rather be in Iraq or the Sudan than with
me . . . but its hard. And i want you to choose me.*

OÙ EVE!

———

ASHA HELD MY KITE string, in the way that is almost always good for a kite. Or really—she was the string, the security against fears of drifting off the planet, and I felt safer to have her knotted to me wherever I went. She was stuck to a place, though—in America—and I couldn't imagine being so stuck to any solid ground.

After nine months apart, it was infinitely clear that we couldn't stay together long distance if we didn't see each other's faces. I flew to Chicago for a fast week in a small hotel. The world of deep dish pizza and pork sausages and hand-holding in the streets: I was electrified to be with her, and nearly panicked to get home to Abu Dhabi. Like I'd left the kettle on, and it was screaming.

I was sick almost from the first bite of pepperoni until the plane back, uncomfortable with the comfort she offered.

- - - - - -

I DIDN'T FEAR IRAQ as much as I obsessed over it, quietly. And I didn't obsess in the notebook-pages-filled-with-its-name kind of way. It was a name that had reverberated just under surface awareness since we—and it was *we*—began to bomb it—and only since then. And what a good name to do the reverberating!—in with a vowel, out with the hardest of consonants.

As a boy, I trailed in the logic of a country going to wars; now I'd followed it to the Afghan datelines and through to the place where the punishment for our hurt was executed on its most personal scale. Next, I would have to make the logical leap into Iraq.

Two days before leaving for the Eid al-Adha break, I was about as far as I'd get in the brainstorming phase of a week in Iraqi Kurdistan—the final "itinerary" would be a few phone numbers and a general understanding of the east-to-west order of Kurdistan's three major cities.

My colleague Nora swiveled to face me from her desk in the corner of a large floor of loosely tangled cubicles in our new, stark, glassy offices in Abu Dhabi. Originally she was from Baghdad, but her Assyrian Christian family, native speakers of a modern dialect of Aramaic, had sought refuge from extremist persecution by Arab Muslims in the south. Now her family lived in Dohuk, an Iraqi Kurdish city of about a quarter million near the border with Turkey.

"I've never even seen the waterfalls," Nora said.

At points off the beautiful road from Dohuk to the capital of Kurdistan in Erbil, there are waterfalls, *shillal*—or so her family had told her. But they had never packed her in the car to see them, despite the modern Mesopotamian fondness for picnicking in pretty places. The Nineveh Plain, the lush region on the upper banks of the Tigris where the legendary cities of Nineveh and Nimrud poked out from the underbrush of suburban Mosul, was her family's ancestral homeland. But even there, in the autonomous north where Baghdad is despised, Kurdish nationalism and religious persecution of Christians have not made for the most peaceable homecoming.

Since the fall of Saddam Hussein, Kurdish autonomy had increased exponentially. As Kurdish minority status in Iraq became majority rule in Iraqi Kurdistan, hawkish nationalism found new enemies to fill the role of Existential Threat. No surprise, then, that the smaller religious minorities are not champions of the region's new "freedom."

Echoing Antonia from Maaloula at her café in Syria, Nora felt more comfortable with a minority group in power. Though Saddam's Baath Party was founded by Shiites with pan-Arab idealism, it quickly became a party of the Sunni minority (about 35 percent of Iraqi Muslims). And even though other ethnic groups were not invited under this umbrella, Nora's family opposed the full independence of the Kurdish region for fear of becoming foreigners in their own land. Their religion was already a point against them; now, everywhere but in the north, their Kurdish nationality would be, too.

"They want to have their own country. This is impossible," Nora spoke flatly. "I'm really supporting Saddam in it. This is Iraq—it cannot be divided into two."

Ever since her father put her and her little sister on a plane in 2001, away from persecution and toward opportunity, she had been a refugee. He was living now in political asylum in the UAE; she was in the process of becoming an Australian. Her brother Fady, his wife, and their tiny twin daughters stayed behind in Dohuk.

Her Australian citizenship process depended on the plea that it was too dangerous to return to Iraq. She browsed tickets on Etihad Airlines that she knew she couldn't take. Only once she became an Australian could she go home again.

"Take so many pictures," she said excitedly. "I want to see my country."

Danny had written me after an unscripted week in Iraqi Kurdistan. *You've got to go*, he said. His roommate and Arabic teacher in Damascus, Khaled, was a Syrian Kurd who told him just before he left about another student of his.

"She went with her friends to Kurdistan and now she's in an Iranian prison," Khaled had said. But Danny had come back delighted.

I passed our building's security desk on the way out to gather American dollars for the trip. (U.S. currency is common tender in Kurdistan, along with Iraqi dinar, and there were no ATMs.) Ahmed, a guard from Egypt, wasn't happy with my answer about the upcoming days off.

"Why are you going to Iraq? Don't go to Iraq." His eyebrows peaked high above the rims of his glasses. "You need to have a reason." A United Nations worker or a doctor would have valid reasons, he said, but I was just a tourist. I contested unconvincingly, saying something about wanting to distinguish between facts and fears, and seeking connection. "Or maybe I just want to tell a story to a girl at a bar," I offered. Ahmed laughed, and a shrug rolled from his shoulders to his teeth.

He found it distressing, then curious, that I would choose Iraq. "There is something wrong with your thinking that you see danger and you say, 'I'm going to go,'" He wasn't upset. At another moment, he might have been right—there were many moments when I saw danger and teased the gas pedal. But Kurdistan was the opposite: I expected peace.

"You will see they are becoming much better than the other parts of Iraq," Nora had told me. Despite unresolved ethnic and national and spiritual issues, Dohuk was no Baghdad. Kurds had fought the Arabs for hundreds of years, long before Saddam made their persecution a national pastime. For this, "they lived to learn independently," Nora said, and had been rich even before foreign companies settled in northern cities to corner new markets and prepare for a postwar boom.

Ahmed had never heard anyone say this. He admitted that even his hometown, Cairo, wasn't now the tourist trap it used to be, but he wasn't as afraid—he knew more. Iraq was still a great unknown, still one big messy piece he preferred everyone he cared about would stay away from.

"We have a phrase in Islam," he said grandly: "*La tulqu b'ayadkum ila tahluka*." "Don't throw yourself by your own hands into hell."

"Jews don't really believe in hell," I said, and he laughed. My consequences and rewards were terrestrial things.

EID AL-ADHA, the Festival of the Sacrifice, celebrates Abraham's willingness to kill his son Isaac and played the role of a long Thanksgiving break. I offered my parents the decoy stories of stuckness in Abu Dhabi while I made arrangements to go to Kurdistan with Charlotte, a college friend working in Dubai, and her friend Sue, whom I knew mostly from e-mail blasts as our former student body president.

Three hours nonstop and we'd be in Erbil, the Kurdish capital. Of the few facts I knew before takeoff: the seven-thousand-year-old Erbil Citadel, a fortified earthen mound more than a thousand feet wide and a hundred feet tall that UNESCO says "may be regarded as the oldest continuously inhabited settlement in the world," sits at the very center of town.

Nora's brother Fady and his friend Makh picked us up at the airport to spend the afternoon exploring the countryside just outside the capital. Fady, short and stout with a round face and a small snub nose like a grape tomato, appeared almost unceasingly jovial, smiled while he worried, and laughed as a reply to English he didn't understand. Makh was as quiet as Fady was talkative.

At an intersection near Pirmam, home of the Kurdish Democratic Party's political bureau, a strange edifice poked out from behind roadside trees, surrounded by low, crumbling walls of some porous material. I thought they really might have been stacks of skulls and femurs. The outer wall of an ancient ruin no bigger than a 7-Eleven, it featured knobby tan and gray stones piling into a tall peak that nearly clipped the telephone wires overhead. A firm overhang shaded the room of an old house or church. Inside, a group of children shared a cigarette, inconspicuous. Out front, a pond of dirty, green water.

Kids scrambled up the rocks. Fady and Makh weren't exactly sure what the ruin might be—monuments weren't always well preserved in areas of conflict, what with a revolving cast of bureaucrats responsible for creating agencies of preservation. "Maybe four thousand years ago," said Makh. It didn't seem impossible—archeological research had confirmed sedentary presence in the area far earlier.

Content with our analyses, we tromped back to the car, nodding to a man who looked local. *What the hell*, I thought, *maybe he knows something.*

"How old is this? Maybe eight . . ." he threw his head toward the bony piles, remembering. My ears buzzed. Eight thousand years of mankind, here! No travel advisory would keep me from the Cradle of Civilization! My heart jumped, in those milliseconds before he spoke again, in the breath before ". . . or nine years."

Through tears of laughter, I wondered how many of my other gut feelings influenced by a little local confidence had been 99.6 percent wrong. Fady and Makh smiled, too, embarrassed a little about their tour guiding. "I am not from Erbil," said Fady.

We drove a little farther on to the town of Shaqlawa. On the right, one side of a huge valley slopes up into a sharp slablike ridge. To the left, across the brown and yellow space sprinkled lightly with stubby trees, the opposite escarpment looked like a long cut of pepper steak sliced into thick strips to reveal a deep, smooth red. We turned back toward town.

ERBIL'S MAIN STREETS are concentric orbits around the Citadel, which looks down on the fountains of Shar Park from the top of the massive hill covered thoroughly in steep stone slabs. The hill was home to Muslims, Christians, Jews, and Zoroastrians through the millennia, claimed by the Third Dynasty of Ur, Assyrians, Alexander the Great, the Roman Empire, Muslims, Mongols, Ottomans and now the Kurdish government.

Two hundred feet away, the Rubenesque singer at the Erbil Tower Hotel's second-floor bar was squeezed into a skin-tight pink evening gown with a sheen like thinly striped wallpaper, a long slit running up her midthigh, and she thumped to the music and crooned a few notes when breaks from her repartee with tables of dark-haired men allowed. I wasn't sure if I could call her voluptuous, Iraq being, as I thought, a conservative country. If I could, though, she was.

Tresses of straightened black hair framed an image of heavy white makeup lit irregularly by rotating disco lights of primary colors, flaming sparklers the men would buy from the pink lady, and the unmistakable sound of Arabian pop synth when the keyboardist felt like playing. We were sitting in the back on red velvet couches. "We have another beer from Turkey," the bartender suggested, and presented Heinekens from Amsterdam.

The singer spoke deeply into the microphone. "Here are my friends from Falujah!" Howls from the front. "Anyone from Basra?" Cheers. "Baghdad?" Bigger cheers. They couldn't care less where the beer was from.

She never cooed *Philadelphia?* or *The Upper East Side?* or *Detroit?* And so I sat gladly and conspicuously on the velvet with Charlotte and Sue, watching this room of outsiders from the outside.

One of the Erbil drinkers shouted to us over the noise of the bar and the fizzing of the sparklers his table had bought. He said he was having a party on Tuesday. (On Tuesday, just as he said, he called with an invitation.) He paid for our Heinekens. Beer was liberty; the noise was liberating, and the farther these tourists had come—in distance, in difficulty—the happier they were to be in Kurdistan.

OUR TRIPLE ROOM on the ninth floor was the pink of a faded skirt. The bathroom was pastel yellow. We had worried about room-sharing rules for unmarried men and women, but the hotel asked no questions despite our name that mismatched far beyond the possibility for claims of kinship (Chinese, and German-Jewish sounding). It hardly ever mattered. In restaurants we were always seated in the family section (as groups with one or more women always are) and we were treated warmly everywhere as a blend of long-lost relative, zoo animal, alien, and celebrity.

Minutes after we rode the outdoor escalator into Hawler Mall (Hawler is the city's Kurdish name, Erbil is Arabic—and with whatever we Anglophones called it, we made a little political statement), I felt the weight of universal public curiosity. The gaze was hot, my neck hairs spiked, my skin moved as if I were connected by strings to everyone I could see.

I pointed my camera at a couple of groups of mall-trawling guys with a standard pairing of gelled hair and leather jackets, but soon the tables turned. Crowds sensed action and gathered, almost everyone pushing to have their picture taken with us, *the foreigners*, or pushing their friends in as if on a dare. On the mezzanine of this mall that sold nearly identical Western-looking merchandise from nearly identical stores manned only by silvery mannequins with no faces and, maybe, some of the curious we were posing with, we obliged as long as we could and kept snapping, with our cameras or with theirs; the product didn't seem to matter. We hardly ever spoke. We said we were from America. I'd never felt so famous.

When we rode down, they seemed to follow and lead, a tight circle of dozens and dozens of Kurdish teens and adults thronging toward the escalator, out of the mall and across the street, chattering, praising the USA, and halting traffic like a small protest fueled by fascination. Occasionally, someone would present himself as an envoy, suggesting with body language to follow him, to escape from the riffraff. We'd follow for moments, not to escape, but to adventure further until, muddled into lanes of slow-moving cars, we realized our ushers had nowhere to go either. Still, the group lingered. *Who were we?*

My female companions were more uneasy. It was possible to feel their attention-gathering as something of a different sort. After dark on this crisp November night, there were only men on the Saturday streets of Erbil; there were only men in the malls and at the bar. Only by the fountains in Shar Park, dead in the center of the city, did we see a few small groups of women in headscarves gathering around the fountains lit from below with colored lights. A woman in her black abaya sat with some kids, playing. Everywhere else I looked, women had simply disappeared.

I CALLED FADY after the morning azan. Staggered from every corner of the city, the sounds of the call to prayer were richer than I remembered hearing anywhere else, evolving in a lilting weave and dissolving into the sounds of streetside banter. Mosque megaphones broadcast morning sermons that overlapped with other calls broadcast to those in bed, wafting in gentle cacophony from a hundred minarets up to our pink room on the ninth floor. An hour or so after the first call had sounded it was quiet again—only a handful of mosques were still active in the distance, fading. A car would whoosh by every now and then and disappear.

Fady answered my fourth call. He had decided to leave the night before, abandoning us, and was already in Dohuk. The city felt deserted, too—it was the morning of Eid al-Adha, the Greater Eid, the holiest of all Islamic holidays, and Muslims were busy commemorating Abraham's obedience. In reverence they would make sacrifices of their own, on the creature substituted for Abraham's son. I watched drainage ditches and street gutters trickle bright red with sheep's blood.

Sue and Charlotte didn't feel forsaken. I hadn't even thought it was possible to rent a car in Iraq, but it was, and soon we had one, because Sue was from Detroit, Motor City, and having a car was like packing a water bottle. Free for the moment, we sped off on clear roads to the north.

HIGHWAY 3 RUNS FROM ERBIL about 180 kilometers to the Iranian border, and is known by many as the Hamilton Road, named for its New Zealand engineer who completed it in 1932. In between, on one of the five mountain ranges of varying severity, I noticed something humbling out the back window of our Hyundai: a man in a brown T-shirt and shorts, protected from nippy autumn winds only by simple gloves, was cresting this couple-thousand-foot climb on his bike. He had a shaved head and an American military look about him, wearing a hikers' backpack and smiling as he pedaled. He wore black horn-rimmed glasses. We wished one another well through the window, and Clay—he told us his name with breath to spare and an accent just like mine—pushed on uphill.

Hours later we were parking at the Gali Ali Beg waterfall. The pride of all of Iraq, Gali Ali Beg is printed on the back of the blue five-thousand dinar note (about enough to get kebab nearby). In one of its did-anyone-actually-come-here moments, our *Lonely Planet* had given us cause for dissatisfaction: the "80 meter" cascade they describe is really on the much shorter side of 80 feet (more like 50–60). Still, Iraqi tourists, who came from all across the country, were genuinely wowed—unspoiled like us natives of waterfall-rich countries with easy road trips.

Clay appeared to his usual welcome of excited locals and visitors giddily trying to make sense of his choices. (Where cars are not taken for granted, and solitude is more pitied than celebrated, a bike seemed an odd pick for a long, voluntary journey—especially for a foreigner expected to have every flexibility.) It was always like this when he coasted into town, he said, and the four of us Americans went to drink hot tea sweetened with cardamom and eat meat on skewers with chewy bread and onions. Clay was an ex-Marine who had done tours in Afghanistan and Iraq. Now, he typically chose vacation spots amenable to bike trips: France, Italy, Jordan. In Kurdistan, he was a tourist like us, taking time off from his job teaching English at a school in Egypt.

"I wanted to come back here," he said. "It's nicer to get to talk to these people instead of having to fight them."

Days later in a small town a hundred miles away, we thought we saw Clay once more. He didn't see us—maybe I was just delirious from the driving. Maybe it was the image that stuck with me, the image of a soldier on his first tour as a tourist, working his way through former battlefields looking for a chat.

He had been to war, right here, and he felt the urge to reconnect. He knew things I would never know. He had seen Iraq from the ground while I had seen it only from the air and through the veil of news reports and eight time zones—and still, we had all come to see this place outside the frame of war. His presence was an affirmation: there are answers to find here.

We kept on driving, hurried like first-timers. On a road that hugs the cliffside above the waterfall, the Gali Ali Beg Canyon unfolds in deep ravines into the wild. Honey from the area is prized, and hushed salesmen offered amber jars out of their cars for the startling equivalent of fifteen American dollars, and, at least at that moment, a gentle unwillingness to negotiate. At the vistas over the gorge, fitted with tables and plastic chairs fashioned to look like tree stumps, Kurdistan presents one of the strongest cases for its reputation of calm normalcy: Domestic tourism is booming like few places in the modern Middle East. Visitors are not only Kurds, but busloads of Iraqis from Mosul and Tikrit and Basra.

Two buses had come from Baghdad, and everyone seemed thrilled to be outdoors. The crowd of a hundred or so danced and cheered while a small band struck up pulsating tunes on trumpet, snare drum, and tom-tom. They wore lanyards with yellow cards that said *Al-Balid Al-Jamil* in big letters: The Beautiful Country.

A man in a purple sweater handed me his trumpet and let me play. I think he offered with his eyes, and I must've accepted with mine. Absurdly, a microphone was produced out of nowhere with its cord trailing unplugged, and they conducted a brief and enthusiastic interview. I was American, I said, and watched faces sour—interest replaced by resentment. "*Laa yastatiia'a*," the tom-tom player objected. *He can't be.*

I had let my comfort in stereotypes about the north carry me away. Americans were now liberators in Kurdistan, where Saddam was forever a genocidal menace. In Baghdad, we'd hear again and again, life is not better, the streets are not safer, and people are no happier in the war's wake. The band didn't look pleased.

WE STOPPED ON A SUNDAY in Aqrah, a famous town built into a gritty hillside in Iraq's modern Ninawa governorate. The houses cover the lower hills in a blanket of tan brick with rare pastel highlights: key lime, yellow, purple. Once an Assyrian town, Aqrah is now mostly Kurdish Muslims. Mosques had released hundreds of children from their Eid al-Adha prayers, and they were pouring through the streets in turtleneck sweaters and suits waving ice cream cones (a Kurdish favorite is a mix of six neon-colored flavors) and toy guns. Many had returned for the holiday from new residences abroad, in Stockholm, in Russia, in Canada. "Do you speak Swedish?" kids asked expectantly.

The town was celebrating. A pair of policemen carrying rifles guided us up the road with kids following behind and twentysomethings in shiny suits striking model poses and demanding to have their pictures taken. Four pairs of girls shrieked and flew in happy circles on a mini Ferris wheel operated by a hand crank. If I had learned anything about Kurdistan, I could appreciate their love of amusement parks—the drive from Erbil passed at least three giant Ferris wheels in the middles of nowhere.

On the way down, with a train of fascinated and apprehensive children, we bumped into fifteen-year-old Umar from Volgograd. "They are following you because you are girls . . . to see what you are doing," Umar said to Sue and Charlotte of his fellow townspeople, presumably those who weren't in frilly dresses. "All will follow her and try to get her."

They were also curious, Umar said, because there were only ten female drivers in all of Aqrah. Sue drove our big Hyundai unapologetically.

I still thought of Sue the way I'd known her first—as president of the Student Council, and because I never knew what "Student Council" really meant: as *President*. Charlotte called her "*The* Sue Yang."

There was a comfort in having Madame President at the wheel. And when we drove, I grew into the role of the backseat—and because I thought of backseat driving as a cardinal sin, I became lazier as a matter of principle.

Here: the freedom of traveling with the fixedness of a small group— as detached from our environs as a pinball, but as tightly podded as three pips of cardamom. I didn't need to fight every second for connection. But maybe that was why I didn't take notice of my companions even as much as I would a houseguest—moving together, I assumed a kind of closeness that made Charlotte and Sue like parts of me, and me like parts of them. I became more selfish, but I liked to think the self was all of us.

I traveled more comfortably not alone, but more dully. And when I noticed the dullness: a new discomfort, a feeling that I was not doing enough.

Umar was celebrating the Eid according to village traditions: 6 A.M. prayer followed by house visits and gift giving—chocolates, cakes, *pepsi* (a catchall for any dark soda in Kurdistan)—to other families in town. His family would stay and chat for ten minutes and then move on to the next house.

And what about the Christians? we wondered. He didn't know much, but there was a church near his house that he had never been inside. We were curious about the minorities in the secessionist state.

Umar offered to guide us to the plain stucco building behind a gate with a crucifix on it. He spoke quietly in Kurdish on our behalf to a few men outside and we were all invited in, warmly; we encouraged Umar to poke in with us to the services held on the small second floor. A dozen or so congregants sat in pews. Umar looked nervous, standing with his back against the wall. He was afraid of "talk," he said. The village had eyes, and if they saw him at a church, he'd never hear the end of it.

The priest was delighted. He showed us scripture in Syriac (the modern dialect of Aramaic written in an ancient script that looks one part Hebrew, two parts kooky computer font) and invited us to come to a full sermon he was about to give half an hour away in the town of Malabrouan. Umar left the church for the first time in his life and bade us farewell—he wouldn't go further with this crowd. Happy to have practiced his English, he was relieved to watch us go, grateful to be free again from the fear of gossip. We followed the priest's pickup truck in the darkness to a stocky yellow building swarming with car lights, took off our shoes, and fell into line behind the regulars.

I couldn't follow the service—in Kurdish with passages in Syriac—but I liked being a nonpracticing Jew in a Christian service on a Muslim holiday. And when that smugness faded, I settled in to the atmosphere, ancient and magnificent, nurtured by the reverence of the parishioners. The priest in long robes spoke to a full room. Charlotte, half-Jewish, half-Christian (wholly Christian to the congregation), was half-pushed, half-invited to give a short speech in Arabic. She was a traveling Christian, and to the priest, this was the only sensible thing for her to do before the services returned to normal. When the congregants rose, I rose. When they sat, I sat. When they sang, I hummed a tune of my own devising.

Something always drew me to religious hubs. I wasn't here for divine salvation, but I felt beneath any conscious logic that there was potential in these churches, in the mosques, in the spaces where synagogues were and might have been. Politically, I knew these houses of worship were lighthouses along the sectarian borders that divided the country—there was no denying that the identities that had brought people here mattered. But political curiosity wasn't what had drawn me here.

In Hawler Mall, I performed the Tall White Celebrity show. In the canyon with Clay and fellow tourists, I was a stand-in for the American military. And yet, if I disconnected from those identities, I was as rootless and aimless as I had been by Osama's cricket pitch. But if I could sneak up on deliberate, voluntary connections, maybe I could slip into one with lighter baggage.

Here was a chance to bear witness to gatherings that had nothing to do with me. They were prime locations to pan for connection. "Friday" and "mosque"—*jumu'a* and *jaam'a*—come from the root "to gather."

Arabic words for synagogue and church, *kaniis(a)*, come from an old Semitic root: "to assemble." For good measure, the English *synagogue* is Greek, from *sun-* "together" and *agein*, "bring."

After the sermon, we gathered with the priest in the dark parking lot to finally introduce ourselves. It was easier for my nationality to fade as we unwound from Arabic, a mutual second language, in French, a sort of third. Jean-Jésus had studied in France and spoke the clear French only foreigners can manage. "*Où Eve!*" he asked me when he learned my name. *Where's Eve!* He translated his joke proudly to his followers in Arabic. It was a joke older than many civilizations, but it made me imagine a time when it would have been fresh, like we were two old friends shooting a three-thousand-year-old breeze.

I took that moment to tell him I was Jewish. He hardly paused. It was finally getting through to me: it was pointless to try to find my footing by seeking the borders my Jewishness hit. I'd never find an identity in a space bound by prejudice. In blood or language or faith, "Jew" was a nametag I wore largely for the right to rebel against some vague outside pushing in. If I wanted to find an identity that connected to the whole world—I couldn't look for it in a box defined by what the world was not.

All this time, I dropped "Jew" like a sounding line, waiting for some kind of bump that would tell me how far away the other was. I always lost those lines in the sea.

This was a great thing I should have remembered: the marvelous capacity of human beings to Give Zero Shits. Sure, *love's opposite is not hate (but apathy)*, everyone told me at the onset of text-driven flirting; but it took a long time to understand the B side—that love is not necessary to prove a lack of hatred. Over time, past points of difference turn wonderfully unremarkable.

Jean-Jésus waived good-bye to Charlotte, and then to Sue. "Say hello to China for us!"

FIFTY MILES TO THE WEST, as the story goes, the town of Lalish was transplanted directly from the heavens. According to the Hymn of the Weak Broken One, one of the most important sources of the Yazidi creation story, "When Lalish came / Plants began to grow," and the world was set in motion.

We parked outside the town in our dirty car, abreast the heavy metal stanchions; no roads continue through Lalish. The holiest site in the Yazidi faith, Lalish sits in a lush valley, one turn off a quiet stretch of highway. It shares its effect with corners of Damascus or Old Jerusalem, old mortar over even older stones, replicated by the newer buildings in shades of gold and tan. Tiny houses pile up the hill on top of one another behind a central courtyard. Large cobblestones fade into hard, packed dirt.

To the right as you enter is the sanctuary of Sheikh Adi ibn Musafir, a Sufi mystic born in the 1070s in Lebanon's Beqaa Valley. Sheikh Adi traveled to Kurdistan and developed a following in Lalish, where he died and was most likely buried around 1160. For Yazidis, he is accepted as the avatar of Tawusi Melek, the Peacock Angel.

In the 1840s and 1850s, the writing of British supertravelers like Sir Austen Henry Layard and G. P. Badger introduced Yazidi culture to the west. Yazidi belief structure and traditions reflect an affinity with branches of all three Abrahamic religions, especially Nestorian Christianity and Sufi Islam, and a deep connection to Zoroastrianism, Mandaeism, and Manichaeism. Belief in reincarnation is fundamental. But when we arrived, none of us knew much more than the stigma: for a millennium, Yazidis have been defamed as devil worshippers.

It was our first audaciously sunny day in Iraq and children would occasionally push past to chortle up the path around the sanctuary carrying picnic trimmings to the top of the hill. A holy man was playing with the squirrels. He was dressed entirely in layers of simple white with a black sash tied around his waist. The soft white band of his hat separated its black cap from his equally black, thick hair and beard. A heavier gray robe with red lining draped over his shoulders all the way down to wool slippers checkered in orange and black. When he held out an almond, a squirrel would stretch itself upward on its back legs to paw it from him—if it couldn't, it would latch on to his hand and hold on for a ride.

With the squirrel waiting for its chance to pounce from the entablature, the man introduced himself as Baba Chawish and offered us the grand tour. "Muslims?" he asked, in Arabic. "I'm Jewish," I said. He nodded in his placid way, oozing calm. "Many Yazidis have Jewish friends on the Internet."

AS INSTRUCTED, we took our shoes off before entering the sanctuary complex, but I made the mistake of stepping directly on the threshold. Two girls giggled, half-hiding behind the corner and motioned for me to step over. Down the first set of stairs, there is a second courtyard. In the far corner is a high stone arch, decorated with small treelike adornments like little spiky teeth. A religious man leaned faithfully against the plinth, wearing brown robes and a black coat under a red and white keffiyeh. A wooden door was propped open beside him, the entrance to the temple proper, and we shadowed close behind the guide that Baba Chawish had charged with leading us three Americans through the mazes.

The long entrance chamber is supported by a span of arches whose pillars are wrapped in lustrous cloth. The wrappings are made of smaller and larger pieces in no strict pattern—the first pillar was dressed in a big swath of electric pink with a shoulder covered in a shiny green, the next in overlapping drapery of purple and yellow and red and orange. A row of tombs stands against the wall, each one fully covered in bright colors. On these fabrics, and the slack hangings that run from pillar to pillar, Yazidis tie a knot and make a wish.

There are no windows in the shrines, and as we followed deeper into the rounded tunnels through tiny doorways it grew darker and darker. On one tunnel's mural, a woman in an Indian sari gazes intently at a bronze depiction of a peacock. A few naked lightbulbs stick out from a cable fixed to the wall. Underneath, in a trough along the walls of some sacred chambers, are hundreds of ceramic jugs, Greek amphorae. They hold locally made oil used to feed the holy lamps in and outside the sanctuary. On the path up to the top of the hill, there are dozens of *nishan*, smooth niches in hollowed-out stones painted white for lamps to be lit.

From the top of that hill, two conical spires shoot upward from the roof of the sanctuary. The tallest is directly above the tomb of Sheikh

Adi; the lesser tops the room holding the remains of Sheikh Hesen, the third leader of the following at Lalish after Sheikh Adi, and the incarnation of the Angel Darda'il. A local man was standing by a second exit from his chamber—from there, a damp staircase descends underground into the cramped "Cave," which is linked by tunnel to the larger "Cavern." Philip Kreyenbroek and Khalil Rashow, devoted scholars of Kurds and Yazidis, mention these spaces with little detail in their definitive book *God and Sheikh Adi Are Perfect*: "These caves are felt to be extremely sacred, and their existence is normally hidden from outsiders."

But the man at the top of the stairs beckoned impishly and I ducked into the staircase. (Archeologist-spy Gertrude Bell described just the same thing a century earlier, departing from a group to sneak down into the caves in her visit to Lalish in 1910.) At the end of the tunnel I could hear the sound of water gushing into a pool. The man moved toward the sound. The Cavern is pitch-black but for one lightbulb that reveals rippling water, undeniably clear even in the dark. I could hardly tell how large the space was, and I could barely see the source: a fast-moving cascade roars chest high out of the back wall, filling the room and channeling out through somewhere I couldn't see. The man bent and splashed his face, inviting me wordlessly to do the same. My time in Iraq had been almost exclusively cold, but I closed my eyes and splashed too, feeling the crisp bite of my first attempt at bathing in Kurdistan. Then he dipped his hands into the pool and slurped a cupful, urging me to follow.

This was the Zemzem Spring, named for the miraculous well that appeared to Ishmael and Hagar, Abraham's second wife, as she ran back and forth through the desert near Mecca. According to legend, this life-giving water is sprung from the same source, a thousand miles away.

I was really, really thirsty. And to drink from a sacred spring . . . but I held back, on an impulse I almost never have. It was still Iraq, I remembered, and there was a lot I didn't know.

Back above, the tightening passageway through the sanctuary opens into its final chamber. I moved slowly behind a small group of Yazidi visitors, who kissed each doorway as we passed from room to room. In this stark marble space, square under the high spire, the sarcophagus of Sheikh Adi is alone and covered like the others in a bricolage of knotted linen. Airier than other spaces, Sheikh Adi's tomb doesn't have walls so black and suffused with the throaty smell of oil fumes. We took a moment to breathe.

In three years, the sanctuary would be overrun with refugees, escapees of the siege on Mount Sinjar and other acts of genocidal violence in the province. ISIS made a particular target of the non-Muslim villages, killing thousands of Yazidi men, selling thousands of women as slaves.

In a plain room toward the outside, I joined the group crowding around a lumpy wall like basketball players around the key before a free throw. Fellow visitors, Yazidi Kurds making the pilgrimage from their home in Sweden, knew what to do, and I watched as a man in a gray sweater closed his eyes and tossed a blanket with one hand (remember: underhand) with his wife and small daughters looking on, riveted. A girl in a striped Hello Kitty shirt was standing partway up the wall to retrieve it. If the blanket stuck atop a rounded shelf about ten feet high, the thrower's wish would come true. Three tries. Mulligans allowed.

Success! At least for the Swedish family; Sue and Charlotte were less lucky, and I remember opening my eyes to watch the blanket slide cruelly off the wall's protuberance after each of my vain entreaties to the Yazidi angels.

So we traded answers to prayers for answers to questions, reuniting with Baba Chawish at the edge of the sanctuary. Only later did I learn what his name meant: it was an office, not his given name, and it established him as the guardian of the sanctuary. The Baba Chawish is appointed by the Mir, literally "prince," the highest Yazidi authority in matters both civil and religious. According to Kreyenbroek and Rashow, "Theoretically, at least, the Mir is the supreme living source of spiritual and temporal authority, the earthly vicegerent of Melek Tawus and Sheikh Adi." The home of the Mir is in nearby Baadre.

He brought us into a comfortable room with an upright air conditioner and uninterrupted couches along all four walls. A man appeared from a kitchen carrying a tea tray.

"When did the religion start?" I asked—a softball as if I had a fastball.

"We don't have any certainty," he said. I could have listened to him read the Terms and Conditions of a thousand banking apps. In his Arabic, it seemed he had shaved away every harsh sound and replaced it with butter. "We don't know when the world was created, or Adam's age. We don't know."

In Yazidi hymns the word *mystery* is an exclusively positive term that refers to the souls of the angels or other holy beings, or sources of divine power, or the absolute understanding man seeks. Because Yazidi texts are written in Iraqi Kurds' native language, the Kurmanji dialect of Kurdish, the use of their word *sur*, "mystery, secret" (a cognate in Turkish and Arabic and Persian), seems to imply an acceptance of the incomprehensible. In my discussions of faith with new acquaintances, I knew I could always rely on this uncertainty: *Well, no one can say they fully understand God, right?* Across the Middle East, everyone always agreed. There is great solidarity in mutual confuddlement.

The district of Sheikhan, "Land of Sheikhs," where Lalish is nestled, is the Yazidi homeland and heartland. "Before it was all Yazidis," Baba Chawish said coolly, with a Northern Kurdish accent. "Syrian, Turkish, Iraq, Irani, Kurds—before it was all Yazidis. But the attack of Islam—what's it called, '*al-Fatuhat al-Islamiyya?*'—replaced the religion and it became Islam, but the language stayed.

"We stayed. In caves, in mountains, in areas they didn't reach, we stayed. All the rest, killed, and the religion became Islam." Metal spoons clinked in armud glasses of apricot tea. Charlotte translated simple summaries for Sue.

"The four nations of Kurdistan, all of them were Yazidi. And Islam came and said . . ." Baba Chawish didn't finish the story. "Violence of the sword," he explained. There was no sadness left in this destruction; he spoke as if this were something he thought about always, or not at all.

There is no absolute data for Yazidi populations. A report commissioned by the UNHCR cites worldwide estimates ranging from less than two hundred thousand to more than a million. Communities in Iraq, mostly in Sheikhan and the Sinjar District near Mosul, are the majority, with numbers in the tens of thousands in Turkey, Syria, Armenia, and Georgia. Baba Chawish also mentioned Russia and Ukraine. He didn't claim that Yazidis were ever the only population in Kurdistan, but he distinguished them from non-Kurdish Christians—descended from ancient Iranian roots rather than ancient Mesopotamian ones. In fact, the sanctuary of Lalish (since destroyed and rebuilt) was once a Christian monastery. Kreyenbroek writes that the Baba Chawish "represents" the monk who oversaw that cloister.

He recalled that calm moment in history. "They were there, Christians, Jews, even them. Everyone just did his work; there was work. Each one was on his way—all that's important for religion is God; each religion is a path, but every path worships God. It's all the same path."

While the Yazidi origin story is unique, the Bible and the Quran are both considered holy books and the lion's share of Abrahamic stories are compatible with Yazidism. Yazidis deeply respect Jesus and Moses and Muhammad ("124,000 Prophets have come and gone," it reads in the Hymn of Babeke Omera). These traditions are protected by the same seven angels, our host explained, rattling off their names automatically. Azra'il, Jibra'il, Mikha'il, Darda'il, Shimna'il, Israfil, Azazil.

Although I could find no cognate counterpart for Shimna'il in other traditions, the other names are familiar in Hebrew and Arabic. But the source of much confusion—of the eighteenth- and nineteenth-century Western obsession with alleged "devil worshippers"—can be traced to the Yazidis' relation to the first and last angels on Baba Chawish's list. While all seven are linked with a particular Yazidi leader believed to be their incarnation, Azra'il and Azazil—names affiliated in other religions with the Angel of Death and with Satan—may be one and the same, both used as monikers for Melek Tawus, the Peacock King. Melek Tawus is certainly the character Muslims recognize as Iblis, later known as The Shaitan, the worst of all creatures that defied God. But their stories have one crucial difference. God reacts differently in the Muslim and Yazidi tellings. Baba Chawish started from the beginning:

> Tawus Melek is a king at the side of God. He is a deputy of God, Lord of the Worlds. Before Adam, God said, "Do not worship anyone but me." The Angels were worshiping god. After

400 years, God made Adam and said, "Worship Adam." God said to the angels, "You must worship Adam." Six of them knelt to Adam, but Tawus Melek said "I will not kneel."

So God, Lord of the worlds said to Tawus Melek, "Why do you not kneel?" He said, "Before 400 years, you said to us 'Do not worship anyone but God, Lord of the worlds.' This is what is in my mind." He said, "You created Adam from clay. I do not kneel to that which is from clay—I kneel only to Your Name. Prostration is but for you, for the Lord of the worlds. I do not prostrate to things made of Clay." And Adam was made from clay.

And God said, "You are a guide, to be leader of angels."

Charlotte made the connection—in mainstream Islam, Iblis answers God, "I am better than he: Thou didst create me from fire and him from clay." In this seventh Sura of the Quran called Al-A'raf, "The Heights," God responds, "Get out, for thou art of the meanest [of creatures]."

For Muslims, this fall from grace is crucial. Iblis was not an angel—he was a jinni, a spirit that God once held in special esteem. (Melek Tawus was also created apart from the angels.) Islamic tradition says jinni and men are given free will, while angels are not, and Iblis, the original shaitan, was eternally punished for willing against God. The Arabic *shaitan* is borrowed from the original Hebrew, *ha-Satan*, "the Opposer."

The only difference is that for Yazidis, this opposition is not such a bad thing. The Peacock King may have *satan*-ed, but he was no *Satan*.

Baba Chawish held his glass steadily on the plate. "You say this, but this word is a mistake if you say it to him—he is an angel. This word is not good. The story in Islam, Judaism, and Christianity, the word they say to God is an error if you are consistent with the Truth. Why is it an error?" The guardian of the sanctuary didn't pause for us to answer. "He is an angel. If one is bigger than you, it is an error to say something like that to him, no? How can you call someone bigger than you a bad word like that? It's criminal."

Sir Layard never heard this word in Lalish during his nineteenth-century exploration: "The name of the Evil spirit is, however, never mentioned; and any illusion to it by others so vexes and irritates them, that it is said they have put to death persons who have wantonly outraged their feelings by its use." (He continues to use "Satan" to describe the object of Yazidi affection.)

Melek Tawus is a king, approved by God and superior to our judgment. Yet his thought process is not beyond our comprehension, and his resistance is considered deeply important to Yazidis. Melek Tawus's choice indicates the power each individual has in making his own decisions; here are strong traces of Manichaeism, the binary struggle of light against dark. "I know a path not good and good," Baba Chawish said. "Everyone is in his own hands, the issue is with the individual."

In Yazidism, this is especially true. The religious experience cannot (and arguably should not) be communalized as it is in the practice of many other faiths. Rumors of the existence of sacred texts began to swirl around the community in the wake of the first Western explorations. As curiosity mounted, texts miraculously began to appear. A Christian dealer of old books began dealing Arabic translations of the intriguingly titled Jilwe ("Illumination," or "Revelation") and the Meshaf Resh ("Black Book"). In the early twentieth century, a Catholic priest claimed to have discovered the originals in ancient Kurdish, and they were promptly published by a German scholar and disseminated in various renderings around the world. But they were forgeries. The "original" language was a Kurdish dialect unknown to Yazidis, and while many of the stories rang true, their status as scripture was rescinded.

The heart of the written tradition today is in the Qewls, the sacred hymns that were documented over centuries as Yazidism was codified. These are recited or performed to music by a Qewwal, always an unordained Yazidi from one of two particular tribes. Until recently, only the Qewwals had access to the hymns—literacy was discouraged among the general population, supposedly by virtue of a cultural taboo against the common folk gaining access to higher truths. For the community, Yazidism was a wholly oral institution.

Most hymns allude to narratives known as *chirok* that have no written basis and are passed down from generation to generation through story-telling. Rashow and Kreyenbroek explain: "Both genres come together in the mishabet or 'sermon,' in which a Qewwal normally recites part of a hymn, tells the relevant story in prose, and generally draws some moral conclusions."

Still, the belief in the two ersatz holy books has not fully dissolved. Yazidis themselves may now believe in lost or stolen texts by those names. In 2006, traveler and journalist Michael Totten spoke with the Baba Sheikh, the high authority of all mystical teachers, appointed by the prince and known as the Old Man of the Sanctuary. Totten recounts his assertions: "Our book is called The Black Book. It is written in gold. The book is in Britain. They took our book. That is why the British have science and education. The book came from the sky."

As Kreyenbroek told me:

> As to the fact that the Baba Sheikh believes in a lost Black
> Book, it is typical of largely oral cultures (at least in the
> Iranian-speaking sphere) that they believe that the ancients,
> who were so much better that they are, naturally had written
> books. Many traditional Yezidis believe this, but that does not
> necessarily make it true.

The Quran is read by many Muslims as the exact word of God as revealed directly to Muhammad by the angel Gabriel (in Arabic). Muhammad, who grew up illiterate, would memorize the chapters and relate them later to a scribe. The Torah has similar origins: God dictated the Torah directly to Moses to transcribe. While all religious Christians would believe the words in the New Testament are divinely inspired, branches of Christianity differ in their exact assessment: in 1978, American Evangelicals issued the Chicago Statement on Biblical Inerrancy ("Scripture is without error or fault . . ."), while the Presbyterian Church around the corner from where I grew up taught that the Bible can still be infallible without all the details being factually correct.

For Yazidis not pining for that certainty, the lack of an absolute text read in public and private is twofold: it encourages the Sufi ideal of individual closeness with God and it unites the community in mutual understanding that is refreshed every generation by living people. But as literacy expands, and young Yazidis avoid the archaic profession of a Qewwal, the written word becomes increasingly important.

IN LALISH, HISTORY IS still more tangible. Yazidis in the diaspora are called to visit Lalish at least once in their lifetime, just like Muslims are to Mecca. Yazidis around the world once even prayed in the direction of the sanctuary. (They now pray toward the sun.) At one time, the Yazidi scholars say, "the early community may have regarded Lalish as 'essentially' identical with the holy places in and around Mecca in the same way as two distinct historical figures may be seen as incarnations of the same 'mystery' or 'essence.'"

The "mystery" of Mount Arafat, where Muhammad gave his Farewell Sermon, simultaneously sanctified Mount Erafat in Lalish. On the day *hajis* visit this mountain in Mecca, high Yazidi religious officials climb their Erafat. The Zemzem Spring, then, not only sprung from Mecca—it was the same as the Mecca well. (And after my rejections at every Saudi visa attempt, I accepted this as a small consolation.)

"I am a lover of the Tariqa, a guide to Haqiqa," it says in the Hymn of the Mill of Love. This is written as if taken directly from the mystical Sufi Islamic playbook: an individual Sufi order is known as a *tariqa*, "path," whose members strive toward *haqiqa*, "truth." (Lalish is also nicknamed "The Truth.") But according to Sufis, Sharia, "(Islamic) law" (also translatable as "path") is the first step to Truth; for Yazidis, Sharia is mere "law," divorced from the Truth at the time of creation and symptomatic of Islam's misguided worldliness. Sharia is based on regulations derived from the Quran and Muhammad's example and teachings, and is considered infallible by those who subscribe to it— Yazidis discard that level of absolutism entirely.

Sufism bloomed in the seventh and eighth centuries, at the time of the expansive Umayyad Caliphate (whose second caliph, Yazid ibn Mu'awiya, is the Yazidis' generally accepted namesake). In the time of Sheikh Adi, Lalish was likely another *tariqa* seeking truth and responding to local traditions. Instead of sprouting directly from an Islamic community, however, this Sufism would have been superimposed on eons of Kurdish, Zoroastrian custom. Since then, the path seems to have wandered very little.

"We don't affect any one," he said. "Everyone has their religion— God made you Jewish, stay Jewish. God made you Christian, stay Christian. God made you Yazidi, stay Yazidi. This is for you personally the word of God." It makes sense that he wouldn't proselytize—Yazidis do not accept converts. "It is closed," Baba Chawish said matter-of-factly. "It is forbidden for anyone to become Yazidi."

Our host spoke plainly. "From the first day until the last day, a Yazidi remains Yazidi. From a different place, they cannot enter. For example, the origin of many Muslims before were Jews or before were Christians, no? Or Yazidis, for example. But from Adam originally—those are Yazidis." The first of his dramatic pauses, and then: "Yazidis remain Yazidis."

This is different from a species of tolerant Chosen People elitism. It is not simply because God has picked an individual path for everyone that Yazidis do not accept outsiders; instead, they see themselves as cut from a different cloth, or rather, sown from a different seed.

Yazidi legend traces their lineage neither to Isaac nor Ishmael, nor to any fabled child of Abraham. As the story goes, Adam and Eve deposited their seed (or spit, or blood from their foreheads) into separate jars to see if they could make a child without the other (the remainder of humanity issues from mutual offspring). After nine months, Eve's jar was full of vile insects, but Adam's held the ancestor of all Yazidis, Shahid ibn Jerr—Shahid son of the Jar. The preservation of this bloodline is vital to the community.

They hope Yazidis remain Yazidis when reincarnated, but this may not always be the case. "Of course there are differences," he said when I asked how spirits returned to the earth. "Everything is in the hands of God." If their path is a different one in the next life, it will still be what God chose, unlike straying by conversion.

Meaning continues to be made from difference. The boundaries are enforced from within—in 2007, a seventeen-year-old girl named Du'a

Khalil Aswad was murdered by her own community for her connection with a Muslim boy—and from without: in 2014, ISIS began its genocide in earnest. Unlike Christians and Jews, Yazidis were not even considered *people of the book*, the Quranic tag for pre-Islamic Abrahamic faiths.

"They have made destruction. Our religion—most people, they do not want killing. Ever. One brother kills another human—he has a son, a mother, he has a father, he has a family. This is an error, by God."

In a moment that fleeted like a second thought, he added: "The world has developed some from the time of the conquest."

The Baba Chawish looked to be in his fifties, or forties, or early sixties. He could have been centuries old. *Çawush* is in modern Turkish a military word for "colonel." One linguist's camp suggests that the "Baba" titles do not come from Persian *bave*, "father," but rather from the Aramaic/Kurdish/Arabic/Persian for "gate." And it is perhaps because they are this kind of gateway between divine and profane worlds that they held to higher standards of purity: the Baba Sheikh abstains from alcohol, though wine is a religiously significant part of Yazidi culture ("Oh friends, drink up, it is part of your duty!" says Sultan Ezi in a *chirok*); our host was chaste and unmarried, as required by his post.

"On earth there is marriage, but in the afterlife there is no marriage," he had told us. "Why? Jesus was not married, true or no? Moses was not married. The angels are not married, true or no?

"In heaven there are no children of marriage," he said.

In the cyclical nature of Yazidi tradition, it made sense that heaven—for those who transcended the cycle of rebirth—would echo creation: Shahid ibn Jerr was no child of marriage either. Like this, its tombs and shrines remembering men whose "mysteries" were those of angels, Lalish mirrors a kind of Platonic form, perfect in the heavens and printed on the earth.

The venerated leaders are considered divine, but the angels themselves are superior. "All of these are degrees," said Baba Chawish. "There is nothing bigger than God. After the protectors and the prophets . . . the last thing is us!" He laughed a hearty laugh. As a sheikh recited in a Yazidi sermon at the turn of the millennium: "We are deficient. God and Sheikh Adi are perfect."

Slowly, the conversation came back to earth. Would Jews accept converts? Were there good doctors in Israel? Sue was from China, how many religions do they have? How many millions of people? He clapped his hands when he heard the answer. "*Mashallah!*"

And why did we come to Iraq? "Someone told you Kurdistan was good?" A friend did, I said, and I had to see for myself.

"The *baab* is open any time," he said.

The Baba Chawish walked us back through his dominion; a delegation was gathering in the inner courtyard of the sanctuary. The German consul was visiting, escorted by the prince himself. Embassy vehicles and attaché cars clogged the area at the foot of the hill, where the most divine of all men on earth had just found a parking spot.

As we exited the temple, I noticed something—I couldn't imagine how I'd ever missed it. On the right side of the entrance, there is something prominent and peculiar: a black snake zigzags upward in low relief, the tip of its tail in an orange-sized hole in the mortar. For Christians, Satan is manifested more directly than anywhere else in scripture as the trickster serpent in the Garden of Eden. For travelers, this image was a mystery. Layard writes in 1849: "The snake is particularly conspicuous. Although it might be suspected that these figures were emblematical, I obtain no other explanation from Sheikh Nasr, than that they had been cut by the Christian mason who repaired the tomb some years ago, as ornaments suggested by his mere fancy."

In some religious traditions the snake is cursed, substantiated by its slithering and undeniable scariness. But in the Qewle Afirina Dinyaye, the Hymn of the Creation of the World, a snake plugs up a leak in the ark that was carrying the very first creatures, man among them, across the ocean. Not a trickster, but a savior.

Yazidis have woven threads through a world of stories, deliberate or not, acknowledged or not. As long as you aren't hell-bent on converting in or out of Yazidism, you are fine by them. As long as you seek truth and follow your path, you do right. Beliefs of the believers are all close enough. But alas, the devil is in the details.

AT EVERY CHECKPOINT we had passed through as passengers, I watched the driver and the guard drown out each other's pleasantries with more pleasantries, never leaving time for an answer to a question. *"Salaam aleykum choni bashee?"* ("Peace be upon you, how are you, good?") the driver would say, partially rolling down the window and waving his hand. Now in the driver's seat myself and detesting the car searches that followed most disclosures of our citizenry, I began to try the same thing.

Salaamaleykumchonibashee, I mumbled, partially rolling down the window and waving my hand. The occasional squint from the soldiers . . . and like a charm they motioned us through.

The murmuring smoothed the borders between languages as we left the dominion of Sorani (the Central Kurdish spoken in Erbil and to the east and written in a variety of Persian Script) for Kurmanji territory. I could suss most Sorani letters out from Arabic, but I got vowels wrong all the time, and often spoke past the limits of my reading skills. Kurmanji, Northern Kurdish, is written in the Latin alphabet and is far more widely spoken outside of Iraq.

In a place where political borders are perfectly satisfying to almost no one, I saw the linguistic lines as extra meaningful. We drove westward toward Norah's brother Fady, and his home in Kurmanji-speaking Dohuk.

FOR LESS THAN A DOLLAR, any juicy chicken shawarma stuffed into a crescent-shaped pocket of fresh, chewy bread can be yours. On the side, the vendor offers "Family Sauce," an inauspicious brown condiment bottled with an ambiguous label of fruits and vegetables that is, without fail, sticky and stained. It is magical. From the U.S. military to Robert from Baghdad waiting in line behind us, nobody didn't love Family Sauce.

The ingredients are hardly secret: seasonal fruits, coconut, vinegar, onion, garlic, seasoning, dates, water, mustard, thickening agent, caramel, salt, starch, tomato paste, black pepper. *Seasonal* fruits, we joked: *there's the secret.*

Across the street a colorful shop squeezes fresh fruits, Kurdish custards, ice cream, and that three-millennia-old treasure of Mesopotamian desserts, likely born in the swelling Neo-Assyrian empire around the time they were conquering the Kingdom of Israel: baklava. A string of plastic bananas hangs from the awning.

Sue raced to the airport, and back to work. We lost our president. And still, with Charlotte, I was far less alone on the road than usual, sharing thoughts with native tongue to native speaker in a way that left less unsaid. I was better able then to live the moments as they came; less scribbling and recording and documenting as if the experience would be nothing without carving it in stone.

I reminisced out loud, I think, so Charlotte would remember with me. So that her brain would pair with mine like a backup hard drive. *Fady blasting Rihanna . . . the hours of café backgammon in a smoke cloud . . . remember that lamb* quzi, *comically oversized and served over rice and raisins?*

My memory of Dohuk is sparse and disjointed—above the city there was a dam that abuts a big, blue man-made lake. On one postcard-esque hillside of long golden grass, a small cluster of whitewashed tombstones decorated in Kurdish and flowers underneath a single tree. Across the road, we drank tea with a beekeeper in plastic chairs high above the water. He stirred the pot for us and his friend over a solid campfire, and white pigeons flapped through the smoke.

Properly stuffed, we rebounded toward the far east of Kurdistan, from Dohuk back to Erbil, and then on to Sulaymaiyah. We passed two of Dohuk's several amusement parks on the way to the highway, waving good-bye to Mazi Mall, *ila al-liqaa'* to Dream City.

As we drove, I remembered the ubiquitous NO GUN signs—in hotels, at the carnivals. No Glocks. No Kalashnikovs.

THE NORTHERN ROUTE to the capital runs parallel to the Turkish border from scenic overlook to scenic overlook, past picnickers and illustrious cities. I hunted out the window with my camera. The eyes and movements were something to study, and I aimed out the window as if to ask how I looked to them. As we snaked through the tight streets of Amadiya—an ancient city-cum-summer-getaway sitting high on a pedestal of sheer cliffs—a boy craned his neck to follow us, away from a foosball table that had been dragged onto the street, and framed from behind by the posters of soccer stars. I didn't take a picture, but that image stuck with me as a freeze frame—his look, the game and the reality, the dream. If I didn't write him down, I'd lose him soon.

Somewhere in the greasy control room where I file these images away, a connection was offered: the girl from Dragon Valley—black mascara and shaved head, red dress and blue eyes-like-sapphires—*remember her*?

Near Amadiya, a side road leads to a small monastic village; a blue highway sign declared this in Arabic, Kurdish, and Syriac on top. We followed until the road went no farther. There: a church remade recently of large sandy stones hid from view in a thick grove of walnut trees, and a spot to park our car and venture inside.

A diminutive woman lived in the monastery complex—the two-room church about the size of a school bus and its one adjoining building— and she shuffled to push open the metal door, guiding us silently from room to stone room and waiting while we looked. She wore black socks rolled up above black slippers, a long black sweater draped over a brown dress that stopped at her shins, and a faded cloth tied tightly around her head. Light leaked around heavy window curtains.

The woman pointed to an object propping a door open. It was a solid metal cone, maybe forty pounds, with grooves on the base to screw into something else.

A rocket.

Through hand gestures, she explained that the church had twice been destroyed by rocket attacks. "Saddam," she said.

His anti-Kurdish, anti-Christian campaign destroyed four thousand villages in Kurdistan in the late 1980s. Underneath the stairs to the church, they had stored other souvenirs of war—another rocket cone, some warped missile casings, shreds of metal, a faded church bell. She pointed again, smiling weakly.

All my chasing the scent of violence; this was its wake, in one form.

From the early 1970s onward, America had a habit of encouraging the Kurds to fight Saddam, and then flaking on promises for support. James Akins, former attaché at the American Embassy in Baghdad, has called this relationship "one of the more shameful stories in our diplomatic history." It had always been like this: "they came to us, and the position that I took was, 'You're great people. You're really awfully good, and you really should have your rights inside Iraq, and probably other countries. But you'll never get any support from the United States, because we have great interests in Iran, and in Turkey.'" It's amazing Americans are still such welcome tourists.

The churchkeeper walked us through the church kitchen to the porch where her husband sat in a blue plastic chair, cracking walnuts with his eyes nearly closed as the late afternoon sun hooked into the crannies of his cheeks. We drank tea. The man was jolly, wearing two sweaters and a mustache, placing walnut after walnut on plates for us to eat.

Soon, it was dark, and we got lost easily. We knew we would have to cross back over the Great Zab, a river that comes from Turkey and joins the Tigris south of Mosul. For hours, we attempted to match the headlights tracing nearby hills with the shape of the roads on our maps. After a few bouts of desperation and only walnuts as sustenance, we belched from the dark underbrush onto the highway north of Erbil, reseeking the refuge of the faded pink room.

THE NEXT MORNING we preloaded phone maps and stapled crumpled paper ones together for the simple journey east. Our only creative choice was to take the faster southern route that skims the outskirts of Kirkuk, a city that has remained at the very core of Arab-Kurdish conflict since before Saddam's time. With a population estimated at around a million, the city may sit on 7 percent of all the world's oil reserves.

For a half hour, we had been outside official Kurdish territory as recognized by the 2005 Iraqi Constitution—as soon as we'd entered the Kirkuk governorate, we were in a disputed territory under central Iraqi government control. Whatever had changed was invisible from the highway, like crossing a state line.

Especially since the Baathist government returned to power in a military coup in 1968, policies of Arabization had been enacted to reduce the number of Kurds in the area. Kurdish civil servants were transferred and dispersed in the southern Arab governorates of Iraq, neighborhoods were renamed in Arabic, major roads were constructed that destroyed Kurdish homes for very little compensation. After 2003, though, Kurdish numbers may have doubled. No one knows. From the *New York Times* in 2010: "The number of Arabs who have left since the American invasion in 2003 might be 250,000, or not; the number of Kurds who have since arrived is said to be far higher, or not. Turkmens once made up 60 percent of the city of Kirkuk, compared with 30 percent now. Maybe."

The 2005 Iraqi Constitution outlined solutions for the "disputed territories," all to be accomplished before the end of 2007. First: "normalization," the reversal of ethnic redistribution policies. Next, a "fair and transparent" census. (While Kirkuk was last tallied in 1997, Iraqi census numbers have been disputed since 1957.) Finally, a referendum; disputed territories would be allowed to choose their own destiny, Iraq or Iraqi Kurdistan. After countless delays, the census has yet to happen.

As we rounded a bend in the highway, I saw the city sprawl, flat without a single tall building. There is very little security in Kirkuk; violence, kidnappings, car bombings are still all too common. Fire glinted at the refineries, and black plumes puffed from the smokestacks of oil wells like tall candles on a cake.

But no sooner is the city revealed than the ring road jerks away over an overpass. We were too curious to take it. *Just a little farther*, I thought.

There was Turkish on the signs now, the written language of Iraqi Turkmen. There were signs for the Baba Gurgur oilfield a few miles away, once the largest in the world, where Iraq's first oil gusher was struck in 1927 and the contest for Iraqi oil took root. Natural gas had been flaming in the fields for thousands of years at Baba Gurgur, where expecting mothers came to pray to have baby boys, and where, as a kind of party trick to light Alexander the Great's walk home for the night, Plutarch wrote, the Babylonians had set a street on fire. In the Book of Daniel, the Babylonian king Nebuchadnezzar throws three Jews into a "burning fiery furnace." Legend has it that was in Kirkuk, too.

The knowledge that this was too far for foreigners was scary and indulgent—I had goosebumps on my arms and vinegar in my belly, pushing us forward. If I wasn't held back, then I would follow infinite directions for infinite lengths. Without a barrier . . . why stop when there is road ahead? It's the nemesis of honor and all good things, isn't it—*giving up?*

CROSSING THE BORDER into a wholly separate country invites a change in interpretation: whereas Kurds in Kurdistan enjoy certain parliamentary rights and freedoms, Kurds in Kirkuk, though they may have the same history, exist in a vastly different political climate. Though they all have survived Saddam's genocidal campaigns, Kirkuk's uncounted have yet to see peace.

Kurdish flags flew here, as they did everywhere in Kurdistan. Red, white, green, the yellow sun. Our visas, guarantees of our security and freedoms as Americans, were valid only for Iraqi Kurdistan. We passed through the first checkpoint. The guard asked no questions.

Suddenly, on the houses overlooking the highway, I saw that the flag's green had turned black—and the yellow sun was replaced with three green stars and the words *Allahu Akbar*. I had only seen the Iraqi flag on government buildings in Kurdistan, and then always side by side with the Kurdish ensign.

Soon, a second checkpoint. This guard wore a different blue, camouflaged uniform that read "US ARMY" on the lapel. His face and voice were Iraqi, and as we feigned confusion, he showed that he had no English to offer. We didn't want to go farther, but we didn't want to get arrested either. Pretending that we thought we were still on the road to Sulaymaniyah (despite the WELCOME TO KIRKUK highway sign) seemed like our best bet.

The soldier was bemused. He waved his hands at the territory in front of us, making identifiably "dangerous" motions and struggling to convey to idiots what a wrong turn was. We mimed idiocy (perhaps it wasn't miming) until we knew we weren't in trouble. If we revealed that we had knowingly trespassed into Iraqi territory, we faced unknowable consequences. Had I really been that stupid?

A blue, camouflaged arm waved in a U-turn. Giving us our leave, the guard tried once more to explain.

"*Ghalat*," he said.

It was a word I didn't know. Charlotte translated, one ripple of a laugh of relief caught in her throat: "Big mistake," she said.

Black smoke seemed to be coming from everywhere. Yellow containers of gasoline lined the roads, available for purchase by the jug. Retracing our steps, I pulled over at a small grocery to treat a hunger that had come to fill the space where my nervousness had been, and, after long deliberation, we left with a package of bone-dry wafers, a sheath of chocolate sandwich cookies, and a banana.

A crowd of children and an older man looked in through the car window as I put the car in drive. We waved, and took the first exit out of town.

IN THE SUMMER OF 2014, the Iraqi army fled their posts in Kirkuk as ISIS mobilized nearby. The more cohesive, arguably more committed Kurdish forces seized the opportunity to assume full control of the city; the Disputed Territory Under Iraqi Control is now a Disputed Territory Under Iraqi Kurdish Control.

Yet all over Kurdistan, whatever transformation may be under way, at shawarma stands and cafés and salad bars, we and the local populations exercise our freedom to put the magical cocktail of Family Sauce on anything and everything as we damn well please.

Although the condiment is made in Erbil, its label is written only in Arabic. Its ingredients, those *seasonal fruits*, are mysterious and immeasurable. At the very bottom of the squeeze bottle, there is a rare stamp: "Made in Iraq." Just above this, a disclaimer: "We are not responsible for poor storage."

WE MET REBAZ at night outside Azadi Park, the biggest and brightest of Sulaymaniyah's obligatory amusement parks. I'd reached out to him on Couchsurfing, like a free version of Airbnb with a mission of international hangouts, and he'd invited us to stay with him in his parents' house. Before we met, Rebaz listed Suly's—the five-syllable city goes by its nickname—major attractions. Azadi Park ("Freedom Park") was "the place of torturing kurdish ppl but now its a good park to rest and breathe." Suly is bleeding with this kind of history; the deepest scars of war and Saddam's genocide are in the city and province of Sulaymaniyah.

Ali, a friend of Rebaz's, was waiting for us at a chic, spacious café in the center of town. He was tall and thin with a lean face and closely cropped hair. Rebaz was much shorter, in his late twenties and a pink cable-knit sweater. It looked like you could order alcohol, but we followed our hosts and ordered exotic-sounding teas.

For some reason, maybe because Suly is thirty miles from Iran, I had expected this eastern edge of Kurdistan to be more strict. It was the opposite. "In Suly it's more open than the other cities. It's like that from a long time ago," Rebaz told us. If it hadn't been Eid, the city's massive outdoor bazaar would've been buzzing. As it was, Suly was taking the week off.

With museums and art galleries closed, we had spent part of the day cajoling our way into the courtyard of Amna Suraka, Saddam's nightmarish Red Prison. On each side of the black, gutted entry, three columns of dirty white brick ran ground to cornice, overlaid and capped with rows of heavy orange-ish concrete, every inch pockmarked with bullet holes. As one of the city's major tourist attractions, the prison was closed, too, so we did not see the prison chambers themselves, or the famous hall of mirrors, where each of 182,000 shards of glass remembers a victim of Saddam's genocidal al-Anfal campaign.

"My cousin is there," Rebaz told us. "He was executed. His portrait is there."

Targeting mostly Kurds, this place for political torture, interrogation and unending imprisonment was the northern headquarters for the Iraqi *mukhabarat*, the secret police. During the fight for Kurdish independence in 1991, the Peshmerga put an end to the operation for good. Our lenient soldier guide, keeping an eye out for superiors, led us around back to where tanks are parked rusting in straight lines, adorned with chains that say "Made in China."

Rebaz had just finished a biology degree and was looking for work. He initiated us in regional history like he was catching us up to date with a TV show. "It's a bit tough in this region, like, all the guys around us. For Kurds, they just consider them an enemy—all of the Kurds living under the tyranny of Arabs, *Farsi*, Turks. Like when you talk to any Kurdish people, they say they are Kurdish. They are not proud to be part of Iraq."

While Erbil is the political capital of Kurdistan, Suly is its cultural heart, at the frontlines of the fight for Kurdish independence, and so it was unsurprising that we had arrived so quickly at the topic of Kurdish statehood that popped up so frequently in conversations around the country. I was probably stirring them up by reflex—everywhere I was fascinated by identity and nationality and language. I often thought of nations like people, butting heads and saving face and connecting just like we individuals did; territorial constraints on the national identity, then, were like an affront at the most personal level—a restraint on the freedom to define oneself.

Since the failure of the 1920 Treaty of Sèvres to establish a contiguous Kurdish state from the remains of the Ottoman empire, Kurds have been divided; there are majority Kurdish regions in Iran, Syria and Turkey, none of them autonomous as they are now in Iraq. Almost everywhere, Iraqi Kurds answered with the same patience and detachment to the question, *What should Kurdistan be?* It had two prongs: *Should you leave Iraq? Should you join with other Kurdish regions?*

Ali said it: "It's impossible." He had just come home from his job in Baghdad. He described the regular bombings in the capital, sounding more annoyed than anything, worn out but good-humored in a *c'est la vie* kind of way. During just one week a month earlier, there had been 250 casualties of suicide and roadside bombs in Baghdad. ("Sometimes I feel it in the morning and it wakes me up," he said.)

"It's impossible right *now*, but it's our hope, right?" said Rebaz.

Ali spoke of independence activists obliquely: "They just want to get rid of the country. It's not logical right now to do that. I mean, you don't have order in some places, like—we don't have sea, we don't have friends. All we have is the United States, our only supporting country."

It was true that Iraqi Kurdistan was not ideally situated to be its own nation; American support, too, has never been a guarantee. When the United States and Israel first encouraged the Peshmerga to fight Saddam in the early 1970s, and then changed their minds, collapsing support drove a wedge between two factions. Conflict between the Kurdish Democratic Party (KDP) and the Patriotic Union of Kurdistan (PUK) still undermines nationalist unity.

"The vision is that it should be the great Kurdistan, all parts going together," Rebaz reported, never adding his own opinion. *It's impossible, after all, so who cares what I think?* Almost everyone invoked *the vision*. I wondered if Iraq's three million Kurds felt they were *supposed* to dream of the day when the world's thirty-five million Kurds would live in a united country—as if it were the more noble ideal—but didn't really want it, or care.

"We are surrounded by enemies, man," Rebaz said. "They don't want Kurdistan to be a—union country. It will be the most powerful country in the Middle East, because of petrol."

I noticed the whir of central air. "They say maybe Kurdistan is going to be a kind of Second Israel in the—you know, man?" As Rebaz said this, his face looked willing to try it out. "The US can stay here and do some foreign policy," he said vaguely. "But it still needs working."

Both Ali and Rebaz spoke clear English; Ali worked with foreigners in the bomb-ridden capital; they had traveled. And it was clear that through these exposures, opinions had been revised. Rebaz had lived for a short time in India, where he reacted first to surprising linguistic communality between Hindi and Kurdish. *Rega* meant street for them

both; "*Panka* means 'fan,' *parda* means 'carton,'" he said, grinning as he taught.

"Before going to India, no—I said, 'I'm a Muslim.' Only me who is being in God, not even Christian or Jewish. But after going to India, no, I said 'No: humanity. Then religion.'"

"I have friends online from Israel," he said. "I have three, four friends, they are coming here."

Like most in Erbil, Sulaymanians speak Sorani, Central Kurdish, written in a variety of Persian script. When I asked what its influences might be—Sanskrit, Persian, Turkish, Arabic?—Rebaz reacted with an uncharacteristic jolt, "No no no no, no Arabic." Rebaz took a terse sip of tea, as if to wash away the mere hint of a suggestion of an aftertaste of Arabic. Kurdishness was clarified faintly for what it was not.

Syria, before it was a government slaughtering its people, had its fault lines drawn along religious borders. The Kurdish population is predominantly Muslim, so the conflict is portrayed as an ethnic one supported by ancestry. Rebaz narrated a variation on a familiar story while Ali nodded affirmation behind his glass: "We are from different roots. The beginning of the story is one old man had three guys, three sons from different tribes. Sami is Arab ancestor, Hami is European ancestor, Ari is our ancestor. They are calling them 'Hindo-European'; this part is Kurdish people, Persian people, even Pashto—Pakistan and Afghanistan—part of the Soviet Union, now Tajikistan, Uzbekistan, Turkmenistan—all they come through same ancestor."

His retelling outlined the story of Noah's three sons, known in the Abrahamic tradition as Sham, Ham and Japheth. Sham (Sami) is the mythological father of the Semitic races; he is Abraham's great great great great great great great grandfather; in Persian and Arabic, *Sami* means "Semite." In Arabic, it also means "supreme."

Biblically, Ham is the son who moves into Africa, while Japheth relocates toward the Mediterranean. Rebaz had forgotten about Africa, but with one minor change the story matched: Ari was Japheth, the forefather of Indo European peoples. "Our ancestor is called Ari—in Kurdish language, in Sanskrit language, it means 'fire.' Born of fire. Because we have even our own prophet and our own religion, which is called Zardasht, Zoroastrian. They are worshipping, they respect fire."

In Sanskrit, *arya* means "noble." These are the world's Aryans. And in the words I could see the migrating populations: Zoroastrian *Aryans* brought fire temples to Persia, giving *Iran* its name. Later, when Zoroastrians moved into South Asia, they were dubbed *Parsi*—the word *Persian* in Persian. The word for the people became the word for the place. Then, the word for the place became the word for the people.

Nationality invoked a mythical lineage and language evolved to support its supremacy. Words and identities and religion aged in constant feedback with one another, and soon, the seams of this social stitching were cloaked in imagination and history.

"It's not about belief," Rebaz said. "It's about story." But, he admitted: "Even I don't know much about it because I'm into science more!"

Kurds consider themselves the indigenes who survived Islamic conquest, even though the Islamic influence stuck. Rebaz described a familiar case: "My uncle is Muslim but he believes Zoroastrian religion more than Islam."

Whatever Rebaz's uncle called himself, he was a marvelous proof of how impossible "Kurdish" or even "Iraqi Kurdish" tradition was to simplify. He was a true citizen of the country that didn't exist yet, a landlocked nation both separate and linked, Iraq and not-Iraq, a piece of Greater Kurdistan and standing-on-its-own-Stan. Against the backdrop of ten millennia of visible history, everyone was free to construct his own narrative—and to redact it at any moment. The narrative was being constantly written and read, and spoken and heard, and remembered and rereremembered and forgotten. It was as if he could change his mind in an instant. And it was beautiful to see borders between identities collapse, but then . . . the absurdity . . . what were we? I was back in the Emirates Palace, flitting about the golden seats, pretending I was anyone I wanted to be. Was I anything but the story I told myself?

The more Iraqi Kurdistan became this *and* this—not this *or* this, or this *but not* this, or this *and maybe someday* this—the more it frightened me with the excitement of a world blown open.

———

FOR REBAZ, LEARNING SOME Hindi helped blur the fences he had drawn around himself. After the linguistic wall fell, others followed.

"When you go, when you read, when you deal with them you come to know they have a great story behind them, this worshipping—it's not just statues right? They have amazing stories."

I LOOKED UP FROM our table and saw that we were the only ones left in the room. The café was closing.

"Shall we make moves?" Rebaz said.

We scuttled back into the cold car and thought of sleep, of tiptoeing back into the home of Rebaz's parents. We would never meet his mother and father, whose approval he'd solicited for our sleepover. Individuation came late here in all its forms.

But before we snuggled up for tea, we fired up the heat and followed Rebaz's directions to an idea for the night's last stop. "Whenever I get upset or have tension after reading, I want to get relaxed, I go there. I have my own place that I'll show you."

The road climbed up into Azmar Mountain, past the land and gardens and new houses owned by Saudis who weekend in Suly during the summers. Ali thought he saw a wolf dart through the headlights. Suddenly, there was no more hillside to block the view, and we saw Suly as if from a plane landing.

"Whoever comes here, I just take them to a prison—maybe they had an idea about those places," Rebaz said. "Finally I take them to the mountain to see Suly and they say 'Wow, we should have come here at the beginning!'"

We stood on the exposed hillock of the Goyja panorama, or squatted for survival by a small log fire someone had left. But we bore the cold for beauty: in the darkness we couldn't even see the mountain we were standing on, and I felt as if we might fall off the planet, and yet we could look down on the gold and green lights of the entire city without so much as a neck swivel. The bright outline of the highway wrapped around all of Sulaymaniyah.

A native of nearby Halabja, Rebaz didn't seem to mind the lunar cold or the wind whipping up over the mountain's shoulders.

"During my bachelors, my nickname was Tarzan because I used to shout same as him."

"When you were happy?" I asked.

"Anytime. Even when I was sad." The wind had made our eyes wet, and Rebaz's caught the light of the fire.

He howled.

JUST AFTER DAWN the next morning, we drove east as early haze baked off under the sun. The road is straight; the scenery marries geometric power lines and autumn streaks. Leaving Suly, the hills were burnt red and smooth, growing taller and greener as we shot toward Iran and the fringes of the white Zagros Mountains.

The first glimpse of Halabja is the hundred-foot-tall sloping cone of its major monument, topped with the struts of an angular orb curled around a wire sphere. The base is a single-story circular building, with the outer rim layered in giant fake pebbles. I thought the cone looked like giant forearms stretching skyward, wrists pressed together with the fingers making a protective shell, or housing an offering. Two modest Kurdish flags flank the driveway, those stripes of red, white and green with a bold yellow sun in the center.

On the evening of March 16, 1988, Saddam's Iraqi planes conducted a dozen bombings over five hours. First came the rockets, the shelling, the usual. And then something different—silent, smoking bombs filled with chemicals that killed instantly upon inhalation, or slowly and torturously. Others, as a university student named Hewa said in 1991, "died of laughing." Many thousands were injured, and five thousand civilians were killed in an act of genocidal madness.

Some say the bombing of Halabja was disguised as a wartime attempt to drive out Iranian forces. (On March 16, 1988, no Iranian troops were in Halabja.) During the Iran-Iraq war, many Iraqi Kurds did side with Iran, as Iranian Kurds sided with Iraq. Each group had good reason to reject its own state. But this made it clear: whichever identity Kurds chose, they would lose friends even among their own. These are people with a history of abandonment and they have a saying to prove it: *Kurd dosteki naya ghayri chaya*, "Kurds have no friends but the mountains."

Compensation from the Iraqi government was more symbolic than useful, and targeted families only of the deceased. Survivors are very often delayed victims of the long-term effects of chemical weaponry: respiratory diseases, deformities, miscarriages.

The golden Halabja Memorial, built in 2003, fifteen years after the attacks, offered no more solace than it did a solution. The first building the regional government had constructed in a decade, the monument stuck out like a trophy for broken promises. Foreign and domestic aid for local reconstruction was funneled and misfunneled through aid agencies to corrupt politicians, and Kurdish representatives leaped to exploit solemn occasions. Visiting diplomats who made this first turn off the highway never witnessed the destruction in the town itself. Iraqi journalist Mariwan Hama-Saeed was clear: "They were paying a visit to the dead people, but neglecting the living." In 2006, townspeople revolted in riots that left a boy dead and others injured; the memorial was burned but didn't fall. (The building has been reopened, but the exterior is plain metallic silver now; they didn't repaint it in gold.)

In the entryway, leafy plants spring out of upended rockets that have been poetically repurposed. Black and white pictures show the town in its heyday: a parade for the last king of Iraq in 1956, dancing primary schoolers, mustachioed soccer players—"The strongest team in Halabjah in 1970s."

The next room is a brutal diorama. Visitors to the museum walk through a re-creation of the March 16 evening. Papier mâché corpses lie on the floor with blood trickling out of their mouths, lips blue or black as they were reported. A famous photograph is modeled here, of an old man shielding his grandson in vain. Over the loudspeakers, an eerie soundscape.

A friendly guide met us at the door leading out of the room, where a sign reads in Kurdish and Arabic and Persian and English: LIFE AND VICTORY FOR ALL NATIONS / DEATH FOR ALL KINDS OF RACISM.

He led us pleasantly to the next hall, where the museum takes another turn for the unsparing. Here, there are real pictures of the dead, collapsed, frozen, in piles. He pointed out members of his family. He repeated something I had read, something that became a twisted trademark of the Halabja massacre—that the smoke that came and the death that followed were coupled with "the smell of sweet apples."

Charlotte courageously followed him through toward the TV screen showing footage of the immediate aftermath; I slumped onto the floor, staring across at a wall of pictures that blurred into abstract colors. Red, white and green curtains hung from the tip of the spire above the central hall. Names were engraved in white on reflective black stone like a small, circular Vietnam Memorial, grouped together in families. The man identified his relatives again, distantly running his finger along their names. He was used to this. He seemed gratified, almost contentedly showing us through the museum and sending us off with gifts of literature and a grim pamphlet, smiling and shaking our hands. We signed the guestbook, and took the turn toward town.

HALABJA LOOKED LIKE many other small towns along these roads outside Kurdistan's major cities, assuredly smaller than it once was. Scaffolding stuck to the side of a mosque painted gray, and children rode Big Wheels by the walls of houses. A sign was fixed to a telephone pole at the entrance to the cemetery in Kurdish, Arabic and English: BAATH'S MEMBERS ARE NOT ALLOWED TO ENTER.

In this last resting place of the victims of their genocide, it seems understandable that supporters of Saddam's party (banned in Iraq in 2003) would not be welcome. The Halabja attacks were a piece in the "anti-insurgency" al-Anfal campaign of the late 1980s in which an estimated hundred thousand or more Kurds, and significant numbers of other ethnic minorities, were murdered in systematic bombings, firing squads and concentration camps. The murders targeted able-bodied

men. Almost no village in Iraqi Kurdistan was spared Saddam's attention; the name al-Anfal, "loot" or "spoils of war," was borrowed from the
title of the bellicose eighth chapter of the Quran. The word derives from
a root that means, "to do more than is required by duty or obligation."

A wide brick walkway curves around the plots with green-brown
hills as a backdrop, whitecaps farther away. There are mass graves here,
for as many as fifteen hundred bodies each, under short, white marble
monuments. And there are thousands of tombstones, most written upon,
some engraved, some with prayers, some with no names, some colored
blue or pink, some decorated with the flowers and greenery they say is in
paradise. There are spaces where sharp stones appear scattered on the
grass, but serve as markers nonetheless. There are many aboveground
tombs with a tall headstone and footstone, and a layer of soil along the
length. We met Fatima at one of these, picking out weeds from the soil.

She was with her sister and her cousin, and two girls younger than
the tragedy. Fatima came three or four times a year from Suly fifty miles
away, and she was smiling as she pulled out the weeds on the grave,
crouching in her black dress, black leather jacket, lustrous black headscarf pulled back to let her hair show. Her sister in all black leaned forward over the footstone, holding her phone loosely.

At the neighboring tomb, the much younger cousin was silently
resting her elbow in a nook of the carved stone. A dark, floral headscarf
hung down over a light blue sweater as she stared out at the mountains.

I had my camera out in the cemetery, and couldn't resist framing the
scarves against the stone slabs against the Kurds' only friends, snow-
capped in the distance.

The kids watched their mother work. They smiled at us shyly and
grinned at my camera, one all in red with a long overcoat, the other in
a pink hoodie that said *Beautiful!* across the front. We walked toward
our cars, talking about important things and trifles, and Fatima invited
us to tea.

NOT EVERY TIME YOU CAN EAT ICE CREAM

———

ORK EXPECTED SO LITTLE of me that I often forgot I had any other job but to seek and dive down rabbit holes. I was getting closer, I thought, to what I wanted. If I had spoken with more of the region and felt no calmer, I figured I must be homing in on the places where answers were kept.

Just as my first weeks studying Arabic planted the nerve to leave for Abu Dhabi, and the possibility of Pakistan planted the nerve to fly to Afghanistan, the experience of Iraq gave me the nerve to wangle into Iran. And nerves are so many things as they flit back and forth between brain and gut, affected by and affecting our energy, our confidence, our perception of what makes sense and what does not.

"Iranian visas for Americans are not a thing," Danny wrote me from Syria. I knew that, but I felt I'd ask, in case the response revealed cracks in that certitude.

I called the Iranian Embassy in Abu Dhabi.

"Sure we have visas!" he said.

"For . . . Americans?"

"Of course!"

I was buzzing.

"*Tourist* visas," I clarified. "For Americans."

"Of course."

"What are the chances that I'll be able to get one?"

"Maybe . . . one percent!"

He was laughing.

I digested that rejection, and scouted for next steps. I brainstormed with Neal, a new Iowan import to Abu Dhabi, who was similarly antsy. (I always seemed to gravitate toward the unsettled, the disaffected, the angry.) We met at a gathering high in the skyscraper for Purim, aka Jewish Halloween, and together we tried to face our fears of sitting too still. Even though it was expected, it was hard to be told "no" so firmly (as I had been only at the Saudi and Sudanese embassies) with no place to push back.

Except—there was a bizarre travel agency across from Foodlands shawarma that I had always passed too hungry for more than a cock-eyed glance. I had always thought that if a travel agent could help me, then I was asking for the wrong kind of help, but this building looked like a mess—plastered in flight routes and airlines and names of places I hadn't heard of. That was what I needed: to throw myself off the map.

Kish Travel could arrange that in half an hour.

There are two Iranian islands in the Persian Gulf: Kish and Qeshm. They are "free trade zones": each island operates like its own duty-free shop, watching people come and go and buy things. No visa from any country is required to enter, except for Israelis and those with Israeli passport stamps—they're barred from every part of Iran. Kish is a vacation spot for Gulf shoppers and scuba divers and day-trippers from Dubai; Qeshm is the opposite. Flights are infrequent and irregular. There was no mention of Qeshm on the U.S. State Department website. *No news*, Neal and I thought, *was interesting news*.

Whatever school of going-with-the-flow Danny had gone to, Neal was the valedictorian. There was a combination I couldn't quite understand: My urge to travel was so fueled by restlessness that I knew only how to hit new ground and run—but the world's Neals had some way of *wanting to move* without *needing to*. Neal was calm like a picture of an Iowa cornfield.

In the months we would spend together, I never knew if he was capable of raising his voice.

Our journey to Dubai's Terminal 2 for Forsaken Airlines began early in the morning on an empty bus that would get a flat tire somewhere on the emptier stretches of desert highway from Abu Dhabi. The driver, who had been in an accident a week earlier, attempted to wind the car jack without using a protracted index finger the size and shape and color of a large carrot. At the airport, the flight was unlisted, but we hadn't missed it yet. The airline had no counter. We waved our irreplaceable paper tickets; representatives at the Miscellaneous Desk directed us to a back office where we paid a fifteen-dollar "airport fee" and tried to confirm that the island still existed.

"You fly in here," said the agent, as if everyone were in on the farce: he pointed to the one of Qeshm's two airports that was abandoned years ago. Even the airline had a name to match: *Fars Air.*

I converted dollars to rials at a window in the terminal, and we became instant millionaires. The fifty thousand rial bill, a new issue from 2007, bore a picture of the late Ayatollah Khomeini, as required by law, and the atomic symbol, as a deliberate *Eat shit!* to international opponents of Iran's nuclear program.

We waited by the gate, though it never appeared on the Departures screen. After hours without announcement, other passengers assembled as if secretly in tune, and we filed in behind them onto the bus to the plane, underneath the sign that read BASRA.

It was a thirty-four-minute hop from Dubai in a Yakolev Yak-42, a Soviet-era plane discontinued in 1981. In case of emergency, above us where oxygen masks might have been, there was a small plaque in Russian and English: ESCAPE ROPE.

QESHM ISLAND LIES seventy-five miles along Iran's southern coast at the mouth of the Strait of Hormuz. Every day, more than fifteen million barrels of oil are squeezed through the tightly regulated waters. We landed over a shocking desert moonscape: sharp-sided mesas snapped like LEGO pieces onto completely flat ground, fire burning over the oil refineries.

In Dayrestan Airport, Americans are fingerprinted with office supply stamp pads and offered sugar cubes to help scrub the ink off while other foreigners file immediately to the one van to the one hotel we were allowed to stay in. We passed our luggage through the outbound X-ray, where the checker kept a bottle of Pimm's, that ginny summertime English liqueur, hidden poorly on his desk. Perhaps it had been confiscated (alcohol is forbidden in all of Iran); the bottle was still in its protective duty-free leggings.

Many Iranians stop over from Dubai on a more economical route to major cities, but the rest are neither tourists nor businessfolk—aside from us two Jewish sightseers, the rest of the van carried disappointed-looking men and women from Central and South Asia to the limbo of the Hotel Diplomat. This was where the noncontract workers of the Emirates came when they switched jobs and their old visas expired, to wait until new paperwork came through so they could return to Dubai. We had come on vacation to purgatory.

Most guests of Qeshm couldn't care less about the scenery. Even the name—sometimes *Geshm* or *Qushm*—is pronounced with an *m* that nearly disappears, as if everyone always realized midthought that it was a mistake even to mention it.

After pausing for indifferent, free-ranging camels to cross the road, we were there. The Hotel Diplomat is part hostel, part minimum security prison, with comfortable enough dorm-style or single rooms and televisions and a sprinkling of channels all from the Emirates. Our roommates were from Tashkent and spoke little to one another. One said that he had learned all the English he knew, conversational and easy to understand, in the last fifteen days. The other snored louder than the Persian army.

The hotel seemed to wake up between noon and 4 P.M. In the evenings, national delegations stuck mostly together either around the hotel's two shishas—the African table, the Arab couples perched on benches—or mingled by the pool table with tattered felt. A woman from Tajikistan in a bright blue headscarf was shooting pool as she did most nights, waiting for her work visa, against our roommate, who had just gotten his. No one dared challenge the quiet, skinny man from north-ern Iraq. He had been there for six months.

Next to Neal, I looked far less American. He is the kind of ethnic Jew who is a marvelous likeness of "white people." But as we bounced our thoughts off of each other out loud, our English made meaning even for those who didn't speak a word.

Traveling not alone again, I was less blank, less able to hide behind a huge nose and the vagueness of tan skin. I also felt less like I needed to, and I relaxed away from the constant strain of choosing how to define myself at every turn.

But—so much of the way I understood a place was based on the way I saw it seeing me. Sure, with a scene partner now, I didn't have to per-form as hard. But I was worried that I'd be less sensitive to all the lasers of other people's perceptions zipping around the room.

Neal was challenged to chess by a burly Russian who performed the same, predictable opening three games in a row, and then demolished him. He asked Neal what he thought of George Bush. Neal was relieved to have a geopolitically sensible answer for the man who could nutcrack his head with a bicep curl.

"I hate Bush, of course. What do you think of *Putin*?" This was supposed to be a moment for hate-your-president solidarity.

The Russian locked eyes. "Putin good. Putin I commander in police before."

Neal swallowed. Then, the ex-KGB patrolman displayed a picture on his phone—Was it proof?—taken in front of a bathroom mirror, of himself without a shirt on. Later he showed a picture of his daughter. We wondered if there was anything on this island we would understand.

There was hardly any food, too. A little shop by the pool table sold chips and ice cream and the restaurant on site offered something at select hours of the day (breakfast of a hard-boiled egg, honey, and a tea bag). But still, almost no one wanted to go into town. "Yeah, it's bad here," our roommate said. "Outside is worse."

In Arabic, Qeshm is called *Jazirat at-Tawila*, "Long Island." Down-town Qeshm centers around two large malls selling clothes and bags and smuggled IKEA for cheaper than anywhere else in Iran. For the same reason we as Americans were allowed in, because the island is classified as a Free Trade Zone, there are no taxes and domestic tourists pop in to shop, either in the town of Qeshm or in nearby Dargahan. Shawarma stands deal in long hoagie rolls and little kids peddle chewing gum and locals gather in the town's park by the sea to smoke nargile or, because it was nice out, to prepare camping tents for the night. Benches in front of a television were set up like a kind of outdoor movie theater.

Resplendent with spiky hairstyles and too-shiny pants, the Long Island of the Persian Gulf even has signs for the "North Shore." Winter is the busy season, when mainlanders show up for sun and more shopping.

We flirted with the idea of a trip to the mainland, one short illegal boat ride to the port of Bandar Abbas, about ten miles away across the strait. Farther down the island, Qeshm came within two miles of the Iranian coast. *Let's do it*, Neal said.

Between the bright lights of the fruit and ice cream stands and the twinkling of boats out in the oil-rich strait, the park at the edge of town had the air of a small carnival. Families and twosomes were strolling along the water's edge. Dark waves rolled in softly and lapped at their feet.

AFTER DARK, we found teams of young people at Nemat's Ice Cream, offering fifty-some flavors from hazelnut to melon to something that tasted like spray paint (beware the four-scoop minimum). Our hands oily from plates of *tomshi*, like crispy Persian crepes—that was where Maral took us second.

Maral was from Shiraz, one of the island's four Couchsurfers, and an immensely eager and delighted tour guide. She'd seen my post on the Qeshm message board and come to rescue us strangers. She was studying physical therapy here at Shahid Beheshti University of Medical Sciences.

There wasn't a whole lot, but what there was in Qeshm was relaxed and (sometimes) lively. And it did beat the Hotel Diplomat. Maral's friends and the other young women around Nemat's were unveiled, wearing bright, patterned scarves that left much of their hair showing—

but Qeshm was less free than Shiraz, Maral said; in Shiraz, she would hardly readjust her headscarf if it fell. If I had expected Saudi Arabia in Iran, I was mistaken. Foreign is welcome: Maral was an avid downloader of *Grey's Anatomy*. On Facebook, she lists Woody Allen as a favorite artist.

She took us by taxi (twenty thousand rial, less than a buck, for anywhere in town) to the Portuguese Fort on the northern tip of the island built in 1507 and destroyed a century later by Persian "liberators." The fort is surrounded by one of the poorer neighborhoods of Qeshm locals (as opposed to mainland workers or students); Maral classified them as ethnically Arab. "I ask if they celebrate Eid-al Fitr or Nowruz," the Persian New Year on March 21. "They say, 'We celebrate Eid al-Fitr . . . that's what we've always done.'"

As we navigated around the stumpy castle to a Zagat's-worthy restaurant on the sea, the driver shut off the headlights. "So they wouldn't see the garbage," he said to Maral. He was visibly embarrassed. "The government doesn't want it to be beautiful."

This part of town does look forsaken, garbage piles collecting in corners of the medieval ruins. It is hard to know how much this can be attributed to the federal government. Religious freedoms, though, may come with a price—one that is levied not only externally, but from within. Those backed into corners at risk of losing their traditions put up walls, becoming conservative out of necessity. A woman in a full black robe and a niqab that covered her face shouted at me from a distance, waving a finger and warning me not to even think about lifting my camera.

I wasn't going to, I didn't know how to say—and I was suddenly ashamed by that truth: Was I so biased that I cherry-picked the memories I wanted to have? So committed to contesting the darkness that all I saw was light?

AT THE RESTAURANT on the sea by the Portuguese Fort, the waiter brought a mixed selection: fresh shrimp, squid in a light, sweet tomato sauce, and shark meat, minced and spiced, dry and pungent and delicious. We talked about Iran and religion and ethnicity over the waves. "I hate Arabs!" Maral said, beaming. She loved the West, longed to emigrate, and hoped for lasting peace and stability in Iran, but she hated her neighbors—or rather, she hated her neighborhood. But still, the brazenness of this—Was it racism?—hit me like ice cream on a sensitive tooth. Maybe what she hated was not a people, but the influences of the strict cultural and religious rules of this Arab-identified island on her personal life. Or, I had read her all wrong.

Beyond that, the girls seemed to enjoy ranking foreign countries like *American Idol* judges. USA? *Great.* Europe? *Wonderful.* Pakistan? *Good.* Maral's friend's sister Azade, visiting from a town closer to Tehran, said she loved Israelis (but would never go to Israel because "it wasn't allowed"). Over the course of our visit we began to teach them some vernacular English words . . . that all happened to be Yiddish. ("I am sorry for being *schlep*," Maral tried out on us.)

And then, we bought embargoed goods in this embargoed country and outed ourselves as allegedly embargoed people. Toking on Cuban cigars, we came out to Maral as Jews. She was delighted. Her parents in Shiraz had Jewish friends who traveled discretely to Israel via Turkey, and now she did, too. When you hate your neighborhood, it's easier to love the world beyond. And Maral did hate Qeshm. Like the hotel's clientele, she had come to the island for one reason, and dreamed constantly of leaving.

We wiled away the evening in a gazebo on the beach, playing card games and abandoning card games and laughing, joking about little nothings and trading the worst words in our home languages. *Motherfucker*, she taught us in Persian. *Asshole.* Ahmadinejad was a *schmuck*, while the man who brought us seaside snacks was a *mensch*. Police were less likely to patrol this beach, a "private" one with a tiny entry fee, to scan for improprieties; otherwise young men and women giggling might have earned a small inquiry. The girls asked how I got my hair so curly.

Maral said goodnight to hurry home before her school's 9:30 curfew. It was easier than dealing with the reprimands and dirty looks if she didn't, and in return for her degree from the prestigious medical university, she would sometimes have to play by the town's rules.

I whispered again to Neal about Bandar Abbas or Bandar-e Pol or anywhere on the mainland, stones' throws away. Boats left under the cover of night, and we might be able to bribe our way across and then scuttle up to Shiraz. Maral made it sound so wonderful. It was *right* there.

I would have done anything to keep the adrenaline charging, to create novelty where there was none. Boredom—I smelled it but didn't taste it yet—would prove that this was a place like any other, interesting and stupid and comfortable and terrible, not a prize witness in my case against bad reputations.

But I remembered what I learned about the Taliban tollbooths on the roads south and west out of Kabul, situations that had no margin of error. And I remembered the hikers in Tehran's famous Evin Prison. With one misstep, we'd be cellmates.

EVERYONE WAS EXACTLY where we had left them, frozen in visa limbo at the pool table. I rotated into the Uzbekistan-Tajikistan doubles game and miſſed a few shots. The woman from Tashkent laughed, and translated a phrase from Uzbek she thought germane to my frustrations: "Not every time you can eat ice cream," she said.

I nodded. I'd have to think about that.

I FIDGETED in the morning soundscape of Uzbek snores.

The girls came to attempt a rescue; outside of town, colorful wooden boats with outboard motors and captains for hire lined the beach, and Maral haggled for one to take us to nearby Hengam Island. The boatman pushed his ship into the surf. Dolphins chased us as we got close.

A couple of miles over the water from Qeshm, some of the area's first inhabitants live in thatched huts and sell handicrafts to passersby. They looked African and wore brightly colored and patterned clothes that would have befit a Pakistani wedding. Elsewhere, the dark sand on sheltered Silver Beach glittered with mica. Except for the dolphins that circle playfully around the island, tiny Hengam also seemed like a place the rest of the world had just let be; aside from the septic tanks

and we tourists with our cameras and the concept of tchotchkes, almost nothing spoke of modern times. One moment, Maral remembered that Hengam might be outside the area authorized by the stamps in our passports, and cautioned us to keep our voices down. If there were any overzealous police, we might have been accused of encroachment into other Iranian territory.

Qeshm is one of the poorest parts of Iran, and Hengam is one of the poorest parts of Qeshm. It seemed as if the country's indigenous had been ignored by every larger social order they are technically a part of. For us, if we were illicit in our presence on the island, it was lucky—it was a place we could be ignored, too.

Maral's sister's friend Azade was the most vocal opponent of the hijab women are obliged to wear in Iran, and when she saw the beautiful beaches surrounding the island, she cursed both the Iranian government and Islam for preventing her from sunbathing.

The effortless beauty of the island made it easy to ignore everything we weren't seeing. "Azade said Hengam has the highest female suicide rate in Iran," Neal told me as we got back in the boat to leave. "Rampant poverty and polygamy."

We parted ways with the Persians on the beach, and hired a fifteen-dollar taxi to take us the length of Long Island and back, about an hour and a half between the farthest points. We blasted Jennifer Lopez music videos front and center on a screen above the air conditioner. The car shook in sync with JLo's hips.

We drove past the mangrove forests like Venetian neighborhoods, canals of hara trees sprouting their yellow blooms from the sapphire bay. We felt the paved road turn to dirt, on the rocky red hillside along the dusty road from Dustku to Salk. We coaxed the driver on, despite the machine gun he charaded with his hands and worried eyebrows. We found the *Ghar Namak*, the Salt Caves most locals know but have never visited. Cavernous walls marbled in red and brown swaths, dripping with pure white salt stalactites like an old freezer, and heaping piles of salt crystals on the ground. Across the flats, water pooled into a tiny Dead Sea, seeping back into a cave. The driver was mystified as we shucked our shirts and shoes and ducked inside to float.

The bottom half of Qeshm was quiet, gorgeous, and we roared through it. At sunset, we found ourselves at the dry dock of a dhow yard, long wooden beams resting on the dirt. No power tools in eyeshot, we climbed the fifty-foot ladder up and over the bulwark onto the deck of a gorgeous ship. I was sure of it: these were the guys who made Noah's ark.

The expanse looked back over the empty island. A dark man pulled up below on a motorcycle and sputtered away, and we were alone at the stern of an incomplete boat drinking in the sherbet skies.

At the Hotel Diplomat, we gave the cabbie nearly all of our remaining rials. The hotel staff on behalf of the police asked the driver where exactly we had gone and what we had done. Our Uzbek roommates welcomed us as if we had been gone for days, and as if we had known each other for years. Our day trips were incomprehensible to them. And when they greeted us with their only two salutations, we never had answers: "No problem, no problem," they would say, in the space *hello* might have gone. At other moments, they were more existential: "Where are you?" they said, standing face to face. Some moments, I felt that was a decent question.

IN THE MORNING, the biweekly plane wasn't there. With a flash, the fabricated stresses became real ones, and we were trapped, too. We didn't know if the delay would mean another week on the island, or more, and the truth of the place began to trickle out and into us.

With no money, we had lost the major advantage of being American in a place where nationality is meaningless.

All it took was a moment of being stuck, and in a flash, I was aware how much I had forced greatness on the place: As if my life purpose depended on it, all strangeness I labeled unique, and uniqueness meant discovery, which was good. The mundane was proof of normalcy, which was good. The flight delay was a welcome beat of adventure, which was great. I multiplied local kindness into sainthood. And if I was frustrated, I would frame it as my fault, a lack of forbearance; or I might blame a deviant individual who I plucked from representing the place.

In Damascus, I had celebrated street-stand juices as if they negated the war. Facing the muzzle of a Kalashnikov in Karzai's driveway, I made sure there was good where danger could have been. Was my maddening day with Marwan in mosquito-haunted Lebanon all my doing, or ours together? As if only positive prejudice could counter the negative, I moved fast, flitting across *The Middle East* in a blur of novel inputs. But when the rush slowed . . . when boredom hit . . . there was no stimulation to keep my gaze from the messy, the stupid, the bad. The shuttle to the airport continued not to arrive. It was nerve-racking—and if my nerve had fractured, I might have seen the place the way everyone else saw it.

Masha was coming soon, for a winter break visit from law school, and she could bring me home with her. That felt like exactly the wrong direction. I needed some other way *in* . . . some way of seeing and being where I didn't need everything to be great.

And then, only twelve hours behind schedule, the shuttle came and took us to the plane. And the Yak-42 dropped us in Dubai after thirty-four minutes, and I lacquered "Iran" in the bright polish of memory.

I have had the EXACT same worries. . . . I used to worry
so much about not being able to imagine my future,
I was sure I would die young. Maybe that's why I'm
scared of death. And now I can't see ahead either, I cant
imagine . . .

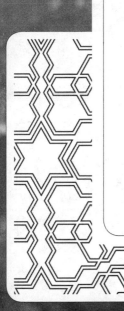

PART THREE

ببدأ شعب أخر
ANOTHER
PEOPLE BEGIN

I don't know
what I want.
How could I know
what I want
when I always
say yes
to everything?

—THERESE BELIVET,
Carol

BAP BAP BAP BAP BAP BAP BAP

———

WAITED FOR MASHA in the shadow of the Great Pyramids as the last weeks of my job contract waned. I was quitting.

I needed to move—even though by that point, I had honed the performance of diligence to where I was able to show up to work about forty-five minutes per month, rushing through the two buildings on our campus with a phone to my ear, jabbering as if I were under-pressure-but-handling-it (and that's why you hadn't seen me), as if I were too-busy-to-talk-but-I'd-sure-love-to, and catching eyes and smiling to nip suspicions in the bud.

I could collect Indian food and the company of good friends and a paycheck all by direct deposit, and I still itched. I had shot out from Abu Dhabi because I wanted to feel the world's heartbeat. I was close enough to hear it pounding, but too far to feel it, to know how or why or what that meant. I had told the Abu Dhabi rabbis I'd work on self-transformation toward a better me, but it was the region that was transforming, and I was unsettled enough to face the fact that I hadn't found any deeper understanding of what the world was going through—as if I weren't a part of it.

Iraq gave me the fire for Iran, but Iran pushed me toward anything—everything.

Slowly but surely, as I ran away only from what I knew, with little motive but lusting curiosity, I made the classic young man's mistake seeking a place to put himself: I lost sight of the thing I sought to place.

Revolutions had raged for a year. Protests exploded. I had watched friends studying in Cairo evacuate while blood hit the streets. The next month, the Supreme Council of the Armed Forces, known as the SCAF, dissolved the parliament and suspended the constitution. Hosni Mubarak, the domineering president since 1981, who had been angling to bequeath the democratic post to his own son, was dethroned.

But—fairy tales never seem to hold up in the epilogue. As quickly as the army had come to give muscle to the voice of the people, they pivoted to squeeze the people with the same force.

Soldiers and civilians clashed; the army killed hundreds, injured thousands. The Friday protests ran under the banner of the "Second Revolution." As it had been in the first stages of the uprising, Tahrir Square was ground zero and a symbol of something larger. It was a simple calculus: The larger the crowd, the more powerful the message. The SCAF forced the area clear the only way they knew how, but crowds returned and grew with determination. Coptic Christians and Muslims united against a clear common enemy. Again and again, Cairenes would insist on the force of the protests by invoking the fullness of The Square.

Now, the parliament had been reestablished, and elections had begun for its seats. In a month, guidelines for the presidential elections would be released. There was an atmosphere of cautious hope, of the kind that still smelled of gunpowder.

MASHA. AFTER ALL OF THIS TIME APART, I would be traveling alongside the girl I felt closer to than anyone in the world. Months and months had passed easily when I had accepted our physical distance as a fact of life, but now that I knew she was coming, I was desperate for her. The combination of *probability* and *proximity* hijacked my centers of self-control. Nearer and nearer a border, I ached for the other side. Nearer and nearer in time to her arrival, I pulsed with impatience.

Her flight was delayed an entire day because of blizzards in America. I remembered that snow still existed—and then raged at it for keeping us apart. It was only a day's wait, but adrenaline had made each second an hour, and each hour like a maximum sentence in the solitary confinement of my own stifled excitement. Like that, I thought in overly dramatic sentences. Like that, I surged with a child's restlessness.

I needed her to come and understand me. Egypt was a place where our reasons for coming would overlap—maybe she'd be close enough, then, to understand my other reasons, to see why I needed to crawl around the world's heart. Maybe she could explain it to me, help me, save me, bring me home.

Soon, she was there, and we were there together—two kids in a triply discounted luxury hotel, in a city visitors had deserted, looking out over our balcony at the last standing Wonder of the World.

AT THE GATE to the pyramids, the teller was convinced enough to sell me a half-price student ticket for my expired-but-dateless French *étudiant* card. The ticket taker refused to accept it. I protested. He grumbled something so unintelligible it could only have one meaning, and I handed him an extra ten pounds, relieved. He still blocked the way. I protested. Frowning, he moved. It was like a game of chicken— his hands were dirty now, and confrontation would do neither of us any good.

Four-hundred miles south, throughout the magnificent tunneling stairwells in the tombs of Luxor's Valley of the Kings, watchmen peeked out from behind the curtains of the off-limits chambers. Most were no different from the splendor of the three millennia-old passageways we had come from, lined with hieroglyphs still vividly colored with triturated gemstones, but the draw of the velvet rope was too strong, and so we ducked under.

"Take photo," invited the nervous guard. Photos were absolutely prohibited inside all of Egypt's monuments. We did. They came out terribly. The guard coughed on the way out and we shook a bill into his hand. He wouldn't call after us—and we didn't look back to see if it was enough, clomping quickly down toward the sarcophagus of King Tutankhamen, where we would do all of this again.

So long as the *bakshish* is received as satisfactory, though, everything feels less scummy. I didn't feel like the magnanimous colonist, the chalky Sahib, the khaki-clad lord of the bush—I just felt more complete, unashamed, like I had successfully completed a social transaction: expectation, execution, satisfaction. Not, as it usually goes in Egypt: expectation, attempt, expectation, rationalization, supplication, dismissal, resentment, dissatisfaction, discombobulation. A dash of nausea.

I WAS TRYING NOT TO idealize anymore; every interaction was not caked in charm. There are opposing sides and disguised agendas and feelings of success and satisfaction to be won and lost—it was less a game than a battle. To our antagonist, ten pounds is dinner, or five lunches, or three keffiyehs, or shisha and tea and two coffees and another tea. To us, then, it was a principle and a precedent.

It was nicer to offer than to be taken from, even if it was all the same in the end; it was simpler to adhere to some constant standard than to be hostage to mood and guilt, in the murky middle ground where there is no force and only feeling.

"Give me whatever you like," we heard from cab drivers after long drives, or boatmen who accepted anything silently. Oh, the onus!

Hospitality could take turns, too. A glass of tea offered, putting us at ease. Then, perhaps, a charge: betrayal. When money was caught sneaking into innocent interactions, we'd lose our trust, and for this, the next innocent vendor felt the brunt of our retaliation. Knowing that we were often seen less as guests than as opportunities, I could never process this place in the same way again. I began to shun connections I might have embraced naively before. Sometimes we rejected interaction all together, and floated through ancient cities in total detachment.

Later, we developed a technique: in the cliffs of Deir al-Bahari in Luxor, outside the Mortuary Temple of Queen Hatshepsut known as the "Holy of Holies," there are gift shops. Dozens of them, with proprietors who cry like bees: "Pashmina, alabaster! Sir! Best price!" It was too much. We started yelling—not at anyone in particular—like recently escaped crazy people.

"AAAAHHHHHHH!" we said.

The shopkeepers stared, slack-jawed and silent.

VERY QUICKLY, our mental energy for constant bargaining ran out. We'd escape the crush of the capital to somewhere less famous for its Things To See. Fish, we had heard, was great in Alexandria.

A first-class ticket was only seven bucks instead of five; the deals felt good and we felt okay taking them. So when a cab offered to take us instantly from where we stood to the sea, for only triple the price of a pair of tickets—no schlepping to the station, no waiting—we jumped. I lugged a wheeled duffel bulging with a backgammon board and an open bottle of Kazakh vodka into the taxi. For 130 miles, we'd be relieved of all hassle.

At the limits of twenty-two-year-old imagination, this was the best of all possible worlds, and there was something beautiful about that perfect convenience: a *con-venience* is a "together-coming" of things. I often found it worth the price of forty teas to feel, just for a moment, that everything had come together.

In the cab, we were a willing audience to a lecture on waxing techniques and romance. Drivers loved to broach topics with us that might have been more questionable with local fares—marriage, sex, cosmetics. Maybe the same conversations took place with Egyptians in the backseat, but it seemed more likely that our foreignness invited discussions of love and pudendal grooming.

"We make 'sweet,' the Egyptian woman," said Muhammad, explaining *halwa*, in one of its varieties. *Halwa* is the name of both a dessert (made from sesame paste), and a natural wax. The wax is made from boiled sugar and lemon juice, spread on hairy body parts and then yanked away.

"Any supermarket, you go inside and tell him I need sweet, she bring you sweet. The lady, most of the lady she do this. She get out all hair, leg hair, pussy hair—everything. But *she* didn't," he said of his long-distance American inamorata. "It's like, 'What's this! Why you didn't get it out?' She said, 'No, that's my hair! I like!'"

That was only the beginning of his disenchantment. "Most of the time she ring me, 'How are you I love you. Come to me.'" He was not the only one he knew getting calls from Kentucky. Other Egyptian men got calls just like he did, he said, from tourists who wanted to take home more than memories—then packed a bag, went to the airport, and left. He felt the pull, too. "This time, not a lot of business, not a lot of tourists. I want to leave Egypt. But I didn't want to go there with *her*. I didn't want to live my life *with her*.

"I wake up in the morning, I see ugly face. Also, I didn't like American—the black. I like the white, nice hair, nice eyes, like *romancy* lady, not too fat. Fat for the women not good, my friend—you understand, not make you happy."

In the end, there was no enchantment at all. The longing caller in the faraway land had none of the things he wanted—except that she was far away. (Just as Muhammad predicted, Masha would see many couples at airport check-in in this narrow category: black American women and Egyptian men. The women were large, the men small. No children. Multiple carts piled with luggage.)

Masha and I took all this in. She was more open, more reactive, more willing to laugh. She was comfortable. I hesitated to react for fear of affecting what he was about to say. She was transparent. But mostly we made noises only to keep him speaking, smirking at each other when he said something unseemly.

I still rationalized forgiving him his type ("not black") because I still wanted to listen with ears that didn't dislike him. Muhammad was on the darker side of the average Egyptian. He was ethnically Bedouin, "from the desert," descended from the traditionally nomadic Arab tribes that have adapted with varying degrees of friction to urbanizing societies across the Sahara and Arabian deserts. "Romancy" whiteness was an ideal, like something out of the airbrushed magazines I remembered my Tunisian Arabic teacher showing us.

If his life were a movie, Muhammad would've been a relatable protagonist, despite his seeming colorism and vendetta against pubic hair. Like Copts, Nubians, Jews, the other four hundred thousand-odd Bedouin in Egypt and fellow minorities, his life was defined in large part by his ethnic and traditional roots. He had grown from them, and then decided he didn't like at all where he was planted.

"What's wrong with Egyptian girls?" I asked from the back of the cab, half-joking.

"My father, he forced me. I married one of my family, a cousin—close cousin," said Muhammad. "My father say to me, 'You must marry this girl.' I said no, I didn't love her, I didn't want. He say, 'No, if you didn't want marry her, get out, don't come in my home, don't come in my family, get out, go to hell.'"

The girl, eighteen, was onboard; she didn't want to give him time to fall in love with another woman. Now, Muhammad has two boys, sixteen and eighteen. "I married her. Not love her. I divorced her. My mother she take her, my boys with me."

"I didn't do this with my son," he said. "I tell him, see what you need, what you love and go ahead, marry. I'm not force you, not like what my father do with me."

There was less judgment in the backseat now. Muhammad looked at me. "That's your girlfriend? Very good. Lucky. Take care of her, yeah? Inshallah." Masha was everything he said he wanted, and I was holding her hand. The young tourist, gleaning lazy impressions from the backseat of a taxi.

"I love the American people, I love the tourists," he said. "Also the head—big head. European women, like *open*. Not like the Egyptian lady."

He glanced at Masha. "If you have a sister, I marry your sister and I give your father fifty camels? Fifty camel for pretty woman."

"What's the most you've ever heard of?"

"Thirty or forty. Fifty is the highest thing."

No belaboring, but he wasn't joking either. If I had offered a viable prospect, we could have made a deal right there, halfway to Alexandria, sight unseen. Yet even though it was Masha's nonexistent sister on the line, the deal was mine, the man's, to facilitate. Certain traditions were more resilient than others.

He had been performing for her the entire trip, but I relished the chance to watch from the outside. I felt so well wired to Masha that I thought I could absorb what she was absorbing, too. And she brought out so much more from the men who spent so much of their lives with men. It was a kind of immersive surround sound: as she listened and I watched her listen, Egypt and I shared more points of contact.

"If you find one lady for me, I give you good commission, two camels one donkey," Muhammad said. "Two camel one donkey."

And like this, we picked up the brass tacks of the matchmaking business. And then, he offered the single most valuable and concrete nugget of information I hadn't known I was seeking: the camel-to-donkey conversion rate.

"Maybe ten donkeys per camel," said Muhammad.

Soon, he might be making those calculations for his sons. The average Egyptian groom is twenty-nine, the average bride twenty-four (up five years over the past five decades)—the burgeoning youth populations across Arab countries are delaying marriage simply because it is too expensive. Sixty percent of the youth polled in a Cairo survey reported "marriage expenses" as a main hindrance. "Mismatching?" Four percent.

Both men and women in Egypt seek to marry younger than the averages. Men peg twenty-six as the ideal age for matrimony. Women picture a wedding before they turn twenty-two.

Muhammad glanced back again at Masha and me through the rearview mirror. "Maybe you married her in the future, why not?" He laughed. We smiled. He laughed again. "You're still young."

ON TARIQ EL-GEYSH in Iskandariya, Army Road in Alexandria, a man was waiting for a communal van taxi. We waved, hoping he would know where the famous fish souk was.

" 'Aarif feyn suq as-samak?" I asked.

He smiled blankly.

"As-suq . . . ?"

A nod.

"... *as-samak?*"

The man readjusted his keffiyeh, thin and white around his head. "*Samak!*" Fish! he exclaimed. Then he looked us over, curious—or disinterested. I tried to think of ways to use our understanding of "fish" to some mutual advantage.

Just then, a young "Can I help you?" sounded behind me.

I heard this in the Cairene accent in which *p* becomes *b*, *j* becomes *g*, *q* disappears and vowels are rounded like luxuriant smoke rings. Two friends in their twenties smiled at us—one big, one small—with the blamelessly chiding look you'd give a baby who stepped in a bowl of oatmeal.

"Why you pick this guy?" they said. "He can't speak Arabic. He speaks, but not this language." The old man was Sa'idi, an ethnic group comprising a fifth of Egypt's population hailing from the south, Upper Egypt. Literally "of the plateau," the Sa'idi can usually understand others' Arabic far better than they are understood.

The friends knew where a few good seafood restaurants were, where the menu is the day's Mediterranean catch laid out on ice, and after only a little coaxing they agreed to join us. We crossed the street and stuffed into a van taxi heading down Army Road. My new seatmate insisted he bear my duffel on his knees.

THEY WERE BOTH wearing black leather jackets over black sweaters. (Bright colors outed us immediately as foreign—Lebanese at closest.) Hisham was at first more talkative, built like a high school football tight end, smiling through the stubble on a kind face. Ahmed was thinner, with slightly receding short hair. Within a few weeks, we'd all be twenty-three.

In one direction, Army Road runs straight southwest down the edge of the sea. Men in twos or threes blasted music from the speakers of rented motorcycles and wove in jerky zigzags through traffic, yanking the handlebars so abruptly that the bikes nearly fell at every turn. On the beach, a couple of boys flung handfuls of sand into the water. At its southern end, the road curls like King Tutankhamen's false beard, and

at its tip: the fifteenth-century Qaitbay Citadel, built on the remains
of the legendary Lighthouse of Alexandria. The fallen lighthouse was
once a towering four hundred feet of wheat-colored stone, another of
the world's so-called seven ancient wonders. Now some of the rocks
that formed it decorate the end of a long jetty popular on pleasant evenings. We thought to head that way to find some shisha.

"Shisha, I do!" Hisham would smoke with us, but Ahmed would not.

"No, no cigarettes, no shisha, no drinking. No exercise."

"I do everything! You like something, I did it before. He didn't do it."

Ahmed smiled cordially. "I have rules and principles."

We sat in ductile chairs around a red plastic table at the end of the
promenade with the seaside castle in front of us. The sea blew lightly
against the rocks where couples were sitting taking pictures, and cats
pawed around unnoticed. As fish soup was delivered, and then cala-
mari, and then something fresh and local, they guided us through
familiar teenage and postcollege points of concern that were in so many
ways similar to our own—money, sex, politics, our parents, the origins
of the universe, Paris. The backdrop, though, at least this year, was a
little different.

One week earlier, the votes of the first two of three rounds of parliamentary elections had been cast all across Egypt. Turnout had been
"the highest since the days of the pharaohs," said one electoral official
famously. Ahmed had voted for the expansive Islamist alliance with ties
to the Muslim Brotherhood—he admitted their faults but felt that he
shared the same pure ideals. This Freedom and Justice Party won the
plurality of seats, just ahead of the more orthodox option that sought to
establish Sharia law in Egypt.

Hisham voted for the liberal bloc that was Seabiscuit to Western
hopefuls. They came in last. And we were weeks away from January 25,
the one-year anniversary of the explosive protests throughout Egypt.
A week earlier, Cairo had seen the largest demonstration of Egyptian
women in a hundred years. The next day, Hisham took to the Alexandria streets for a women's march. "Really, when I saw these pictures on
the Internet"—of a protestor beaten and stripped to her now-famous
blue bra by soldiers in Tahrir Square—"it's a human being! You don't

do this. We did a revolution and you did this to the people?" He liked addressing the regime as if they were at the table. "Plus, it is a woman, it is a lady, you must respect her."

There were protests in Alexandria as there were in Suez, in Luxor, and up the Nile. It was just like in Cairo, he said, only smaller. "They shoot we fight they shoot we fight they shoot we die."

If change came, it would come slowly. "Not in one year, not in two years . . . five, six years. You know, they start to take something, something, something—after ten years you will find us like Iran."

And then it would be time for another uprising. "I think so. Another revolution, another people begin."

I PULLED FISH BONES out of my teeth and set them on the plastic mat covering the table. It was still warm outside even in the last days of the year, and Army Road was crowded beside the silty shore. Fully veiled women passed with shopping bags; a young guy with dangling headphones pushed a handcart loaded with bread. A thick stone wall separated the sidewalk from the sand and a little girl in pink walked along the top, her father holding her hand from below.

Our conversations braided in the way they do in four-person squares, kitty-cornered and sideways, coming together and pairing away. Face time with *Americans* prompted questions about sex, gay rights, God and gods and godless-ness (or was it just speaking in a second language, bypassing certain filters hardwired into the first?)—and if it didn't, and if I felt energetic, I might steer conversations in that direction. Who knew how long we would have access to our comrades in age, and to the things we call their "worldviews" and the trains of thought that ran through them?

A man brought four glasses of crimson black tea, and after making certain several times that we wouldn't be offended, Ahmed assumed the mantle of religious explanation.

"Where do you think this all comes from?" Ahmed asked. "Imagine that we don't believe in God, where did this all come from? It's big. It's huge."

Our paired-off conversations reunited—there wasn't room on the table for the whole universe and another chat. "There's only one answer, but you keep on denying and I never understand that: that someone has created this world," he said. "If you read about, I don't know, planets and astronauts and things, *y'ani*"—the all-purpose filler word that means "it means" or "like" or "you get the picture" or "you know" or "I dunno"—"these things are so accurate." Ahmed talked louder to muffle the roar of a looming motorcycle making its way toward us like a drunk slalomer. The truth of Creation was proven by all things created.

"If all this was another way," I said, "then it would be another way. And that would be perfect, too." The tinny sound of tambourines and ululation approached.

"The universe is not, how I say, *fouda, y'ani*—chaos."

At that exact moment, the motorcycle for two rounded the narrow pedestrian cul-de-sac, swerving deliberately. The driver stared me square in the eye. In an instant, he lost his balance and slammed into the ground with the bike's full weight on his right leg. I saw it buckle as he fell.

A crowd circled around him. Everyone issued orders. The friend who had been on the backseat righted the bike, throttled the engine, and disappeared. Masha and I were far more excitable than our Egyptian friends. Here was a kid who had very ostentatiously pulled up and broken his leg in front of us as if he wanted a tip. We owed him at least a call for an ambulance.

"Actually if you do call an ambulance, they will hang up on you," Ahmed said. "They don't care if someone fall—they have bigger catastrophes."

"This is not the kind of thing I want you to see in Egypt," Hisham said, upset.

"It's very common, to rent a cheap thing and they play these stupid, very stupid, songs and then fall. It's very common here in Bahari," Ahmed explained.

"As we were saying—how much sugar?" Ahmed lifted a container of grainy, off-white crystals. "This is not real sugar. It's very not sweet."

—

POLITICIANS FEIGNING MIGHT, SUGAR feigning sweetness, stupid bikers pretending to be fearless while the ladies are watching—there is posturing in Egypt in all things. Though he would have mocked the bikers were he alone with Ahmed, Hisham didn't want us to see Egypt's stupidity. *We have that, too*, I could have said, but it wouldn't have made a difference. The pain on the injured biker's face was matched with shame on Hisham's.

Soon, I took a jab again at dorm-room philosophizing.

"Before, people thought the sun went around the Earth, and they said 'Perfect! That's great, of course it is!' and they said 'How could it be any other way?' and then we discovered the other way and we say 'Great, of course! How could it be any other way?'" I rambled on, hoping something would stick. "If I think of the name 'America,' that's how it should sound, right?"

"Yes," said Hisham.

"But if I was raised for twenty years hearing people say 'ama-*Reeka*,' I'd go, 'Of course that's how it has to sound.'"

"You'd say, 'This way is the right way.'"

I left the analogy's loose ends on the table, and listened to Ahmed against the noise of the evening.

"We have been given brain to think," he said. "And I think, and I choose what suits my brain."

Would those choices be different if he didn't grow up in Egypt?

"Maybe. It would be harder to find."

"Everyone says, 'I was lucky. I got the right choice,'" I pushed. "What are the chances that we were all born with the right choice?"

"Yes, yes," said Hisham, nodding at me. I knew that religion had a weaker grip on his politics and options for nights out than it did for Ahmed, and yet he seemed able to agree firmly with his friend on every point of faith and sympathize with me on every relativistic objection.

His brain could continue to suit itself to whatever it liked. Faith was so deeply rooted that it was safe from doubt and statistics; everything else was up for discussion. In a realm where human logic was inadequate, so much depended simply on comfort.

Maybe I was more comfortable being uncomfortable. "I say there's no answer. And I say, 'Okay! There's no answer.'"

"I think that because we don't know, I think God sends us prophets, sends us a book that may guide us to what we don't know. *Ey rayik?*"

"Isn't that too easy?" I asked. "A book with all the answers?"

"Not all the answers; the answers that we should know. I believe that there are many things that we should not know. We know only a few things," said Hisham.

"Why seek for the hard answer, which you will not find?" Ahmed asked.

"Because it's a possibility," I said.

And it was such a common refrain, that in a universe where everything is possible, doubt prevails and proof is nowhere. It's a wonderful fuel for endless seeking. But for Ahmed and Hisham, proof and possibility had nothing to do with each other.

"If there's physical proof, what's the point of religion?" Ahmed asked. "God would never lift a mountain for you. Because if he did, you would believe in him. Where is the difficulty?"

I thought I was the one defending difficulty, but I flip-flopped. (The Christian faithful in Cairo had a tenth-century legend to match: when the caliph challenged Jesus's claim that mustard seed-sized faith could move mountains, a committed crowd prayed Mount Muqattam right off the ground, just a bit.) "Why does it need to be difficult?" I asked.

Life could be difficult, without being complex, Hisham said. "He give you the rules—"

"And then he test you. You fail the test, you go to hell," said Ahmed. "You succeed it . . . life is not—it's just a small test. A person can live hundreds and thousands of years—he *will* live hundreds and thousands of years. But this life itself is just a small test."

Masha looked for a summary: "So you're saying God created us to worship him, that's why we're here?"

"Yes," Hisham agreed.

"Isn't that selfish?"

Ahmed didn't care if it was or wasn't a good enough reason to make a planet. "If he created us, he can do whatever he wants. I have a car, I can throw it over the mountain."

At first they seemed like the ones who needed certainty, assurance, answers. Ahmed said he "couldn't imagine" life—this terrestrial installment of it—without a clear, greater purpose. But at its dual core, faith depended on an absence of certainty. What gave life meaning was its meaninglessness. What made all the uncertainty worthwhile was the certainty that it was.

Beyond that, we were trespassing into the kinds of uncertainty that can never be reconciled. Hisham chided me, "You try to think like a god! Why you do this?" He was right that there was some hefty seed of arrogance in all this seeking—in the need to quell my own doubts on my own.

Masha looked back to the biker, still contorted and grimacing silently. "Does he want Advil?"

"Happy pills?" Ahmed joked. "I know, I know—painkillers." He didn't think the man would accept them.

"If he were drinking . . ." I offered.

"It would make the pain go away," said Ahmed.

WHAT IS BAD for dough is good for friendship—after kneading our most deeply held beliefs for hours, we were lighter on our feet with one another. We didn't have to tiptoe around potential sensitivities. The sun dropped and we walked to a man-filled café down the unstraight city streets. Over more shisha and more tea, we could refocus our brain trust from the purpose of human existence and the ramifications of chaos theory on predetermination back to handholding and sex and their values on our respective continents.

The Alexandrian duo delivered us to the train to Cairo, and we exchanged nothing but silly looks and the kind of hugs-without-ego that America's men have not yet adopted. No phone numbers, no Facebook—the *coulds* of connection can become the *shoulds* of Good Friendship, whose neglect brings a special kind of sadness. But it wasn't deliberate. It wasn't that we had weighed potential and responsibility and kept our phones in our pockets—we just didn't think to ask one another for anything else. *We understood one another*, I thought. And there could be no neglect of something so perfectly frozen in time.

Before midnight, we took can-canning pictures in the station as the night train south hissed up to the platform.

CAIRO, AFTER MIDNIGHT. We left our hotel to take in the misty night air on the east bank of the Nile. I ate the breeze like energy and lived the moments as if we were walking through a painting. I believed in the grandeur of *The City of a Thousand Minarets*, and so I saw it.

In the empty roundabout that circles Tahrir Square, a few men held cans of paint and flags in an orange pocket of light under a streetlamp. It was December 30, cold, and the wheeled furnace where yams baked during the day was no longer puffing sweet, sticky smoke. The men moved quickly to meet us in the middle of the road. Paintbrushes immediately followed handshakes, and we surrendered to the welcoming face masks they made. In the reflection of the yam cart, I saw that they had drawn neat Egyptian flags—stripes of red, white and black— from cheeks to chin, and something like the number 2 and a heart on my forehead. We took pictures together against a falafel cart. Whatever we represented to them, to me they were totems of the revolution. I felt the imminence of something important: this was Tahrir Square— *Midan Tahrir!*—and the fact that I was covered in paint with my back to a pile of radishes belied nothing at all.

Despite its grand name, there was once nothing special about Tahrir Square by the KFC and the only metro in Africa. Before the revolution, it wouldn't have been a place to gather, ever really, let alone to ring in the new year. But this plot had earned its place in international history the same way the protestors had, scarred and beaten and resilient.

One day earlier while we were pleasantly touring, Egyptian police had raided and shut down ten NGOs, including four American organizations. If it was a sign of anything more than an autocratic tantrum, it hinted that the Supreme Council of the Armed Forces didn't care so much about Americans anymore—even with $1.5 billion in annual aid money earmarked from the United States to Egypt, and all but $200 million of that for the military. The SCAF, also called the Military Council, had seized power in the vacuum left by Mubarak and broken its promises to return the government to the people. And those twenty officers were mad for theater.

Illegal graffiti repeated on the walls around the square drew the lines of argument most succinctly. "Fuck SCAF," it said.

As the paint dried on my nose, a man in a trench coat led us into the heart of the square, a small circular embankment now covered in muddy grass no more than three hundred feet across. The circle is sometimes called *as-Saniyya*, "the Tray."

A tartan scarf burst from the neckline of his taupe coat underneath perfectly parted hair and a dark goatee, and he invited us to sit with our backs against a canvas tent. Three revolutionaries wafted over. There was a protective atmosphere about the whole thing, and they quietly assumed the role of guardians while we listened. I scanned the empty roundabout and wondered if there really were any threats, or if they were acting for the theater of it.

For all the tension I expected, wanted, searched for—it was quiet. A gun might have been drawn. The army might have come through to raise trouble, or to level the place with guns and camels as they had a year earlier. It wasn't; they didn't. There was only talk, and a kind of talk that might have sounded self-righteous if I didn't want to believe in their ideals. I wanted only to engage, no matter what they were saying, and so we did, listening for hours.

"Do you want a democracy like in America?" Masha asked into a black cowl that hung over a thin, chiseled face, almost skeletal.

"I need justice," he said, in a voice high and light, almost evaporating before it reached us.

"What does that mean?"

"It means lots. That's why we are standing and still fighting."

"Eighty percent of the people are worthless for a revolution," said

Tarek, the trench-coated from above his Burberry scarf. "Like I always give the example, if Benjamin Netanyahu came to rule Egypt, 80 percent of the people would say, 'Come on, we know the guy!'"

That was what we were: desperate for change and desperate for the familiar. We fought to raze everything to the ground and to hold on to everything we ever wanted. And when push came to gunpoint, would it always be the familiar that won?

"It's a matter of time, right?" Tarek said soon. Eventually, another people would begin to make the right kind of progress. I wanted to hear how to take steps forward, too, how to have renewed hope, how to find direction when my past protests had brought me closer to nothing.

And then I thought: *What on blue earth am I doing? How absolutely fucked do I have to be to project my* Bildung *onto the narrative of the world's* roman? *How self-centered did I have to be to see a four thousand-year-old country as a metaphor for myself?*

Just then, we heard shouting coming from the tents near KFC. Everyone stood. Someone had thrown a glass at someone else. Our hosts were quick to offer protection, insisting we remain calm.

"Think we're suicidal? We have these fights every hour."

A little charge ran up my ribs. It was late now. Tarek warned us of treacherous taxis that whisked people from the square straight to the police—a doctor had disappeared that way—and offered to walk us home.

"Are they walking so far?" the bone-thin man said with real warmth.

Our double-upgraded room at the Shepheard's Hotel was close. Tarek's was a little closer—he was staying at the $240-per-night Inter-Continental. We made fun of him for saying that he liked having a view of the square, where he could "look down and make sure everything is okay." Maybe he was a better organizer because he slept on three hundred-count long-staple Egyptian cotton sheets.

"You know, some hotels don't know how to even market this revolution. I'd make revolution tours, like you guys man. You get a little can of tear gas, you get a mask and you see all the action."

I felt my face paint crinkle. The red, white and black and the rough heart on my forehead were tightening like a second layer of skin. Was that actually us—vulture touring for want of a cheap thrill?

"It's Disneyland!" Tarek beamed.

THE NEXT EVENING, bands played on a huge stage that had appeared in the last day and cheer songs broke out in intermittent eruptions. The first New Year's of the new era, the night was a celebratory warm-up to the first anniversary of the revolution, January 25. The lampposts and flooded patches of dirt remembered the last year's violence, and, in still existing, modeled a kind of stoicism for the future.

I don't remember how we met Nevine—the Professor, the Organizer, the Mom. She was just there, keeping an eye out among the chanting thousands, and she pulled us away from Tarek into one of the many tents that had stood for the past month and a half of second-wave protests, and stored the minimal provisions necessary for life in the square. She sat us in the small circle of friends on the floor.

"How many times did you drink tea in plastic cups for New Year's?"

The black tea scalded through the hair-thin cups that, in other hands, doubled as windshields for candles stuck through the bottom. Every so often when the wind blew, the cup would catch and go up in a burst of flame.

"Homeless!" She beamed. "We are the thugs, we are the homeless people of Egypt."

It was a ten-dollar word in Cairo, in English or in Arabic: *thugs* or *baltagiya*. The baltagiya came typically in packs, rogue but in the service of power. The word is Turkish for "axeman."

Antiregime looters had vandalized Cairo in the early days of the revolution, even raiding prisons and freeing the inmates, but the baltagiya were almost always instruments of the powerful, the ones with extra pounds on hand. They were favorites of Mubarak, and now, of the military. It was grisly how gracefully the machinery changed hands.

The Emergency Law, né Law Number 162 of 1958, allowed the government to arrest suspects "dangerous to the security and public order" without a warrant. The Emergency Law stood for the entirety of Mubarak's reign, and when the square cleared to celebrate his ouster, the protestors who stayed stayed because Mubarak was just the master of those measures. The revolution couldn't end until they were erased along with him. Without that, the transition was almost meaningless.

One year later, on the eve of the great day of expectation, January 25, 2012, SCAF chairman Mohamed Hussein Tantawi announced that the law would be lifted. Citizens' rights would be returned. But he left one important clause untouched: warrantless arrests were still kosher, in those cases of what Tantawi called "thuggery." Anyone, said everyone, could be accused of thuggery.

There was a new addition to the tent, purchased just that day from a market across town. It was heavy, with a tight black leather skin, and metal studs down the length. When Nevine leaned on it, her hands rested just above her navel.

"Do you feel safer now that you have the clubs, too?"

"Not me, because I use my tongue and my brains," she said. "And my tongue secured the Square the past week. I got them to really leave the Square. The first day we were less than a hundred fifty and at least fifty thousand came—the paid people, the hired people." In the Square, numbers were conspicuously round. "Today, less than fifty because of me."

Nevine said the uprising had its own security force fifty-strong. "From poor areas, tough, who are really used to fighting. And then they have a club and they say, 'Go. Out!'"

"Are they paid?"

"*NO!* They are from us."

One of these men no older than me and Masha was in the tent now. He wore a neon yellow security vest and a hard hat. The two revolutionaries posed for a picture. The rebel cop made a *V* with his fingers and looked at me straight, eyes relaxed. Nevine, a black and white checkered keffiyeh tied around her head, wore a devilish little grin.

"We're criminals!" she said.

I felt the weight of the club in a cold hand. I imagined swinging it at someone's head, someone swinging it at mine.

"It's quite heavy, yeah. But you can kill somebody using this one," Nevine laughed. "We arrest a lot of officers here."

"What happens to them?"

"You want to know? We hit them until they die."

"How often does that happen?"

"At least once a week. And more people are scared of visiting us since they know they are killed or thrown out." A pause. "But really, really, people die. They hit them, throw them on the street, call the ambulance—by the time they go to the hospital they are dead."

"We are fighters, you know, people who are born in deserts. Different from people who are born in gardens, right? The weather is enough: very cold nights, very warm days—the weather is enough. Also, the food that the land produces is different, and you have to depend on meat. And this makes you aggressive, it's a fact. We are aggressive, it's a fact. So we are not like people who can be led easily. *Do this*, *do that*. Once we open our eyes, *khalas*, finished."

Artists of the revolution and national headliners took the stage. Music drifted in through the tent flaps and we poked out. A light breeze set Masha's cup instantly on fire, singeing her hair. The men mobilized, some with bandaged hands and canes, broken noses, eye patches and looks of intense concern.

"Are you okay?"

"Do you need anything?"

"Do you need a bandage?"

They made her sit. The man with the cane stood to offer his place.

"No, really . . ." Masha said.

"Sit."

"Are you okay?"

"Do you need anything?"

"We don't want you to get hurt."

She let them seat her, these men with their scars and damaged limbs. There was only the faint smell of burned hair. "It looks fine," they said. "You can't even tell."

It was summer camp here, sitting around a campfire or a flaming teacup and telling stories. And it was a place to kill people.

Blithely, I felt no dissonance. Despite my Quaker schooling, I couldn't bring myself to denounce Nevine's team's clubbings, neither out loud nor to Masha nor in secret. Nevine ordered her men to strike back or they did it on their own. If it were me, surrounded by belligerents and with traitors appearing from the tents next door, I'd have bought a club, too. During the Libyan revolution, I relished the news graphics that showed the Honorable Rebels gaining ground against the Evil Dictator. Simple. Good. In Egypt, no such hope. The battle lines dissolved in Tahrir Square (as they would soon in Libya, too). The Tray overflowed with fake protestors, scattered ideology, thugs, government moles—confusion.

They wanted so badly for us to have a good time—to see the revolution on its happiest day in a long while. And . . . that's all it was. This grand milestone before a grand anniversary at the heart of the uprising, and it was just another night. I chatted casually of murder and brotherhood and joined the *Down With* chants just to yell at someone specific.

All the while, I kept seeing me in the crowds of disaffected youth looking for answers. What I heard when I listened to the small secrets of the square—immediate danger could masquerade as clarity. And then when the threat was gone, the moment's solid footing would slip again.

"If we arrest somebody from the intelligence that is staying in a tent, it's a big thing. So even if I tell him do not hit him, they will hit him and they all go after him *bap bap bap bap bap bap bap!* and use everything, knives and clubs. So he have to die. And sometimes also, more often we arrest thugs. And just between us, two of us, we also have a jail. We have a jail and the thugs we arrested are put in jail and they attack each other inside. Thank you for coming," she said. "A good educational trip, right?"

I did not seek out the supposed counterjails, and I did not scan the hospital for the bludgeoned bodies of police officers. I found no reports of protestors killing the baltagiya—but then again, who would such reports have come from? The SCAF wouldn't have wanted their lackeys to hear this. And unlike Bashar al-Assad in the initial months of the Syrian protests, they had no imaginary "terrorists" to blame for violence. This was no hidden corner of southwestern Syria; journalists and Twitter had brought the spotlight to this amphitheater, and the world could see far more clearly who the regime was fighting.

Masha and I squeezed each other in the shelter of the crowd, and the year changed number.

Since she had arrived at our pyramid-side palace, we had coiled around each other—too close, perhaps, to really see each other. In a connection that skintight, she could only feel my panic reverberating—in my overreactions to her flight delays, in my anxiety about train tickets, in our late nights bouncing compulsively from falafel stand to a one-room Cairene casino looking for more, *more*. To her, the place was the cause of my jitters; to me, it just wasn't the cure.

- - - - - -

AROUND TAHRIR SQUARE, there are falafel carts selling six thin, dry pitas full for a dollar. In Egyptian Arabic, falafel is *ta'amiyya*, "little food." Across from the square, behind the street arrays of T-shirts supporting various uprisings and Syrian flags and the new Libyan tricolor, there is a KFC. It was a KFC that was once shut down with "No Mubarak" spray painted over its glass doors, the revolution's injured and unwell deposited at a makeshift clinic under the awning. In a few weeks, the Mubarak regime would start a rumor that protestors were camping in Tahrir only because organizers were distributing *Kentucky*. A YouTube upload quickly mocked this idea with a joking endorsement—holding a date biscuit over his head, a young man makes his revolutionary demands: "One Kentucky for every citizen! One Kentucky for every citizen!"

For the average Egyptian, the fast-food chain with its American prices is no budget fare. Cairo had made us forcefully aware of our place in the world—as tourists, as Americans, as wealthy children for whom the price of brand-name chicken was a drop in the bucket. With a guilty stomach, I still bought two KFC combo meals and heaps of coleslaw for the overnight train to Aswan, to which we were fleeing under the banner of *exploratory curiosity*. With the sea air in our big noses—Masha and I shared those and were mistaken as brother and sister for it—we'd keep moving, from Egypt's northern tip toward its southernmost point.

On the way to the station, we rode with Hisham. He was loud and funny and erudite in the taxi driver's book of quips.

"Welcome to Alaska!" he shouted, like so many Cairene cabbies did. "Welcome to Hawaii!"

"What-*ever*!" Hisham would say often and for no reason, with perfect Valley Girl syncopation. This was his shout-out to America. He gave us his number, to call for taxi service when we returned to Cairo. "See you later alligator!" he called.

Fellow passengers stared at the mountains of chicken we lugged into our sleeper compartment—I didn't know the sixty-five-dollar fare included dinner, but when I smelled it I was glad I never had. I slid the door closed quickly.

THE CITYSCAPE DISAPPEARED against black windows to leave us with that funny sense of being without context or responsibility. American movies on an American laptop, and in the satisfying postchicken lull—carefree sex on the cot that folded out from the wall as we mounted farther into Upper Egypt.

"Upper" Egypt is the length of the Nile valley south of ancient Egypt's capital at Memphis, fifteen miles south of downtown Cairo, to the frontier of ancient Egypt. All this was *Sa'id Masr*, the "Egyptian Plateau."

When we woozily stepped off the train in Aswan, everything looked different. The main street followed the wide bluffs along the Nile, the sidewalks were less crowded than up north, keffiyeh styles had changed—what had protected against cold shoulders now protected against hot heads.

Aswan was an Upper Egyptian border town facing Nubia, the ancient region that stretched down to Khartoum. Its southern part was the biblical kingdom of Cush famous for the stunning array of pyramids at its capital, Meroe. Greek cartographers included Nubia in the region they labeled Ethiopia. To this day the name is a simple warning to would-be travelers/tourists/invaders. From Greek, *Ethiopia* means "to burn the face." In the summer months on average, highs in Aswan top Cairo by ten degrees, Alexandria by twenty. But every winter in Aswan I imagine weather forecasters are all smiles: day after day with highs in the low seventies.

It took mere minutes on the pleasant riverfront to feel guilt again, and a restlessness that I hid from Masha. Was this what I'd wanted to do in Egypt, lounging in the green leather armchairs of a Hitchcock set-worthy café car, en route to ancient tourist sites? Tourism had left but the tours remained, and there was no real discovery in following these timeworn grooves.

Racist politics had redefined modern Egypt here in the name of progress. In 1899, the British broke ground on the Aswan Low Dam, submerging Nubian territories again and again in two enlargements over the following decades. When Prime Minister Gamal Abdel Nasser ordered the High Dam built at Aswan in the 1960s and 1970s, immense amounts of farmland were drowned in the rising waters of the great river. *Life* magazine reported in 1966:

> This stupendous project was conceived to increase Egypt's cultivable land by one third, double her electric power output, and change the very climate of the Nile Valley. It also would inundate more than 5,000 square miles of a veritable open air museum, rich beyond a curator's dream in art and artifacts, tombs and temples.

The Nubian people were struck an irremediable blow, and they have not forgotten. The three hundred-mile-long man-made lake that filled behind the Aswan Dam is called, aptly, Lake Nasser. Sudanese refer to their small portion of the reservoir as Lake Nubia.

A short drive away up and over the dam, at the loading dock to the tourist extravaganza at Philae (*Fee*-a-luh), a trio of Nubian men sat along a stone wall. Philae itself had to be dismantled and relocated, in tens of thousands of pieces of heavy syenite (granitelike rock named for

Aswan), to nearby higher ground. The men shook their head at Nass-er's memory, pained.

It is generally easy to note this distinction: ethnic "Egyptians" look Semitic, like other Arabs and Jews; Nubians look African. In Nasser's flurry of nationalization, Egypt was taken from the king for the people. But when it came time to unify the empowered "people," religious and ethnic minorities were forced to pull the short straw: the dispro-portionately Coptic bourgeoisie lost its economic and political stand-ing; Nubians, among others, were ignored altogether. The waters rose unchecked, and theirs was deemed a worthwhile sacrifice by those it never affected.

But aside from the "five-star" ferry boats sulking in their moorings, every sign of conflict was hidden. On the sail of a wooden felucca roped to the docks, Bob Marley grinned with a lion over a map of Saharan Africa.

Just minutes off the train, we followed a kind-enough-looking hawker to the water's edge to meet his felucca captain. Ahmed was half Nubian, half Sa'idi. He wore all white and walked barefoot across the planks of his felucca. Under a dark mustache, stubble covered a sharp jaw. While we bargained with the boss, Ahmed disappeared to find food for our short journey and low-quality Egyptian weed. Then, the "organizer" took his large half of our fee, and disappeared.

A felucca can be rented for days or a week for a slow journey up the Nile. For us, away from the constant screeching of Cairene streets, Ahmed's felucca—bought by his father—was paradise. Before night fell and Masha and I clung together to steal each other's warmth, we played backgammon on the deck, smelled the river in the sun, drank tea, and drank tea and drank tea.

When it was nearly dark, we docked on the silent east bank and Ahmed began to cook rice.

Stars poked through. Aswan has a population of less than three hundred thousand—greater Cairo has twenty million. In Cairo, some-times, it is hard to see the sky.

The last night's feast of KFC was all that had sustained us for our day of floating luxury, about the price of a midrange hotel. Ahmed laid out plates of food on a floral plastic mat: brown rice, thick wedges of fresh bread, chopped vegetables in a light tomato sauce. And then, as if it were the symbol of all things right and true in this world, he produced a plate of fried chicken. Breaded, crisp but juicy, soft and succulent and falling off the bone like manna from Louisville. We ate rapturously from clean metal bowls with metal spoons, praising Ahmed through facefuls.

"Mmmmmmph!" I said.

"It's just chicken," he said, and said again.

And then we retreated into his compartment in the shallow hull of the boat to digest. Ahmed slept here, in a space hardly tall enough to sit in, but warmer than outside by two full seasons. He told riddles, illustrated in patterns of broken matchsticks. Then, he rolled an enormous joint.

"Some days I don't smoke. When I'm coming to the felucca here, little money, I bring some like this. I leave it with us." Hashish, which he liked more, could be five times more expensive. He brought weed wrapped in newspaper. There were none of the benefits of American science; it was less potent and more crumbly and less green. The purchase came in long, loose clusters called "fingers." Ahmed looked for matches. The only light in the hull came from a small candle, and the match flame flickering against his face. "This is Bob Marley," he said. He sucked in and waved the match out with a swish. "Bob Marley smoke big cigarette."

It was cold over the river, and Masha and I shivered to uneasy sleep on the deck, clasping each other for heat.

Even in my sleep, I could feel that there were no more paychecks coming. I'd quit the job because I thought the best decisions were the scariest ones—that safety nets made Truth harder to find. It's an old trick, fusing destruction with creation: If I give something up, shouldn't it come with something?

That had been my blind bargain—that doing the unnerving thing would be rewarded, the way a plunge in cold water wins freshness, clarity, a rush of warmth. The way flirtation with danger earns newly leased life.

I had come to the Middle East with a strong desire to connect, and a job to root me to the place. And now, at the heart of the revolution, I was a tourist—a fucking tourist!—unrooted from mission, and unrooted from the job that made that mission less desperate. But no, it was good, and I was with the girl I loved, and I was cold, and it felt good when the breeze died and I could stretch the blanket over our feet.

At 3:30 in the morning, Ahmed had brought us safely back to the west bank of the Nile to join a van convoy pointed south for the temple complex at Abu Simbel, fifteen miles from the Sudanese border. Each convoy is accompanied by police, they say, for security concerns.

Masha was happy here. The new southern landscapes helped thicken our understandings of the region we'd wanted to connect to through the language. And sometimes when I hid my antsiness from her, I lost sight of it. Together with her, it was all too easy to occupy the middle space where tourism fits, between stillness and adventure. I let myself mold to her shape, and together we yin-yanged smoothly across the desert.

Before dawn we crossed the Tropic of Cancer. Thirty-three centuries ago Ramses II—of (historically uncertifiable) Exodus fame—had a pair of humongous temples hewn from the sandstone cliffs at Abu Simbel. Man-made Lake Nasser threatened to crest the cofferdams, and the god-king and his favorite wife Nefertari prepared to hold their breath.

A row of twenty-two baboons looked down from the frieze of the Great Temple. One baboon-headed god, Hapy, is the protector of the lungs.

In last-minute desperation, international planners descended on Abu Simbel. Rescue teams hustled to pump water away from the monuments and masons labored around the clock, dicing the entire complex into blocks weighing up to thirty-three tons. When they finished, twenty-five million pounds of stone had been heaved to dry land, two hundred feet higher and several hundred back from the water's edge. All of the crowned figures of Ramses are safe. He is now well positioned behind excited Japanese girls making peace signs, the breathtaking view of the lake on a sunny morning and a loud American screaming that he had been swindled by the entrance ticket's "Tour Guide Fee."

Modernity threatened and saved the temples. The original stone is refashioned on a conical base of cement. Everything you see is ancient and real, and everything holding it up is modern technology.

While the larger temple has the king's wife carved in miniature, on both sides of the entrance to the Small Temple, a full-size Nefertari is carved between statues of her husband. For the first time, the only documented case in pharaonic art, the queen is equal in size. Perhaps this design somehow served Ramses's own vanity—*Even my queen is bigger than all of you Nubians!* Perhaps he bucked the mold out of egotism, or politics or love. Comparisons came easily as Masha and I basked hand in hand. As it is for any anxious boy made more whole in partnership, the power of my girlfriend was a testament to my own strength: The more equal we were, the more of *me* there was. Her smarts were our smarts, her beauty was our beauty, her jokes were our jokes that we shared and let us be aloof from the seriousness of the world.

But to build us up I had to subscribe to our sameness, even though we wanted different things from this place. No part of her needed to make things difficult, while half of me was tense for feeling no tension.

After noon, temperatures climbed with the tempers of the grumpy and our van convoy prepared to leave. Distant sand turned to mirrors in the shuddering heat. Soon, the drivers turned their engines off again, and we learned we weren't going anywhere.

For two hours, there was "roadwork" along the single highway back to Aswan. Our vanful sat courteously fanning themselves, better prepared with snacks and sustenance than Masha and I ever were. We dug the dregs from a plastic bag of tiny Ghirardelli chocolates her mom had given her, like the most aristocratic of table scraps.

In Arabic, our driver told me that there were protests. Workers were striking somewhere and obstructing traffic, and someone had decided to keep the foreigners sheltered. All of the drivers were doing this.

"What did he say?" a Japanese man asked me from the backseat.

I hesitated. "We should be going soon."

I lied to keep the borders drawn. To hide information from the backseat in order to declare my loyalty: not a tourist. No, I wasn't part of *his* group—cameras-around-necks, waiting to be chaperoned. But of course I was. Masha and I held hands in the convoy. And when the desperation of the year's appetite for understanding became the desperation of an hour's quest for a sandwich, I forgot the point again. I delighted in that starvation, a clear problem with a clear fix. I often kept myself hungry on purpose just for this—so that despite all uncertainty, there would always be a simple solution for a base desire.

With Masha, if I ever let myself, I could truly be at ease. That scared me more than anything—to feel *okay* when I was so close to others in revolt. To choose blindness, numbness, *pleasure* even, instead of truth. How could I be growing without pain?

I settled into uneasy sleep against the van window, dreaming of falafel and fried chicken, and of the hungers that I could sate in a sitting.

I'm not demanding you quit your job, I'm not demanding you come to American for me, I'm not demanding anything. All I'm asking for is to be taken into consideration. Maybe you are . . . I just want you around. I'm sorry if I'm making you feel like shit because i actually want a relationship with you. That's it. I just don't feel like you are taking me into account at all. That's fine, you're 22, you should be able to make these decisions for you and I understand that.

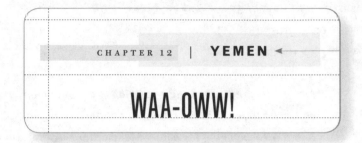

WAA-OWW!

THOUGHT I'D KNOWN WHAT restless meant, but the minute my contract at NYUAD expired, the bottom dropped all the way out. Almost as soon as I set foot back in my apartment in the Emirates, I rented a car the size of a teacup and raced in a skinny circle through all seven emirates, sleeping in the driver's seat leaned back and eating baked beans cold from the can. I hadn't let myself believe it, but that contract had kept me intact, defending the value of each day no matter how I spent it. Now, I could justify my wandering only with discovery.

I was completely unscrewed now, back in an apartment that served no greater purpose than to hold spare shoes and cutlery. Neal was on January term leave from the university and felt hemmed in by the city. Together, we set our eyes on a place with unclear visa restrictions and a reputation as the region's time capsule, isolated from the Gulf by money and dialect and money—Yemen has yet to achieve membership in the Gulf Cooperation Council, which includes the other six states on the Arabian Peninsula. It was the kind of set-apart place I hoped would let me feel like the photographer who first stood on the moon and watched the Earth rise. In my state of blankness, Yemen was the capital.

I was saying my good-byes to people I knew and didn't, people I liked and didn't, as they flitted between the two buildings on the university's temporary campus. It seemed strange to everyone that I'd leave now, as the school had started to settle into its routine, as our expat cohort was finally finding its footing and the beaches beckoned. Brittany understood the urge; she was an anthropologist who studied Yemen and gushed about it at the wooden table outside the cafeteria where I seemed to be holding casual court. "I went overland once all the way south by taxis," Brittany said. "I went alone in Peugots, completely alone in 1999, as a woman, in Peugots filled with men, from Sanaa to Taiz and Ibb and Hudeidah and Aden."

She would entrust Neal and me later with two copies of her thick book intended for a friend, an outspoken journalist in Somaliland. All we had was his name, but if we found ourselves in Somalia's secessionist province across the water from Yemen, she said, it would be lovely if we could seek him out. We said sure.

Like everyone I had ever met who had been to Yemen, she oozed with knowledge and opinion about the place, and wonder. No one returned from Yemen unaffected. "You might want to do the things that in any other place you would consider touristy," she said. "Everything is off the beaten track at this point."

Jamal, a freshman from the Yemeni capital, found me at the table. We'd met first at the weekend where potential students flew in for a last round of the admissions process; Jamal had arrived a week early to escape the violence in Sanaa. "I was in the airplane and I looked down, and you could see these beautiful flower-like formations around all the gas stations that went out for miles and miles and miles. People just waiting for gas."

Yemen retreated into the otherworldly partly because the world wouldn't have it. "It's kind of like a fetishized place, which is . . . cool," he said. "Even Yemenis fetishize it, so we don't want to live anywhere else." It was poetic and lovely, but with a fat caveat: "Except, if they open like visa situation here. Then everybody would move to the Gulf."

When it was time to come to school, he did have visa troubles with the UAE. "So I ran to the ambassador's house and was like, 'Please give me a visa quick, I need to go to university.'" It worked. I loved that kind of administrative mushiness—not for what it revealed about the power of elites, but for showing how a connection between single people could cut through chaos. There was still the promise of discovery through little collisions with one another.

There was that promise, and then there was the planning to make that promise bear fruit. Before taking off for uncertain places, I sought advice most intently from nearby sources. Even though some of them told me not to go, the Pashtun tailors down the block had given me useful advice and clothes for my days in Afghanistan. Iman had picked sandals for me to wear in Pakistan. These meetings gave me a kind of confidence simply by revealing something tangible in my blank predictions—*they are from there, so there is a place.* And there was always the jitter-reducing province of preparation for its own sake, despite how little preparation I really accomplished. If I was still answering a twelve-year-old's questions, I had to stay as much like him as I could. I didn't buy guidebooks or cram regional history or stock-pile toiletries I might not find abroad. And if I went on travel forums to measure the off-ness of a city's limits, I looked for threads that suggested even the faintest possibility (and always found it) that the door was still open, and took that tiny hope as good enough.

It was unconscious sleight of mind to maintain the place's mystery, all while distracting myself from the kind of true fear that would keep me away from an airport. I titrated my ignorance to keep me just afraid *enough*. Travel without fear is nothing, as Camus liked to say, or said once.

The flat winter sun beat down hard around the umbrella and Jamal prepared me with useful Yemeni dialect: *qabili*, "tribal matters," *rubta*, "a bundle (of qat, the stimulant shrub)," *muftahin*, "chillin'." This was practically everything I packed in my head.

Before that, this was all that I knew (and I knew it then in even less detail): on October 12, 2000, a boat rigged with explosives detonated against the hull of the USS *Cole*, moored in the Aden harbor. Yemen materialized instantly in the public consciousness of the United States. Al-Qaeda claimed responsibility and, after September 11, the Yemeni government began to cooperate with the War on Terror, accepting in return tens of millions of dollars (and rising) in military aid.

Arabic students from American universities began to flock to Yemen in small, adventurous numbers. Yemen, now uncovered, was the place for unspoiled immersion.

The Arab Spring and the government's abusive reaction put all of this on hold.

Jamal remembered the *Cole* bombing from his childhood. "I remember going to the TV, like, 'Daddy daddy, Yemen's on the TV for the first time in history!' and he's like, 'Oh . . . that's cool son.'"

That introduction has colored much of the world's relationship with Yemen ever since, however fairly or unfairly or oversimplified or cautious. I asked Jamal what came before all of this, before the students, before the violence.

"Before it didn't even exist," he said.

WE PICKED A GOOD TIME to go to Yemen, between the cease-fire and the elections. The warring factions of Yemen's revolution were holding fast to a period of tense calm, a fuse curling out of the capital, waiting to be lit or doused on inauguration day. Entering its second year the Arab Spring had lowered flight fares to Sanaa, too. Mainly, though, we had visas, and we were Yemen bound even if the time was wrong.

We flew Qatar Airways in the wrong direction, to Doha for a transfer, and then turned back to the south. In the Sanaa airport, they checked our papers as our bags were X-rayed and then sent us to a small room.

"Tourists?" said the immigration officer in his sky-blue uniform and beret, incredulous. His eyes darted between papers on opposite sides of his desk. "We don't have that."

He looked at our visas as if they were stickers from another universe.

In these situations of broken promises and suspicion, sudden moves must be avoided. An argument would mean we had already lost. Recently, four American doctors had been denied the chance to return for a second trip to Yemen. The consul was convinced: *They are FBI*, he said. The officer was shocked and suspicious that we would come now, for our *first visit* to Yemen.

And even worse, we were young—further proof of our espionage. The consul had passed this message to the doctors: "They should come back after they retire."

Our guard's shaded eyes were glassy calm now, no longer straining to understand. "What are you doing here?" he said. His coolness was a sign of our lost ground. Men grow calm when they know they have all the power.

"*Siyaha*," I said. *Tourism*. His eyebrows twitched and I quickly added, "we're visiting friends." We were talking in Arabic now. It was a gamble. Certainly a spy would speak Arabic, but I was betting the country's gatekeeper was warier of the naive than the crafty.

A Japanese man entered the waiting room to stand by us, ushered by a guard.

"There's no tourism here," the officer said to me and Neal, in English. "There's *harb*"—war—"and it's dangerous and you can't go anywhere. We don't have tourism."

"Yes, we know, but there are safe areas. Our friends know," I said, meekly.

Hope sank into my toenails. He was actually going to send us home. He flicked idly through the pages of our passports, hardly looking.

He turned to the Japanese man who struggled to make himself understood in English. I helped translate between the two as best I could—*yes!* They would reward us for this service!—and listened as the situation deteriorated. I had made the right choice: the Japanese man denied all knowledge of instability, a genuine look in his eyes as he cited a trip to Yemen twenty-five years earlier. He asked to come in—the freshman outside the college bar—face full of indignation and entreaty.

"No," the Yemeni said. And turned to us.

We got the tourist visa in Abu Dhabi and we came, I said. For our friends, I said. I was holding a sheet of paper with a few names and numbers from friends of friends of friends and from the Internet, a skeleton of an address book for our wanderings.

A blue cotton arm reached over the metal desk and snatched it. The officer began calling the numbers on the list, under SANAA.

First he called Anoud, a woman we had contacted on Couchsurfing. "Leave me a voice mail to tell me who u r to call back I don't answer numbers I don't know," she had written me. But she did pick up, and they spoke for ages in rapid dialect. And when he asked for her address, she hung up.

The man put the phone softly back in its holster. "She is not your friend."

My heart was squirming to find somewhere lower, considering breaking the way a business considers bankruptcy, pulling my face down so that it could hardly move. *Yemen*, I thought, wistful, as if I had already lost a lover.

The Japanese man offered to change his flights to Socotra, the far-away Yemeni island a world apart from north or south Yemen, unique with wildlife, language, history. He stood, waiting for an answer. In a stroke of luck, as I remember it now, my hopeless face had frozen in an expression perfectly suited to the man I was pretending to be, the one in control, unworried. The officer moved—I flinched—and picked up the phone again. He dialed Tal, an Italian who had lived his entire life in Yemen, the friend of a Sana'ani I'd bumped into once or twice in Abu Dhabi. They spoke for a moment, before the phone was passed to me. Finally, a moment for collusion.

"Yo man."

I'm certain the officer's English was better than my Arabic, but he was unprepared for, or uninterested in, the slurry of mumbled slang and bakery fresh neologism. In Syria, Danny and I had practiced consulting each other in public-secret with a monotone of *ahmnotlike-trynnadothashitbranahmsayin*, where "no" might've done. It was our Navajo. I handed the phone back.

A click.

The man reverted to Arabic, tapping our passports together on the metal. "*Ruh*," he said. *Go.* "Be careful."

We ran without running, new energy surging through our legs as we stood and turned our backs. I passed through the door, praying he wouldn't change his mind, power walking until we were safely out of earshot.

———

WE BOUGHT SIM CARDS for pennies and charged them with a few Yemeni rial as we raced toward the city. Colorful clothing and white *thobes*, a cluster of roadside shops, tree-brown faces overgrown with stubble and highly decorative belts with a curved dagger tucked in front. Memories flashed as everything blurred by, a crowded street in Pakistan, the impoverished outskirts of Cairo. But then we were there, at the thousand-year-old gate to Sanaa's old city, and all similarities ceased for good.

Hilltop fortifications and central souqs, castles and mausoleums, ancient stone synagogues-turned-churches-turned-mosques, each with singular stories and nuanced architecture—the Middle East is ripe with Old Cities. Sanaa's is made from wholly different ingredients. Crammed together on narrow streets, the six thousand houses in the old city are likened often to gingerbread houses of fired brick and rammed earth, reddish brown and iced with white gypsum bands between the floors. They climb as high as nine stories above the valley floor, with rooftop *diwan*—meeting spaces, qat-chewing rooms—looking out at the mountains and minaret tips all around.

Sanaa is one of the world's highest capitals. At ground level, the city is seventy-two hundred-feet high. As we navigated its winding streets looking for hotels that hadn't closed for lack of business, the sun was setting, the light sliding up and off the tops of the sand castle buildings.

Like Fez or Damascus, Sanaa's old city is made to reconnoiter by foot. The first order of business: food. As we found out, Yemeni cuisine was as wonderful as it was hard to find. Whenever we least expected it, we were invite-demanded in for lunch, but when we were the hungriest, restaurants appeared a foreign concept. Even the hotel we finally found had few ideas.

When we asked for recommendations, the doorman-concierge-groupie whispered the name of a famous chicken joint that exceeded his wildest fantasies for quality and elegance. He bent in close, as if he were forfeiting some coveted secret. "Have you heard of *Kentucky*?"

Instead we wandered the dark signless streets off *Shari'a September*

26, a thoroughfare that remembers the Yemen Arab Republic's coup against the short-lived kingdom that ruled the north between 1918 and 1962. It was Gamal Abdel Nasser's rise in Egypt that sparked the anti-monarchy revolution in Yemen. After a minute, we hit Gamal Street.

At the intersection of the two wide roads, long green canvas tents stood in *Midan Tahrir*, "Liberation Square." Following the Egyptian model again, Yemenis camped in their Tahrir Square to call for thirty-three-year-ruler Ali Abdullah Saleh to leave, just as Cairenes had demanded the ouster of Hosni Mubarak. In both cases, protestors insisted power not be ceded to one of the president's sons.

Protestors in Yemen had never been extremely organized—Facebook and Twitter were far less accessible and active than they were in Egypt—and the square had often been flooded with government lackeys bought and fed "because they have nowhere to go."

"There was a very, like, motivated central group of students who were involved with the shit," Tal would explain with Californian cadence, "but there was also people who would just come to voice very minimal and not politically oriented, you know, unhappiness." These might have been paid disorganizers, plainclothes progovernment thugs trading in confusion for a moment, instead of their usual violence; or it might simply have been a by-product of the wildfire nature of the region's revolutions: all encompassing, populist, vague.

"They would just come by and be like, 'I can't fucking like get my car fixed because the guy at the car fixing store is charging too much. This is because the regime does this and this and this!'"

Now the tents were empty. Two months earlier in November, Saleh had ceded all executive powers in return for immunity and the square fell quiet, a cease-fire holding between the government's military and the armed rebellion. One month later, Yemen would unanimously elect the current vice president, Abdo Rabbuh Mansur al-Hadi, to the presidency. Hadi would be the only candidate.

In these interim months, life continued, it seemed, as usual. On the streets, vendors sold shoes and watches and loose ammunition, bullet casings glinting in the light of a laundromat, the photocopy shop, anything but a restaurant. Finally, a young boy made an offer for our salvation in a no-frills cafeteria with picnic bench seating wrapped in disposable plastic.

"Biid?" He said: eggs. *Yes, please.* He brought onions and an omelet and a spicy tomato salsa known as *sahawiq* to put on everything. The other restaurant-goers looked and turned away. The boy watched us inhale ravenously before bringing a plate of something we didn't think we'd ordered: the salsa was here, the Cokes, the bread, eggs . . . and then the fog of hunger lifted, and Arabic that mattered came back to me. As in Spanish, *eggs* may be other spheroids that hang low on many mammals, these, in particular, from the back of a goat. A faint taste of musty liver. Neal abstained. Sated, we began to see the city.

WHEN WE FOUND TAL, he took us to a friend's stately home on the other side of town where he and his friends were lazing after an afternoon of chewing qat. For almost all men and a less huge and more hidden set of women—in sessions generally separated by gender but not always, qat, said *gat* in north Yemen, was an afternoon drug. When we got there, the guys were leisurely sprinkling dark hash into rolling papers.

We dropped into the couches that wrapped around the walls of the *diwan*. "Everyone has one of these rooms in their house. They're basically just getting high rooms," said Muhammad, a Yemeni university student with curly hair and a voice that was relaxed and righteous. (An estimated 80 percent of the population will chew on Fridays, 50 or 60 percent on other days. This includes every living human being in Yemen, up to one out of every five children under twelve.) This room was lit by one lamp plugged into a generator. These days in Sanaa, electricity came on for about three hours a day, one out of every six hours. When the crisis was worse, they said, the electricity shortage was less severe. Maybe that kept people in their homes.

Adam had just arrived with a bottle of vodka. "But now that things are getting better," he said, "the electricity is getting worse."

The beautiful thing about the gat chew, which usually begins after lunch around 1 P.M. and stretches into the night, is the conversation. Yemenis are deliriously social because of it, and with their hospitality, we could tap into the locals' shared information, opinion, gossip and rumor. All of it out in the open.

"After the revolution everything is chaos. They opened up U-turns in the middle of the highway . . ." I had seen piles of rubble cleared to make unmarked Michigan lefts, further allowing amateur traffic engineers to make rules on the fly.

"It's part of the government's grand plan to show that without them everything is crazy . . ."

"We don't have water in Yemen, but we have 3G Internet . . ."

"I heard they boil the beef with Panadol tablets and put weed in the salts to make people eat more. I think it makes the kids sleep better at night I don't know. That might be a rumor I don't know . . ."

In a place where truth is hard to come by, collecting stories is the best first move. "Are there any agencies where you can get straight news?" I asked.

Staggered noes from around the room.

"The opposition and the government, it's all exaggerated. Like none of it is real. It's complete propaganda." He passed the hash in foils to Tal. "The Internet—"

"—on TV it's bullshit," said Tal.

"Bullshit, man," said Muhammad.

"The biggest bullshit," said Tal, looking back across the room. "Give me the papers, too, don't be a whore."

Like this, on Neal's birthday, we were introduced to Yemen. The territory safe to travel was receding, leaving a space rumors filled. The room knew less the farther south we talked, until we hit the bottom of the country, where electricity might have been stolen and held from the people on offshore ships, and where, Jebel had heard, you could hitch a ride to Somalia by boat.

WE WOULD HEAR ECHOES of these complaints and speculation from every echelon. Unwaged revolutionaries and the unwound elite often sounded alike, trusting in a deep mistrust of power. Jamal had explained the hired mobs that clustered around Saleh's meetings just when he was taking pen to his resignation papers. "He paid them to all carry signs that said, 'Yo, we want you to stay.' And then he doesn't sign. He's like, 'Oh, they don't want me to go.'"

He didn't even believe Saleh's November handover was genuine either, in the wake of these last-minute reversals and the fighting that raged on city streets only months earlier. The Arab Spring had turned to summer, had turned to fall. "People have to be hopeful, because, you know, it's been a year."

Tahrir was quiet now, and it would stay that way. "The protests are over," said Muhammad, "like all the shit. The revolution is over."

Minutes later, appliances whirred to life as the lights came on.

"*Allahu akbar allahu akbar,*" Muhammad cheered soberly. "Bring the TV, man, bring the TV! What do you want to watch?"

Tal shrugged. "Whatever."

The future was coming fast whether or not anyone knew about it, but it made no promises of change. The lights would come on in Sanaa, at least. In a month, Hadi would be in charge—the vice president becoming president—and ruling oligarchs would shift their weight accordingly. Despite Hadi's southern birth, Yemen's southern movement boycotted his predetermined election; they preferred full secession, a return to the pre-1990 state of things: North Yemen and South Yemen. Tal mentioned something from the papers—that Hadi was selling electricity to Yemen from Africa.

"You know what I read a while ago? That fucking Hadi—"

Muhammad interrupted. "Who's Hadi?"

WHEN THE LIGHTS finally went off (after two unexpected hours) and the smoke was settling on the ceiling, we had forgotten our politics. Conversation drifted toward the other subject, ripe with rumor and detached cynicism, that locals know visitors are hungry for. It was the language they flirted with when they dressed up with daggers on Chatroulette—the video chatting site that pairs strangers at random— just to scare people. Danger. Acquaintances of acquaintances disappeared and reappeared in a puff of tribalism and statement making.

Muhammad remembered when the Polish ambassador was visiting his grandfather's house.

"—like ten years ago right?"

"—his daughter went to our school."

Kidnappers rushed him off to the countryside where he feasted, spoke with his wife, and gave chocolates to kids in the village. "They set a whole ram in front of him. The village was fucking with the government."

As it turned out, kidnapping was a form of politics: tribal leaders pressured the government with foreigners held in legendarily convivial custody. The government paid ransom to keep its foreign allies. As the friends saw it, these were problems outside the *diwan* and over the high walls, problems too ingrained or too intangible to engage with constantly. If something really mattered, it was probably too late to do anything about it.

A very small number of kidnappings ever went wrong. Deaths of hostages were generally blamed on government mishandling.

"There are tourists who come here to get kidnapped," Tal said. "It's a cultural experience, you know."

We laughed. He shrugged.

I SPENT MUCH of the dawn hours in digestive mutiny in the dark bathroom of our seventeenth-century hotel, a sliver of light finding me withered and broken through a pane of red glass. Neal was separated from this fate only by goat balls. I argued with my guts as the sun rose, hoping to impart upon them some sense of urgency, of the value of time exploring Yemen as it compared with time spent clutching an antique toilet.

On this first morning, we visited the still-functioning Tourist Police to request permits to leave the city limits. A permit application includes passport photocopies (painfully xeroxed from the shop outside Tahrir Square) and exact travel dates. If locations on the permit didn't match the checkpoints we hit, there would be repercussions along the Disappointing-Troubling spectrum.

I never knew if a well-placed bribe would substitute. This fell into the category of *qabili*. Jamal had offered only one simple rule of bribing etiquette: "You gotta be classy about it."

Our first encounter with the Tourist Police was an amicable one. Yousif, one of their agents, was eternally having tea in the courtyard of our hotel. He gave us his mobile number to call whenever. (I did, at ten in the evening, at 7 A.M.—and he almost always picked up and facilitated.)

Yousif walked us to the office, two little rooms with the lights off, one with a phone (disconnected), the other with a bed. Our permits were given immediately with one caveat: the Interior Ministry could always call and reject them. We were told to leave our phones on.

STUBBORN AND NAUSEOUS, I hobbled with Neal through the Bab al-Yemen, an archway with so much character that the Yemeni Embassy in Abu Dhabi had borrowed its look. Castle walls thirty-feet high bound much of the city with colors to match the buildings, but the gate is a deeper brown with a trim of dark gray stones and four thin pillars under the entablature. The Yemen Gate has Yemen on both sides, separated by one archway and a thousand years.

In the knot of cabs outside the egress from the old city, one driver in an ancient yellow taxi cornered us with a good deal. He spoke in clearer tones than the old chainsmokers, with a higher voice that cut through the throng; he thronged best. We negotiated vehemently without knowing what reasonable was, and Abdulkhaliq, who began to call himself AK, never stopped grinning. His grins stuck with me as a Yemeni national treasure.

AK had the face of a twenty-five-year-old to match his even-younger-man's voice, and he bubbled with the kind of excitement that felt trustworthy because it came fast.

We drove with him to the northwest, passing buildings with lost windows like black eyes. AK pointed to one skyscraper in red brick, the blast hole of an artillery shell high above us. These were the only indicators that less than two months ago, Yemenis were killing each other in the streets.

Bloody weeks into the uprising, the Yemeni government began to lose control. In a meeting with religious leaders in February, Saleh was reported to have said, "I'm ready to leave power but not through chaos. I'm fed up now after thirty-two years, but how to leave peacefully? You scholars should say how."

On March 18, unidentified forces killed forty-five protestors with gunfire. In the continuing series of ministerial defections, President Saleh lost support from high-ranking generals. Then came the tribal leaders, among them Sheikh Sadiq al-Ahmar, hereditary chief of the Hashids, the second largest tribal federation in Yemen. The president himself was a Hashid, but the federation didn't act as a bloc. The third time Saleh balked at signing over his powers, in late May, Ahmar flexed. Tribal loyalists and government forces met in the capital, with guns. In the coming weeks, more than a hundred fighters were killed.

With tribes involved, loyalty tended to trump strategy. The International Crisis Group quoted a tribesman who explained the dangers of domestic combustion. "It will spark a cycle of revenge. Secondly, we are all armed. It will not be like Tunisia or Egypt, where only one side is armed and where people are only hitting each other or the security forces only use tear gas. . . . If we were to follow the Egyptian or Tunisian examples, it would be a disaster." Nearly every home in Yemen has a gun. Amazingly, though, as so many Yemeni men were quick to tell me, unaffiliated civilians did not reach for their weapons when the violence erupted. The guns, they said, were not proof that Yemenis were violent people.

Northwest across the Red Sea, NATO was bombing Libya to help rebels in their full-fledged civil war. Yemen seemed on the brink of the same. On the southern coast, Islamist militants had taken advantage of the distracted government and attacked the medium-sized city of Zinjibar thirty-one miles from Aden—every inch of which locals were forced to flee by foot. Ansar al-Sharia took control of roads and towns in the south that were once safe to travel.

Sanaa locals saw war in the capital. On June 3, a bomb detonated in the mosque of the presidential compound. Saleh suffered second-degree burns and shrapnel wounds. The next day, Hadi was named acting president, Saleh left for treatment in Saudi Arabia, and a tentative cease-fire was brokered.

"There was tanks there!" AK pointed, on a street that didn't look wide enough to hold a minivan. Stone walls were chipped and pockmarked.

It was purposefully irresponsible, the way I watched these city scars from the bench seat of an old cab. I was still desperate to find something I could wrap my eyes around that might make my life flash before me.

On September 23, Saleh returned. A hundred Yemenis died in renewed fighting. In November, he finally signed the Gulf Cooperation Council agreement to step down, as if he had intended to do so all along.

AK ran directly over a pothole, as he was wont to. I clenched against puking or shitting myself. The next day, the Yemeni parliament would grant Saleh total immunity.

IN FORTY-FIVE MINUTES, we were ready to show our papers at the first checkpoint. Children were streaming out of Friday prayers in Shibam dressed in formal *thobes* and blazers with curved daggers in sheaths, *janbiya*, on belts at the navel. A darker trio stayed apart from the rest in shirts too small, pants too big. The others eyed us curiously, smiled, jostled into line for pictures they demanded. The most precocious, with a bright teal scabbard tucked under a golden threaded belt, stuck his tongue out.

AK left the car to negotiate with the officers while the kids stole glances from behind their friends, dagger handles glinting. Something was slow. Our permit should have easily let us pass through to Shibam and to Kawkaban, the town perched on the mountain next door.

"He wants to come with us," said AK of the officer. Neal and I were doubtful. We'd be under much tighter guard with the police following us. "He wants to have lunch."

It became quickly clear that we weren't moving an inch farther if we didn't accept. Bilious and grumpy, I trudged into the restaurant the officer indicated, figuring *lunch* was just another form of bribery-for-

passage. He appeared outside in a gaggle of seven soldiers in camouflage and fur-lined hats. We'd been had.

With no tact or class I told the commander how unfair it was to
make us stop and pay for a battalion, that we would not be strong-armed
while precious hours of the short day waned.

"No!" he pleaded, his big brown eyes lifting into his broad face.
"Only me! I'll pay for everything." Officer Naji was crestfallen. He
hadn't wanted to have to say it. This was an invitation, not a demand.
The whole world seemed to sharpen into clarity while my ego crum-
bled with that sad assumption. *Oy*, I thought, *now I'm the asshole*.

Shamed, we climbed the stairs to our private room, beautiful
and empty, lined with cushions along the wall. A dozen dishes came
in heavy metalware. *Fahsa*, a thick yellow lamb stew spiced with
fenugreek—that pea relative often pulverized for curry powder; *shafut*,
bread soaked in yogurt and coriander; plain rice and tomato rice; a
brothy soup spiced with *hawayij*; flatbread fresh off the *taboon*, and
another drizzled with honey for desert. The *hawayij* blend is also used
for coffee, cardamom heavy with various additions to suit the region
and the purpose. Yemeni Jews brought the mixture north to Israel,
where coffee is now sweet with its gingery fragrance.

I could hardly convince Naji that I was still battling the last night's
cafeteria consequences, and so I picked at the boiling pots with a look
of quiet despair. To Naji, that made me a rather dour, inscrutable sort.
Neal ate like a man.

In the highest room upstairs with bright windows on the town, men
were starting to chew gat—after 2 P.M., all of Yemen talks with its mouth
full. The *mafraj* was overflowing with green leaves, stems tossed onto
tables and the floor, sunlight streaming through the windows onto red
couches. Daggers had been removed, laid quietly on the cushions next
to handguns.

The word *mafraj* means "relief, relaxation." The immortal *Hans
Wehr Dictionary of Modern Written Arabic* also offers "denouement"
and "happy ending." The same stem leads to words for "a state of happiness," "removal (of grief or worry)," "opening wide," and "observation." The *mafraj* is often a room with a view where days go to untie

themselves, and to end. Just after lunch, we began to pick the leaves with a man named Max and his friends, all in white robes under suit jackets, light keffiyehs on their heads or around their necks.

The World Health Organization does not classify any of Yemen's four dozen gat species (or African varieties) as markedly addictive, but insomnia and lethargy are common consequences and, as a doctor at the University of Sanaa said, "people who are genetically predisposed are extremely vulnerable to psychosis."

Within a couple days off the branch, gat can lose much of its potency. Every hour counts. The quality and freshness of every leaf is examined by the buyer, savored for its uniqueness, and everyone is a connoisseur. It is like wine or weed or bourbon or theater tickets.

Chewers claim strength, stamina, clarity, while nonchewers report exactly the opposite. An old man might admit to being unable to get out of bed without a few leaves to nibble. A British minister of parliament lamented the quoted ten tons of gat imported and distributed weekly through the United Kingdom, where it was banned only in 2014. In Canada, possession is officially illegal, but a woman caught with seventy-five pounds at the airport was fully discharged. Ontario court justice Elliot Allen said, "I read everything I can get my hands on about it and I find it difficult to be persuaded of anything other than what I was told . . . when I had my first case, which was: 'We think this is almost as dangerous as coffee.'"

In America, the Drug Enforcement Agency classifies cathinone (and any traces thereof) in the same category as heroine and cocaine; the FDA says the plant may be detained, not specifically as a drug, but by invoking the "Misbranding" section of the Federal Food, Drug, and Cosmetic Act of 1938. This is marvelous: its labeling fails to bear "adequate directions for use."

Naji gave Neal and me our first instructions. The stems were not to be eaten, I learned first, though the soft red joints of the leaves where they met the branch were fair game. It was important to chew up front, passing chopped leaves back to the pocket behind the teeth, but not too much, or the fine pulp would slip away down the throat. Or, as some experts did, whole leaves could be stuffed directly into the cheek, to be massaged as a ball slowly over time.

"Chew gat and you'll see America from here!" Max grinned.

If gat was the national drug, and *salta* the national dish, this was the national joke. A gat scholar reported the very same in 1972, and I would watch so many others deliver that punch line again and again with the same expectancy. Were they awaiting kudos for originality, or was it just something you said to be pleasant, the gat-chewers' "bon appétit"?

BY EARLY AFTERNOON, we were packed into Naji's armed police truck with the seven soldiers and AK holding on outside in the truck bed, clustered around a massive armor-piercing machine gun.

Naji's police forces were loyal to the government of Ali Abdullah Saleh. He indicated his units along the road, men at checkpoints under his command. He pointed vaguely across yellow fields at the hills where the revolution had attacked.

"There is shooting, there are firefights," Naji said. But, he explained insouciantly, his men would shoot back and Ahmar's forces would disappear.

"Are there problems for you because of the revolution?"

"No. No! We are not in a revolution. We are in a crisis, a small crisis. The president, Ali Abdullah Saleh—in Yemen 80 percent are behind Saleh. Ali Abdullah Saleh is okay."

The truck rattled up Mount Kawkaban, winding around vast gat plantations. Naji's cheek was puffing. Ours were, too, as we dipped into gift bags of fresh leaves. Naji broke off twigs of his *rubta* when we were empty. We barreled through the entrance of the fortifications around Kawkaban, fifty miles an hour through the narrow, rocky town road. We missed children by inches. At a clearing, Naji roared up to a ledge that fell one thousand feet straight down to the valley floor. He eased the truck forward until the edge was hidden under the hood of the car.

When he spoke, it was in an Arabic accent unlike the city folk, never in English except for one special word, broken into his two favorite syl-

lables, enunciated with every muscle in his face. He turned: a Cheshire grin with the truck five loose stones from death.

"*Waa-oww!*"

From this vantage in the Haraz Mountains, Yemen is splayed out flat like a coloring book. Only the mountain and a pair of small clouds cast shadows on the mosaic of empty fields, copper, wheat, tan and camel browns. A spot of green. Naji smirked mischievously with a cigarette between his fingers, surveying Shibam from above. The blocky tan homes of a few thousand looked like stones that had overflowed the mountains, almost invisible if I forgot we'd come by their roads.

In Thula, an ancient walled city only miles away, a long ladder climbs to a stone staircase that switchbacks to a view of a similar sort. From the unconquerable fort in Thula, the fields along the plateau are Yemen's most deliberate kind: terraced grassland stretches for miles. Brown for the winter, the terraces make long, geometric waves—wholly man-made, but entirely natural. If I didn't look too closely, I wouldn't see a single trace of mankind.

Of all places, Yemen was not where I expected to find hints of the far east, of Balinese rice paddies carved into verdant hillsides. Another distinction muddled and thrown away.

Down below, women descended into an open cistern. Their abayas were bright and colorful in the patterns of older traditions, and they carried buckets on their heads that they dipped into green water. On a stone street the shade of raw almonds, I bought a janbiya—said "jambiya" almost always—with a bone handle and a fraying belt, and a silver bracelet for Masha.

"Made by Jews," the shopkeeper said. "Only they know how to make this silver." When Israel was established, and they left, he said, Yemenis forgot how to make such delicate patterns.

A resident pointed out Stars of David, marked on the older houses in motifs of loosening brick.

ON THE WAY DOWN from Kawkaban I sat untethered in the back holding a machine gun while Naji slammed through town, driving as

though he wanted to dismount his entire regiment. The scrawniest
soldier sat near the back, holding my folded pages of *Lonely Planet*'s
single Yemen chapter and sounding out the only Arabic words at the
section headers. Thirty percent of Yemeni men are illiterate, twice that
figure for women.

"*Kaw-ka-ban!*" he beamed.

The others often called him *yehudi*, "Jew," as a joke. It meant "cun-
ning," sometimes, or that someone was being an idiot. Or it meant nothing.

Neal was keeping Naji company in the front. The only other Jew in
the back was holding a Kalashnikov and feeding a mild amphetamine
into his system.

"I've got the gun now," I shouted through the wind. "You guys can
feel safe."

They laughed. The gunman standing at the trigger wore my aviator
sunglasses. AK continued to take video on his cellphone, putting his
arm around the soldier at his sides. I'd forgotten my bellyaches.

When we reached their checkpoint again, Shibam was getting dark,
and Naji invited us into a small shed to continue chewing. We had
stopped along the road to buy another *rubta* each. AK never partook.

We squeezed together against cement and cinder block walls. Guns
relaxed on the green tarp floor. Balls of chewed leaves grew inside our
cheeks. Despite the soldiers' untroubled warnings not to eat the juices
(*Lonely Planet* counsels: "Only Ethiopians swallow!"), I couldn't keep
the leaves from spilling over onto my tongue and down into my stomach
to wreak whatever damage they would. (Not much, probably—a small-
scale summer fad in Israel popularized gat juice lemonade at cafés and
partygoers' street stands.)

We talked, sipping water. Naji drank Mountain Dew from the bottle,
as he always did, gulping it behind the pocketed mash in his cheek.
"With Jack Daniels, even better!" he said. We discussed our plans, to
head south with AK at the wheel for a few days if we could get the permits. We'd be in Aden just after the weekend, for seafood and a culture
shock in the capital of the south. Naji said he would come. Big eyes
bulging, he smiled from his cheeks. *"Waa-oww!"*

We sat until it was fully dark, waiting to buzz. The soldiers were quiet, entering a different phase of the afternoon pastime—they had been plucking leaves for eight hours. Most people will say the effects never really kick in until a chewer's third or fourth sortie—perhaps for lack of efficient technique, or because the amphetamine-like chemicals haven't built up a sufficient reserve in the bloodstream. All night after we stopped, I couldn't stop clacking my teeth and chewing at air.

In the Sanaa mansion where Tal and his friends came down from their chew, Tal had explained something important. "There's another thing that needs to be established," he said: "Yemen is the slowest place on earth. Because we're the slowest people on earth." I nodded.

But could it have been the other way—that they were slow because the place was slow? Did the energy of the drug match the speed of a racing mind with little place else to run—and, in matching it, let it be still? Too fast in a too-low gear, the engine wails; sometimes gearing up is all it takes to calm down.

I kept nodding, as calm on those plush couches as I was lounging against the concrete.

"Yeah," Tal said. "We're chillin'."

AT THAT TIME, the road into Sanaa was diced with competing check-points. *Taftish*. At one, forces loyal to the government of President Ali Abdullah Saleh. A few minutes later, another group of uniformed men, standing with guns in the near-dark.

"This is with Ali Mohsen," AK said, greeting the soldiers politely at the window. General Mohsen had defected months earlier and urged the armed forces to follow suit, after serving as the president's top military advisor for years. "Like Ali Abdullah Saleh! Same village!"

Jamal had explained very briefly the backgrounds of Ali Mohsen al-Ahmar, and Saleh, and Sadiq al-Ahmar. "It's true they all share the same last name and come basically from the same village and they all want the same thing"—Ali Mohsen and Sadiq al-Ahmar at least—"but I doubt any of them are big on sharing."

These opposing *taftish* made sure no one had full control of the capital.

"Sanaa love Ali Abdullah Saleh," AK said disappointedly. "Sanaa

I think all the people, all the home, there is one person he work in the army." (Yemen has more than a quarter the number of military personnel as the United States in a country one-fifteenth the size. Top brass were all Saleh's tribal allies.)

AK had not surrounded himself with the like-minded. Not only did he live in the regime's stronghold, he also worked in the barren offices of the government's Ministry of Youth and Sport. His uncle worked for the state-run Saleh-loyalist newspaper *Al-Thawra*, "*The Revolution*," named for the overthrow of the religious monarchy that established the Yemen Arab Republic, "North Yemen." (A month after Hadi took office, *Al-Thawra* halted publishing indefinitely.)

AK spoke of his *mudir*, his boss; the *ma'arada*, the opposition; a *masiira*, a demonstration. "I sometimes can't talk about Ali Abdullah Saleh in my work. I think my *mudir* he see me with *ma'arada*, *masira*, I walk with '*Irhal! Irhal!*' "—a sign saying GET OUT!—"he see me, 'You go with *ma'arada*.' I say, 'Yes I do.' I need change. Twenty-three years Ali Abdullah Saleh, why come new four years and come another . . . no good?"

In moments like this, his indignation spewed faster than his English could handle. Everything that AK said was said in absolute honesty, in earnestness that bordered on reckless. He couldn't pretend—he could only choose when to show himself. "I don't talk with Naji anything," he affirmed.

And yet, he had friends who supported the revolution and who hated the revolution. Was it hard to talk openly with them? "No. Not difficult."

I hardly have any friends who vote differently for president, let alone ones who would take opposite sides on the Civil War. It isn't deliberate. Possibly, some combination of political convictions is refracted by more friendship-relevant ideals. Maybe those are just the circles I run in. But something bigger than politics united these Sanaanis as friends, something that shaped their lives far more than the revolution, with consequences far more permanent than the future of Yemen's government. It was a lifestyle choice like vegetarianism or neck tattoos or playing a lot of golf:

None of them ever chewed gat.

IN THE LONG HOURS after sunset, Neal and I walked through the outer edges of the old city looking for lights—a janbiya shop with walls covered in daggers, a *biqala* selling phone credit. Across a four-hundred-year-old bridge built by the Ottomans before they were ousted for the first time, there was a well-known tea shop with unsteady tables outside. Inside, a man angrily stirred milky tea in black iron cauldrons. He scooped the *shai* into glasses with a metal cup and brought them to us, scowling.

Moments later, AK showed up with four friends. We had only just said good-bye, but there really weren't many other places to hang out. Sometimes for a certain type of people—expats, non-gat chewers—the country could feel like a college campus. In other cases, Old Sanaa alone might seem bigger than the solar system.

The friends wore their politics on the sleeves of their blazers and army jackets. On each side there was one Muhammad—AK and Muhammad al-Sukari were revolutionaries; a second Muhammad and Abdullah supported Ali Abdullah Saleh. The fifth, a goalie for a local soccer club, was totally apathetic. "He sees the future and he's okay with anything," said AK.

"You like Real Madrid or Barca?" asked the goalie.

"I like Inter Milan," I said. I'd be neutral, too.

"It's a draw. Two with the *thawra* two with president Ali Abdullah Saleh," AK said. Amazingly, both he and Muhammad were government employees. Muhammad was even in the army.

"Are there other people like you in the army?"

"Five percent or ten percent, like this," he said. He was not a deserter or a man fed up with Saleh as a direct result of the uprising. He was a Zaidi Shia (like Saleh) and part of the Houthi rebel campaign that had challenged the central government for greater autonomy in intermittent skirmishes since 2004. He explained himself simply: "Just Houthi. *Ideologia* Houthi."

"He just want *justice* in all this. But he don't like America," AK said.

"Equality between people. But there isn't equality with this government," Muhammad said.

In 2014, Houthis stormed the capital; soon, they dissolved parliament. Saleh's replacement Hadi was forced out, replaced by the "Revolutionary Committee" and a new iteration of civil war in whose name, heeding Hadi's calls for support, Saudi Arabia would bomb the nation to smithereens.

Houthis are famous for their catchy slogan: "God Is Great, Death to America, Death to Israel, Damn the Jews, Victory for Islam." Shia activism tends to provoke actors on all sides—the Yemeni government; Saudi Arabia, afraid of Shia incursion and effects on its domestic politics; and Al-Qaeda, which markets its terrorism under an orthodox "Sunni" label.

It didn't really follow that Muhammad could actually be a member of the Yemen Army, seeing as his Houthi compatriots had been actively killing them for years. But it didn't have to make sense. Jobs were scarce and he had one, or so he said, for the moment.

"You know why I like *thawra*? Because *this*," AK said. "Some person he have four job, three job, and there is some person there isn't any work, he sleep all the time in the home. There is no any work." In the hearts of revolutionaries, at least, the revolution had at its heart the revival of a middle class. AK was the most vocal about his opinions—the others seemed content just to *be* their characters as the world changed. Muhammad *was* Houthi, and that was all. He endorsed justice and equality for people.

The other Muhammad was a comfortable economics teacher, but AK was most enviously critical of his friend Abdullah. Abdullah did, in fact, hold four jobs: in the police, in the army, for the government's *Al-Thawra* newspaper, and as a doctoral student of journalism. If the regime fell, he would lose three of those.

"This is why he won't change president Ali Abdullah Saleh, because this. Because there is man he have four jobs." Apparently, Abdullah spent a fair amount of time in the Police Club and the Army Club. Supposedly he was the best at billiards.

Abdullah smiled politely and pulled out a stack of ID cards from his wallet. This one showed him in army gear, that one licensed him to report in Jordan. One was for the university.

"You'll still have that one," I said.

Everything about it seemed like a sitcom. The boisterous and silly cabbie-cum-ministerial seat-filler and his gang of activists, soldiers, and goalies who all grew up with one another. The rebel whose movement "officially" cursed Jews. His new Jewish friends.

After lunch, these were probably the only guys in town who moved.

More tea came, sweet with condensed milk. "Like you!" I said to Muhammad. His last name, Al-Sukari, means "sugary." It might have been my most successful joke in Arabia.

After a short back and forth where Muhammad granted that Israelis were no more like the Israeli government than Yemenis were like theirs, he was wondering where I was from. "Citizens are not the government, true or no? *Sah walilaa?*" I asked. "Cor-*rrect*," said AK, rolling his *R*s until they popped.

In my Arabic, they had picked out influences from all over. They knew Egyptian from films, Syrian from the superpopular Ramadan series *Bab al-Hara*. "You talk like *Maghribi*. Or *Lubnani*." Moroccan and Lebanese dialects couldn't be further apart, but they were right. I tended to borrow whatever I could remember, like making do with unmatched socks. Still, I sort of liked the perplexed eyebrow raises.

"Your origin is Arab?"

"Jewish."

"Origin, I mean, country."

It was a delightful change: ethnicity or nearly irrelevant ancestry had always been the goal of the where-are-you-*from*-from question, so refreshingly untaboo across the Middle East and beyond. "America" is almost never a satisfactory answer, especially not after conversations out of English with confusingly named foreigners. ("Neal" is pronounced in Arabic like the longest river in the world; "Adam" is equal-opportunity Semitic.)

"America," I said. And for however much that was meaningful, it seemed to mean something good to them; and for however much it was meaningless, it was great for me—leaving space for a teatime's worth of conclusions to do more than a name could overwrite. And as we agreed our citizenship was a weak indicator of our identities, our sys-

tems of preconception began to fall apart. The army isn't all for the
army, the Houthis aren't all for anything, and we foreigners weren't
always totally foreign.

- - - - - -

SOMEWHERE TO THE WEST of Sanaa facing away from Mount Nuqum,
there is a neighborhood known as Al-Ga'a, "The Plain." If you ask for
directions, a local will always repeat its full name, just to make sure you
know what you're looking for.

"*Ga'a* al-*Yehud?*" they say. The *Jews'* Plain?

Eventually, the chain of finger-pointing leads to a crossroads down
Gamal Abdel Nasser Street near Salta Hut where there is a brown
sign—the emblem of all tourist attractions: ALGA'A QUARTER—حي القاع.

"This was the Jewish neighborhood?"

"Yes," said a young boy, about twelve and aging fast. He hardly
looked at me—he just watched his smaller neighbors watching us.
"They are not here anymore."

Some Yemeni Jews held that their ancestors broke from Moses's train
during the exodus from Egypt, heading south and settling in Arabia.
(In 1992, though, genetic testing showed that Yemeni Jews were far
closer to other Yemenis than they are to other Jews.) Historians posit
Jewish genesis here in the early years of the first millennium AD when
the spice-trading Himyarite Kingdom controlled much of modern-day
Yemen. Somewhere during the reign of their last king, Yusuf Ashar
Dhu Nuwas (named for his curly hair), the kingdom converted to Judaism and began to execute Byzantine traders for apostasy. Soon the Byzantines came with their Ethiopian allies. The *Jewish Encyclopedia* says
this: "Preferring death to capture, Dhu Nuwas rode into the sea and
was drowned." Curly hair and all.

The synagogues have vanished from Al-Ga'a. Within two years after
1948, the vast majority of the sixty thousand Jews in northern Yemen
and Aden and Hadhramout had left their homes to emigrate to Israel.
The portal that first opened was not on the flank of Mount Nuqum—
where local legend predicted a gate to Jerusalem would appear upon the

Messiah's return—but above the staircase to an Alaska Airlines propel-
ler plane. With the cooperation of the ruling imam, the controversial
Operation Magic Carpet whisked Jews away to their scriptural homeland. By 2014, the last of the tiny communities were disbanding; hardly
anyone with sidelocks stuck around to cope with the Houthi insur-
gency (*"Death to Israel, Damn the Jews . . ."*)—these days, Yemen's
Jewish population numbers around fifty and falling.

The streets narrow quickly, always in shadow except for minutes
when the sun is exactly overhead. At the tops of low buildings, molded
into the walls or the *qamariyya*—"moon windows," crescent-shaped
patterns of colored glass—there are clear Stars of David. There is
Arabic graffiti across bolted metal doors and down the alleys blocked
with broken cinder block and empty plastic bags. Other passageways
are neat, quiet. Houses have faces of white plaster and large stones,
unlike the more decorative icing elsewhere in the Old City.

When we were tracing our exit from the quarter, a young man was
hustling home with his father and bread and a clear plastic bag of gat
hanging from the handle of his dagger. If only because of our foreign
faces, eye contact was enough for invitation (and this was a place where
eyes always made contact). We must come and eat with them, they
said, and ducked into their house. Soon, they were shouting into the
street. *Come!*

I bowed to enter and guarded my head from the ceiling, stepping
up to a room where a few men and a boy were lounging against the
walls, waiting for boiling *salta*. This time it was light green, coagulated
hilba (blended fenugreek) bubbling at the edges of the iron pot. *Salta*
is Yemen's national dish, ostensibly derived from the Turkish word for
"leftovers" during Ottoman times when Yemenis made due with whatever they could find. Meat is involved, tomatoes and onions usually,
leeks, spices, garlic, broth. It is different everywhere, most popular in
Sanaa, and ferried scalding hot to the face on folded scoops of pita.
There was *skhug*, too, a spicy condiment I knew from Israel. It had
been introduced by Yemeni immigrants. With the belly warmed, the
digestive system is primed for the gat chew.

Our young host had the kindest of faces under a short beard. He was more religious than the others, the older man said, and they teased him for it.

"Osama! Osama!"

They wondered if I wouldn't like to convert to Islam. I said something like, "not on such a full stomach," and sat back against the wall to digest. Plastic bags were opened.

ELSEWHERE IN THE SWARMING gat market at the Souq al-Milh, casual religious conversations took a different turn. The "Salt Market" inside the Bab al-Yemen is a labyrinth of spices and appliances and housewares and food, and salt, probably. One alley is dedicated solely to the mongering of the leaves of *Catha edulis*. Vendors sit on the sills of their stands, mouths overflowing, beckoning for a sale or waiting carelessly. When I told one man with teeth freshly green that I was Jewish, he beamed proudly.

"Oh, from Yemen?"

"I'm from America."

"The origin of Jews is from Yemen."

"No habibi, I'm from America."

"Before *zamanin* they were from Yemen. Your origin is from Yemen."

I didn't argue. Yemenis often claimed the birthplace of coffee (Ethiopia) and gat (also Ethiopia). It was nice to feel wanted—not simply tolerated or accepted, but *claimed*.

The seller, stuffing more leaves in his cheeks, had refocused on more important matters.

"You want to buy gat?" he said, offering a bundle. "This is . . . our vodka."

The insides of my gums were torn and sore, my jaws exhausted and swollen. All along the street, sitting on the ground around piles of filled bags, men were buying and chewing, cheeks puffed. Hands in camouflaged uniforms, in lily-white *thobes*, reached down to grab bags. It was six or seven dollars for a standard *rubta*, more for something fancier.

While gat chewing was once the province of the rich, it is now everyman's pastime. An average sample of families in Old Sanaa spent more than 10 percent of their salary on gat. Later case studies have found men who spend upward of a third, or, relying on remittances, more than everything they've ever earned.

I remembered Tal and his friends coming down from their chew, coolly drinking tea. Muhammad wondered aloud about the price of diesel. Someone hazarded a number of rial.

"No no, not in Yemen," said Muhammad. "In the *real world*, man."

I thought it was hysterical. But how true was it? How far from "reality" had Yemen slipped, high up into its many *mafaarij* where the windows looked out on anywhere at all. Each single-serving bag of gat requires approximately five hundred liters of water to cultivate. The industry takes a third of the nation's water. Avoiding the consequences by choice or necessity, Sanaa will likely be the first world capital to run dry, possibly within ten years.

THE NEXT EVENING, we finally reached the woman who had told the airport officer that she was not our friend. It had been a bit of don't-talk-to-strangers self-defense. When Anoud heard we were coming, she e-mailed a very warm welcome with her contact instructions:

> *what a kuck i openned my mail today!! NO shit, our friend*
> *Gert just got kidnapped a few days ago and u got a visa!!!!!*
> *Woooooow.*

I suggested the scowling man's tea shop over the Ottoman bridge, but said she couldn't sit there without being stared out of her otherwise expansive comfort zone, and so we arranged to meet on the rooftop of the Dawood Hotel.

The waiter carried a pot and cups up seven flights of the spiraling seventeenth-century staircase to the table outdoors that overlooked the city—the sun had set behind the mountains, leaving a pink-purple sky and a hint of chilliness. Jacketless, the three of us hopped in a cab to the new part of the city. On the way, near a cluster of police cars, someone had set something on fire.

Anoud had thick, dark hair dyed bright red for the moment. She worked for a French company, laughed loud and often, and supported the Saleh regime. The cab bounced toward Hadda Street, the one place in Sanaa where foreigners might be at all numerous. In a pizza place that had electricity all day long we ran into friends of hers, Judith and Boudweijn, a Dutch reporter and her businessman husband. We exchanged contact info as we did with almost everyone, just in case. Expats unite.

Later, in the leafy garden of a coffee shop that might have been grafted from Portland, Anoud, Neal and I drank more tea. It was a shock that someone so open, worldly, foreign friendly would support "the regime." My default assumption for Arab Spring uprisings was that the educated and modern (except those with a direct stake in the current leadership) would support the revolution. Anoud acknowledged Saleh's suppressive tendencies, but defended him nonetheless. Despite her position on the outside of ultraconservative Yemeni society—she did not hide that she was a single mother, living with no male presence—she did not want to see the government change. After all, the attitudes that scorned her were not the attitudes on the chopping block.

The lights were always lit on Hadda Street, KFC and Pizza Hut, Ethiopian food and more pizza. This was Anoud's world, or at least half of it. In the morning, there would still be scowls from crusty cafés, and something on fire.

So many Yemenis saw the malls and franchised glory of Hadda Street as the epitome of class and culture. Our driver felt the same way—but he saw the other side, too.

"There was a German man living in the Old City, I ask him why you not live outside on Hadda Street—big buildings new building. He said, 'In my country I have the best from Hadda Street, but I don't have this.'"

THE SUN APPEARED behind schedule over Mount Nuqum, washing the old city in orange where the mountain's shadow was on the ebb. Purples turned to pink and gold as Sanaa woke up. We met AK in the

predawn alleyways outside the Golden Daar, permits in hand, looking south.

We had spent much of the evening before screaming in the nearby
office of the Tourist Police, or sitting cross-legged and docile in quiet
submission. The man behind the desk had been experimenting with
all the variants of negation in two languages; the road to Aden was dangerous now, he said through green teeth. No foreigners, not in private
taxis, not in buses. As we pushed, he hardened further. More shouting. If we wanted to see the seaside south of Happy Arabia, he said, we
should fly.

The most active domestic Yemeni airline carries this ancient optimism in its name, Al-Saeeda, "Happy," Airways. It was on strike every
day we stayed in Yemen. We might have bought seats on more stable,
less frequent Yemenia, but the forty-minute flight would have skipped
over thousands of years of highland history and the irreplaceable sense
of a place gleaned from soaking up small towns with your forehead
stuck to the glass of a backseat window.

Our window of opportunity was closing. Twice, the man stormed
into the unlit back room to lay on a cot and ignore us. It was 5:30 in the
evening, and our one hope for a permit was descending further into a
gat-fueled fury.

"I stay off the roads then," Anoud had said. "People are crazy then."
As the alkaloids in the leaf kicked in, business dealings grew more
aggressive.

Yousif, the kindly, wandering Tourist Policeman, appeared to medi-
ate. At least officially, the man with the permits was worried for our
safety. Our taxi driver was well seasoned, we said (his license had
expired, we discovered). And we had an *efendim*, and he would protect
us with his array of firearms. We had adopted AK's habit of referring to
Naji in the third person as the efendim (once a mark of formal address:
"my sir").

Yousif coaxed his colleague off the bed and advised us: if we wanted
to use our officer escort as a defense, we would need his paperwork. But
Naji was almost unreachable, and his identification cards were not in
the same governorate as the nearest fax machine.

Finally, we agreed with a wink: *Okay, he's "not" coming.* We proposed our plan the same as when we walked in, we two tourists and our taxi man. Nothing had changed in those hours, except the notary's willingness to submit our application to the Interior Ministry. "We will call you if the Ministry rejects it," he said, like they always did. But they never would. And with that, we shook hands and disappeared.

The men at the other end of the fax machine were asleep now. And we would be gone by the time they were awake, a world away by the time they were chewing gat.

AT 6 A.M. WE GATHERED the efendim from his friend's village on the way out of town. He brought paper cups of boiling tea that we held gingerly as AK swerved around holes in the road. Reprimands were uncouth. Once, as the car nearly fused with a massive speed bump, I issued an *Oh fuck!* in surprise. Naji thought it had been directed at our driver, and wouldn't talk to me for hours.

The southern highway took us high above the valleys, over the clouds that settled sometimes among the terraced fields. Driver, soldier, and tourists—we all thought it was unfathomably beautiful, even without the explosion of greenery that comes every spring.

"Waa-oww!" Naji grinned. He always rode shotgun.

The corners and highlands of Yemen where the edges of the monsoons bring rain, where *Arabia Deserta* turns green and fertile, were once the envy of the world outside. Ptolemy dubbed the entire peninsula *Eudaimon Arabia*, a name popularized by its Latin translation, *Arabia Felix*, "Happy Arabia." Legends of the luxurious smells of the East—of the sensuous resins frankincense and myrrh, of cinnamon imported from India—cast Yemen as a rich utopia. Were it not for the gat industry's profligate use of water, the country might still have a chance to be the region's fruit basket. But for farmers, growing gat is many times more lucrative than fruits, less prone to drought and pestilence. It grows best above a mile high, up to altitudes higher than the Sanaa valley. The crop grows quickly and can be harvested often.

"The happiness of this region has seldom been noticeable, and

its woes have waxed with ripening years until they bid fair to culmi-
nate in a crop which the sword alone can harvest," G. Wyman Bury
opined in his 1915 *Arabia Infelix*. The "crop" were the human strug-
gles, as the Ottomon Empire collapsed and foreign powers swirled
and the longtime religious authorities of the Yemeni highlands prepared to declare their new state's independence. Bury was a scientist
and explorer completely in love with Yemen, but at a loss for solutions
to avoid impending bloodshed. Appreciating its intricately braided
history is essential, he said (mentioning tribes as far back as Moses's
father-in-law). The preface ends: "In any case, that 'most distressful
country' has my best wishes."

We wound down into the flatlands through ramshackle gat farms and
tiny hamlets. Camels grazed along the road, picking their way through
prickly bushes and debris. It got hotter. Women begging in abayas came
to the car windows, fully covered in all black but for their wide straw
hats. It felt like an image from somewhere else—the caps were just like
the woven paddy hats typical in Asian rice fields, with a softer cone that
flattened into a brim. Naji gave a few bills, without comment.

By midday we were in Ibb, capital of the eponymous governorate
nicknamed Al-Khodra', "The Green Province." Summers report triple
the rainfall as in Sanaa, the trademark of the country's southwest and
the justification for its "happiness" in the eyes of early traveling Greeks.
Even in January, the tightly packed hill town was striped with shades of
asparagus and olive.

The city centers around its market, the mouth of which is dedicated to the trading of guns and ammunition, often under imported
umbrellas branded with the Nestle logo and the word *glidot* written in
Hebrew: "ice cream."

Three or four men sat with their wares, bullets and holsters and
Kalashnikov magazines, while a shop owner stood like a mannequin
for his merchandise. He wore a silver Brazilian sidearm with a leather
handle and a dagger at his navel. I started to feel like "dagger" wasn't the
right way to think about it—the way it sounded like a pirate's weapon
and painted Yemen against a romantic, swashbuckling backdrop. The
janbiya—literally "side thing"—was far more style than function; the

guns were both. For handguns from Brazil or Russia, about two hundred dollars, the man said. More for American.

Nearby, atop the hill called Jebel Rabi, there is a community pool with high walls guarded with broken glass, and an empty café where we had lunch outside with a view over the city between the mountains. Hummus came, then kebab, to our makeshift table on a stool, and Neal and I drank cans of Royalty ginger beer imported from the United Kingdom. Naji ate while squatting on the pavement. He couldn't bear to eat when sitting in a chair, he said.

Out of nowhere, there was a man singing. He smiled under a short black mustache, crouched in a blazer and a patterned cloth like a sarong, an oud propped on his knee. Friends gathered. Over the occasional rumble of a motorcycle's ignition, he wove the undulating pluck of oud strings with lines in guttural dialect. My Arabic faltered, and I crouched in with the others to sip at glasses of sweet black tea. "In my wedding, I call him!" AK declared triumphantly.

In the early afternoon, it seemed the entire population—totaling somewhere between Wichita Falls and Fremont—had jammed the two miles of north-south route that cut through town. AK drove us through choking traffic to the sister city of Jibla, like the suburb to Ibb's commuter hell, and Naji produced bags of gat he had procured from the market. With my mouth half-healed from my first attempts, I set in again, putting my gums on the line in hopes of feeling something, plucking dry leaves— drier and more bitter by far than the last time—from a long red stalk.

Naji was always scrutinizing prices, always examining quality—of guns, of gat, of our mood. I spat green juices onto the steep streets, rubbing my face and trying to keep chewing.

Naji guffawed behind me. "My jaw is made in Japan, your jaw is made in Taiwan!"

In the car, his gat energy began to take hold. He drew a handgun from his holster, jokingly, loaded the magazine, and pointed it at AK's head. His movements were like exaggerated pantomime, except that he had a loaded gun as a prop. He positioned it closer, withdrew, and put it back again, watching our reactions ever so curiously in the backseat.

"Abdulkhaliq is not afraid!" said the policeman in Arabic.

AK was laughing in bursts. He took his hands off the wheel and raised them in mock surrender. "Kidnap me!" he giggled, in Arabic.

Naji turned back toward the road, still aiming the gun at our driver. Now he spoke to us in English: "My friend. My friend," he said.

Suddenly, he whipped back around, grinning, in a James Bond pose, gun raised, cigarette in his other hand, gat oozing between his teeth and into his cheeks.

I was squealing, *no! No!* But it was a good kind of squeal. I felt shaken. That felt good. Even though it was all a joke, he was giving me inklings of the danger I craved. And, it wasn't coming from the outside, from the wide world of terror. If someone killed me, I loved the idea that it would be a single unaffiliated guy. That way, the existential terrors of the world would have lost out to the power of something far more human.

The gun lowered. I might have wanted him to keep playing with it. For reasons I never understood, AK made a mysterious suggestion with his sigh of relief. "*Go* my country!" he said, with long vowels.

WE MADE OUR APPROACH to Taiz from the coronet of hills to the flats that bumped and rolled away down below. For a moment, it seemed like we had found a hidden civilization in the shadow of the ten thousand-foot-high Saber Mountain. We slept here, in Yemen's third-largest city, where six hundred thousand people's worth of buildings appear to have grown from the ground like lichens on every patch of craggy rock.

In the morning Naji was wearing the Yemeni version of an off-green Hawaiian shirt, complete with matching pants. Free from the confines of his police uniform, and without a jambiya around his waist, he had wonderfully adopted all the charisma of a duvet cover.

He said something like, "I changed my clothes. Now no one can tell I'm not from the south."

A few steps ahead, AK could hardly keep his giggles dignified. He intercepted not-quite whispers from the sides of the old town market, translating them for us perhaps as payback for the efendim's snoring. "They are saying, 'Who is this guy?'"

I wasn't free from jeers either. I had just had the buckle of my own dagger belt fixed in a nearby shop and I'd put it on over a T-shirt so as not to have to carry it. The jambiya is always a distinguished accoutrement, and a far less common one in the south. To all the Taiz shopkeepers, I must have looked like I was wearing a bow tie over an apron.

I made it a few blocks before I felt self-conscious enough to take it off.

CHANGES IN LANDSCAPE begin to accelerate along the narrow highway between Taiz and Aden. Somewhere short of midway is where the fragile border once was between the nations known as North and South Yemen. We dropped out of the greenery into sandy plains with fewer bushes and more camels to graze at them. We rolled the windows down when the sand didn't blow in. It got hot, hotter.

Before we landed in Sanaa, I never knew that Yemen had once been two independent countries. I figured, like other countries on the peninsula, it had arisen in recent times as a confederation of emirates or sheikhdoms, tribal federations coming together and unifying as a state, perhaps as part of gaining independence from colonial occupation. This was true in Yemen, but in two acts: the northern theocractic monarchy declared statehood from the collapsing Ottoman Empire in 1918, and the last king was dethroned by the founders of the Yemen Arab Republic in 1962.

In the south, warring nationalist groups ousted the British from Aden and unified with its former protectorates to the east, claiming independence in 1967.

According to a CIA report from January 1990: "Despite a sense of common national identity, Yemenis have traditionally been fragmented along regional, tribal, and class lines. Successive regimes in North Yemen (YAR) have coopted support of the country's major Islamic figures to buttress regime legitimacy, while South Yemen (PDRY) has been among the most secular and radical states in the Arab World." No wonder that, in 1970, Marxists had renamed it the People's Democratic Republic of Yemen.

Only as the Soviet Union fell did the halves of "Greater Yemen" unify for the first time in modern history.

Four years later: a civil war. Yemen became the theater for one of the last proxy battles of the Cold War, and a marker of American–Saudi tensions to come. Saudi Arabia backed the south for fear of a consolidated, Shia-controlled Yemen. The United States pushed for unity and the final dissolution of that Marxist state. With U.S. support, Sanaa bludgeoned Aden into submission.

Saleh, the Yemen Arab Republic's president, kept that job; the general secretary of the south, Ali Salim al-Beidh, became vice president. From exile, al-Beidh had recently returned to politics to champion the separatist *Hirak*, "the Movement," short for the fragmented "Peaceful Southern Movement" that seeks secession from the union. There were whispers about the execution of northerners at *Hirak* road stops. A honey trader and his wife told the *Yemen Observer* they'd barely escaped a stop just outside Aden where everyone in the car behind them was killed. But at our checkpoints, Naji always seemed to know the guards; if they waved us through without asking for our papers, he'd get out of the car and lecture them on how to do their jobs.

We rumbled toward the southern capital under a midday sun. When we passed the last checkpoint, I thought I could smell the sea.

IT WAS LATE AFTERNOON when we dropped into Aden on the south coast, humid even in January, and I started thinking about Somalia. At our first night's gat chew in Sanaa, Tal had mentioned whispers about cargo boats that might take passengers across the Gulf of Aden to Africa. Justified with professor Brittany's book-delivering mission, our first trip was to the port.

At one entrance, guards reacted with suspicion but without aggression to the idea that tourists would want to snoop around the industrial loading docks. At another way in, I tried something that I had limited experience with in preliminary dealings with officials: honesty. "We're looking for a boat," I said. "To ride on. To Somalia."

In fact, Berbera, the port we were shooting for, was no more like Mogadishu than Erbil is like Baghdad. It is the second city of secessionist Somaliland, something else entirely from Somalia: different currency, different government, different visas, and a wholly different respect for the rule of law.

But all I knew was rumor. I was told Somaliland had "the fastest Internet in Africa." I had read on online forums that it was far more dangerous to sail in the other direction, into Yemen—this was the only way to see this stretch of sea. We had balked at the option of a four hundred-dollar one-way ticket on the weekly half-hour flight from Aden to Berbera and traded that near certainty for the possibility of something much cooler, cheaper, and potentially more fatal. Yet with that risk came a new ideal, a new best-case scenario. I felt a surge of honest, intestinal belief in the wisdom of fortune cookies: this trip became about the journey—not the destination! This was my chance to travel with the world's original travelers, a ship of traders—the common man's ambassadors and storytellers from distant lands to the neighbors of the faraway.

Ibrahim, the port official, had the blue shirt of his uniform open to the undershirt, black and gray scraggly chest hairs crawling out from underneath. He mentioned an "agency," and gave directions that sounded clear enough—near the Lebanese Grocery and by the American Language Center—and seemed to suggest that boats left multiple times daily with passengers. My heart flew. The likely response I feared—*Are you out of your gat-chewing mind!?!*—never came.

But gun-toting Naji and loyal Abdulkhaliq were soon stumped as we twisted around the apocalyptic main drag of Aden's Mualla neighborhood. An aisle of whitewashed buildings of even height sat on top of decrepit shops and graffitied storefronts and pink plastic bags. A tiny number of people milled about, a few children played with rocks or ran after their parents across the road—this was very clearly somewhere that once expected to be busier. Thousands of gray bricks were strewn almost deliberately like styled bed head, remnants of antigovernment protests the government hadn't bothered to clean up. One bright sign indicated HA'IL WALID HA'IL MARTYR STREET, THE YOUNGEST MARTYR IN THE SOUTH. A constructed barrier three bricks high directed traffic; driving through the parking lots and avoiding the street, we squiggled into fish traps with no way out.

We circled back to the port with some difficulty to find Ibrahim and take him with us. To find the Bamadhaf Shipping Company (in the "Boston Language Institute" building), we were supposed to have pulled into the wrong lane of the functioning part of Mualla Main Street, U-turned again into oncoming traffic, and picked our way left onto a side street where no one had ever heard of any Lebanese anything. Ibrahim picked out the nondescript entrance of the five-story building—the door was already open.

Three women in black abayas manned the Bamadhaf office late on that Tuesday afternoon. Naima and Salma showed their faces under simple headscarves, Naima's completely black, Salma's a bright violet. A younger woman smiled from her cheeks and eyes over her niqab, and told me she was from Hargeisa, the capital of Somaliland. She loved it. She never asked why I wanted to go there.

They considered this a noble journey. "He has to find his friends!" the women would say to anyone who asked, because I had mentioned Brittany's books.

Salma was audibly and visibly of Indian descent and spoke wonderful English, but was born and raised, like many others whom Yemenis would call "Indian" or "Ethiopian" or "Somali," in Yemen. She was studying business at the university and wore contact lenses that made her eyes a sharp sapphire (her e-mail handle is "lovebird"). Her laugh kept rising tempers in check. Naima was the office elder, maybe pushing twenty-eight or thirty-two—I didn't fall for her trap to have me guess. She was "Yemeni Yemeni," as those others would say, and was happy to speak only Arabic.

This staff made copies of my passport and visas for Yemen and Somaliland, found no issue with my American citizenship, and said they would call when they knew if there was a boat. Cargo ships didn't come and go every day, and took a few days to load and unload, but they seemed confident that one would come soon. *Inshallah*, they said. "God willing."

Inshallah is one of the phrases in Arabic a foreigner can understand literally and semantically and culturally, but cannot grasp for lack of belief. For all of my uses of "God willing" as a secular English expression—"God willing pizza still has cheese on it when we get home" and the like—the god is a passive one. The *McGraw-Hill Dictionary of American Idioms and Phrasal Verbs* notes: "[This is] an expression indicating that there is a high certainty that something will happen, so high that only God could prevent it."

The American "prove me wrong or else" mentality is distinct: innocent until proven guilty, free until locked up. Inshallah gives mortal defendants different odds. "God willing" here accompanies every mention of an event or a plan for the future from "See you tomorrow" to "I promise I will win the lottery"; at its most frustrating, it can appear to qualify the past: *Has the authorization been confirmed?* Inshallah. *But . . . has it?* Inshallah.

Implying more than one plausible option, it seems to translate to "hopefully." English speakers tend to run with that toward the unlikely side of "maybe." Really though, inshallah carries no judgment of probability. It is weighted only toward what you believe: if you have doubts, it will strengthen them; if you are confident, you'll remain so. The way you feel in the moment between inshallah and conscious thought—that is your default setting on the spectrum from optimism to despair.

When Naima checked her books and told me *inshallah the boat will arrive*, she said so like a newscaster delivering the unadorned truth. And because I doubted, I heard *have reason to doubt*.

AFTER TWO LONG DAYS on the road, AK and Naji were planning to go straight back to Sanaa, though AK wanted to go to the beach. Without us, it was clear the poor taxi driver was fettered by the efindim's whims. We said our good-byes, but I answered my phone several times over the next few days to hear Naji's voice. Always he asked for Neal. Ten feet away from the phone I could still make out his message, as clear and meaningless as ever.

"*Waa-oww!*"

Feeling their absence, Neal and I took in the balmy January evening air on a block-partying main drag in Crater. The neighborhood that is Aden's nighttime hub is settled in the hollow of the ancient explosion of an eighteen hundred-foot-high volcano, millions of years extinct, with rugged cliffs at its back and an oceanfront view. Now Crater earns that moniker in a different way: the word *crater* comes from Greek for "mixing bowl." In Crater nights, people mix.

Aden is a storybook trader's city that absorbs pastimes and recipes and sundry itinerants. Outside near the Aden Gulf Hotel there are billiards tables and ping-pong, and a line of Somali women and children sleeping on single-layer mats of cardboard. Refugees were fleeing to Yemen at ten thousand per month, and the city did its best to ignore them.

There is a stand for *muttabaq*, "folded," like a savory crepe that would have made phenomenal drunk food if we only knew where to get a drink. There is a stand for betel nut, called *fofal* in Arabic and *paan* in South Asia, to wrap in leaves and squirrel away like chewing tobacco. In the thousand-year-old *Hitopadesha* collection of Sanskrit fables, a king narrates:

> *Betel-nut is bitter, hot, sweet, spicy, binding, alkaline—*
> *A demulcent—an astringent—foe to evils intestine;*
> *Giving to the breath a fragrance—to the lips a crimson red;*
> *A detergent, and a kindler of Love's flame that lieth dead.*
> *Praise the gods for the good Betel!*

All around Aden, its red spit is burned into cobblestones and curbs like blood stains.

"Hey Obama. This is Black Label," said a happy chewer. And Neal and I bought two leaf pouches, because *when in Aden*, and because it was new to us.

The ping-pong table sat on a slight incline, and a ten-year-old smoked me with his Chinese penhold grip while the neighborhood watched. And there, outside a popular sandwich joint, we spotted Judith and Boudweijn, Anoud's friends from the pizza place in Sanaa. For expats at least, the Dutch couple said, Yemen was a small town. Before the next year was up, they would be kidnapped and held ransom under credible threat of execution. Their captors leaked a terrifying, seemingly hopeless video. Judith was crying. They had ten days to live. The Dutch government swore they never pay ransom, but in six months they were free. The tears were fake, Judith says—that's just how they made her play along.

That night in Aden, Boudweijn told us to call him Bo and we made plans for dinner like a sweet double date.

THE NEXT NIGHT, we met them at Ching Sing, Yemen's most famous Chinese restaurant. Fluorescent lighting and a few red Chinese lanterns lit line drawings and Eastern landscapes on the walls. Ching Sing is one of the few spots left in town still serving alcohol unabashedly, albeit in a basement, and our newish Dutch friends ordered a round of Amstels. Bo was struggling to attract Yemenis to the idea of insurance brokerage with his new firm, and Judith the reporter was planning to interview the owner, the founder's son.

The restaurant's founder was a Chinese sailor stranded by war in Aden in the 1940s. Ching Sing had remained ever since on Mualla's ghoulish Main Street, despite encroaching conservatism and tightening restrictions on purveyors of alcohol. "You should blow on the top," said Judith of our Amstel cans. They're smuggled in by sea, she said, and buried in the sand for someone else to collect. Luckily, beer has a shelf life of some months.

But not wanting to bury myself in Aden's sand—muddy on most free beaches and unfairly priced at the Sheraton Hotel—I was still looking for seafaring options to skip town. Next to our piles of dumplings and squid soup and stir-fried beef was a table of pale and boisterous Russian men and a Yemeni associate who let slip that they had access to boats making international trips. They wouldn't say more. Another bottle of vodka came from behind the bar. Happily convinced that they were arms dealers, we watched them climb out of Ching Sing and said good night.

It wasn't our luck that night to get bubble wrapped onto a freighter hauling Kalashnikovs to Somalia, but our Dutch friends—whom we knew only as friends of Anoud, who we had only known from a website for traveling strangers—had met a man named Joseph. Along with Naima and Salma, Joseph was our other last hope.

He was like Aden's Godot, a man we never saw but counted on for our salvation. Bo described him in all uncertain terms: a fixer, a highly connected man, a usual at expat parties, someone who behaved like a local but was really from . . . Bo couldn't tell. He thought that if we showed up at a particular bar before 1 A.M., we'd find him. We went, and didn't.

"Joseph would know," Bo said several times above a Heineken at the empty bar where Joseph wasn't. "Joseph can help you," said Judith.

I REMEMBER A GREAT DEAL of waiting in the days Joseph didn't appear. Except for the Sira Fortress high on a conical hill dangling from the city by a narrow causeway, and the fish market below where a hammerhead shark bled recumbent on wet tile, and the north Yemeni monument locals had taken to calling "The President's Dick," Aden was not a city rife with sights to see. There were the cisterns, an engineering marvel explained by a plaque from 1899 on its restored staircases. The title reads simply, THESE TANKS. It begins the story of their accidental discovery like this: "Regarding the original construction of these tanks of which nothing is accurately known. . . ." Later, folks in town would tell me their guesses that ranged from the sixth to the sixteenth century.

I laughed when I read it. Not a laugh of mirth or mockery, but a puff of relief at the sign that signified nothing at all. I saw myself in it, of course, as if Aden was telling me I was allowed to be unsure, too.

We ate more grilled fish and bread with *sahawiq* and relaxed. But in our hyperactive curiosity, we itched again to leave Paradise.

And then at a café in Crater, I read an e-mail from a kindly bank agent that my entire debit account had been siphoned away for a shopping spree in Vietnam. Back in Abu Dhabi, the Sama Tower ATM next to the new Baskin-Robbins had been hacked. I responded in the only way I knew how—*Help?*—and clicked Send in the corner of one frantic e-mail to the bank. And then because it was an unthinkable problem, I did everything I could not to think about it. I held what little money I still had, felt especially grateful for Neal's company, and returned to running away.

For the Yemeni tourist, there was one El Dorado, called Shibam, just like Naji's hometown outside of Sanaa, whose old city boasted five hundred mud brick houses up to eight stories tall. Its nickname was the ultimate draw: "The Manhattan of the Desert." It was to be our only foray into Hadhramaut, a part of Yemen the professor Brittany and every other returning traveler rhapsodized about like a mythical kingdom. Its name, according to one theory, comes from a simple sentence in Arabic: *Death has come.*

We scrounged for cash to pay a travel agent to reserve a ticket to nearby Seiyun. My rial were dwindling fast, as was the small stash of just-in-case dollars zipped deep in a backpack pocket. Hours later we sat in the airport. We bought a package of butter biscuits and tea to dip them in. Minutes passed. A man hustled over to our bench.

"Seiyun?" he asked.

We nodded.

"The flight is canceled."

"Happy" Airways, in all its unhappy consistency, was back on strike.

Buses were another option—the sixty-minute flight would take about ten hours by road, but it was worth it, and we hailed a giant van cab to investigate at the depot.

We had no permits, but we made our case to the company manager from the doorway of a coach. He was incredulous, and unflinching.

"Al-Qaeda will come on the bus and see you and kill you," he said.

There were checkpoints along the way, territory ceded to Islamists during the last year's Battle of Zinjabar and throughout the uprising, and militants had been known to kill travelers, even Yemenis.

"We could cover our heads," I said.

"No," he said.

Earlier, army guards had been murdered on the roads. Things *were* getting worse in the south.

We lounged defeated along the bench seats. The driver and his almost Jheri-curled friend Adam in the front passenger seat consoled us. And as I always did automatically when I met an Adam, I asked myself, *What if that were me?* What if, in the great prenatal vending machine of Adams, I'd tumbled out for life in that seat and those slick curls?

Out of ideas, we drove together to the Adeni permit office and sat for hours, discussing and rejecting the possibilities. I was amazed at how vastly more humane the Tourist Police were here than in Sanaa. They sat, placid, on cardboard mats outside their office, chewing gat and drinking Mountain Dew. They wanted to help.

But their chief Yousif wouldn't make a permit. He was learning how dangerous the roads were himself, calling for updates, listening to Adam and his friend. Our driving duo was on our side—they really wanted us to get to see Shibam, our frustration was their sadness—but they also didn't want to send us off to die. They would have regretted that terribly, they said.

Through their connections to connections, we found a driver, a private car willing to take us by a different road he knew, free from Al-Qaeda and its affiliates. We returned to Yousif and told him. And just when our efforts were making good, the chauffeur called. The car's owner said no. Al-Qaeda controlled that road now, too. They controlled all of the roads east of Aden.

At that moment, despite my inbred stubbornness and an inability to let go of even the slightest whiff of the merest fragment of a long-shot possibility, I remembered that earlier lesson, in Afghanistan, in Iraq, in Iran: some things truly are impossible. And the relief that came with letting go.

I had been pulled here for selfish reasons; I was not a Marine, I was not a doctor without borders, not a journalist. Without a greater cause, the *me* in these unknown places was freer, and freer still because the few things I really was—an American, a Jew—were like clothing I felt encouraged to wear differently at different occasions. Without a greater cause, danger suggested that I be flexible—but even more that I attend to life as it was lived moment to moment, and that I keep my head close to the ground. Danger gave me freedom without disorientation.

It was nice to know I could actually take no for an answer.

STILL HOPING FOR NEWS of a boat, and itching to move somewhere after spending a circling day in a van, we took off at dawn the next morning. A bus took us in the only direction we could still go and hadn't been, west to the coast, and then back north along the Tihama plains. It was Kerouacking in the most blatant way: "Now there was nowhere to go but back. I determined at least to make my trip a circular one."

We had no plan. We were pushing so hard against the stifling weight of travel restrictions that when they lifted, when we pushed against a direction that didn't push back, we shot off like the hammer of a mouse-trap. North—we could only go north. We couldn't stop. We landed in Zabid, a UNESCO darling—a mosque built in the eighth year of the Islamic calendar with Stars of David etched into the vaulted ceilings, old houses with stained glass windows on rainbow-lit rooms to rival Notre Dame—and kept going. We hit Hudaydah at night, searching for food on the backs of teenage motorbikers who hustled for inflated "taxi" fares. We took off after dark in a Peugeot, climbing six hours into the mountains back to Sanaa, the only place we thought we knew.

The trip that had taken three days southward took one long day to return.

I sat in the front, Neal and a young, legal arms dealer in the back. Seven of us and the driver pushed through the dark. Whenever I fell asleep and the keffiyeh slipped off my head, we were stopped at a check-point. We had no permits. But no one cared enough to fuss, and there was no Naji to force them to touch paperwork. When I stayed covered, we passed through with a wave.

It was in the wee hours of the morning when we made it to Tal's friend's place in Sanaa. As soon as the electricity came back on, I started looking for flights to Aden. And while Neal was hanging with the boys, I was e-mailing him notes he'd never respond to from nearer the router:

so i just checked the yemenia website and it came up with
almost 15000 riyals for a one way and i was like, shit, thats a
bunch of riyals. but nah. it's like seventy bucks.

There was no reason why any of this should have been important. To me, at least. It became an obsession just to make landfall on the shores of Somaliland. Nothing and no one depended on this. I was practically sick of traveling, slowed even more by the heaviness of light pockets. I was ready to sit still. Yet I stoked fixation with daydreams about the seafarers' way across the Gulf of Aden, and with pictures of the pristine cave paintings just north of Hargeisa.

I had seventy bucks, and so did Neal, and Tal brought us to a travel agent so we could buy our cash tickets straight back south. We flew out immediately.

(I could hear Masha's voice, saying what she often said: "You're being a crazy.")

NEAL WAS SMART ENOUGH to see the circles we were spinning. Work called from Abu Dhabi, and though work was flexible, he saw an easy escape from the dizziness and took it, leaving me with Brittany's thick books for the Somalilander with no address. The hotel room was too wide and dark, I noticed, and silent.

I reached Joseph by phone from the Aden Gulf Hotel.

"Yes my dear," he said often, "I will let you know." He spoke in clear English with an accent from somewhere in a voice that was on the dainty side of high-pitched. He always seemed delighted to talk even though he never called back. He would speak to captains of dhows taking sheep and cows across the Gulf. He was going drinking with some of them, he said one day. And if they said no? "My guys can push them a little."

But before Joseph could tell me that no captain was willing to take an American onboard for a fear of legal problems that made a little ticket money an unsound gamble, Naima called to tell me yes. Bamad-haf Shipping had a boat in port named *Al Medina*, and it was stocked with its thirty thousand-dollar load of biscuits, chocolate and soap and ready to sail on Saturday. I needed only the approval of the port general. "He cannot say no," said Naima. "He has no right to."

She put me in an old car with a company man to get the stamp. The general received us with an officer at his side in a bright, windowed room on the highest floor of the Port Authority building that looked like the bridge of a British schooner. He wore the complete naval uniform, all white with golden buttons, and, with all the authority of the surprised and cautious, proved he had every right to say no.

"No," he said.

Six weeks earlier, an overloaded Somali-made dhow capsized and sunk just out of port. Since the Yemeni government still valued U.S. aid and alliance, it would be no good to have an American go down with the cows. My weak shipping company liaison could accept the impossibilities of only sailing legitimate channels.

The general dismissed us to a separate agency, one that might assume liability and issue me clearance. I was losing hope. In a hot room by the docks a fat man wheezed, wedged into a wooden desk chair behind a table piled high with paperwork that fluttered against a fan. It was illegal for foreigners to travel by boat from Aden, he said. He never moved. I proposed that I write an affidavit absolving anyone of any accountability if the boat sank. Tongue jutting into his bottom lip, he struggled to find a pen with meaty fingers, not because he thought it was a valid suggestion, but because he was willing to have us tell him what his job was. Papers whiffled and blew off the desk.

Disheartened, we left the fat man to pass my plea on to his superiors. It looked like for all of Bamadhaf's inshallah-laden yesses, there were the noes where it counted. Private captains were unwilling to face commercial penalties, or delays in port where livestock begin to die in underventilated cages, and commercial agencies were wary enough not to break the law.

The legal injunctions sank in. And then, hand to the car handle, I forehead slappingly remembered my place in the scheme of things, my potential to be a slippery cog in a greasy machine. Benjamin Franklin winked from inside my backpack.

I returned to the office where Naima still sat in monochrome elegance. I'd be happy to bribe anyone of import, I said. *Aha*, she mused, and then gave me a friend.

Imad, Bamadhaf's man Friday, was handling paperwork before *Al Medina* could set sail. Puzzled and smiling to meet me, he confidently disappeared with my passport to make whispered deals. Fearing the anxious quiet that comes with idle waiting, I called Joseph again in a desperate attempt to keep my foot in whatever doors were still open, and within twenty minutes, he had appeared at the door of the Boston Language Institute building.

Soft-spoken on the phone, Joseph George was anything but in person. He looked a young fifty, with a powerful jaw and straight white teeth that gleamed when he grinned. His skin was the darker shade of those who likely settled from parts of neighboring Africa decades or centuries earlier. He was in his every fiber a native Yemeni. There could be no one more Adeni than Joseph George.

Joseph introduced me to a friend he had spotted on the street, a government minister named Muhammad who, it just so happened, controlled the federal government's Department of Inspections. If I'd still had my passport, Joseph said, I could have given it to Muhammad and he'd have it back within half an hour approved for anything I wanted. Civilian officers like the men at the port are "scared shitless of these guys," he said.

In the meantime, while Imad pressed his luck with the brass, Joseph and I cruised the road around Aden in his massive white pickup truck, hoping to grab his friend the boat captain on the way to get a couple lunchtime beers.

Children heading home from school chased us, shouting, and Joseph bared his teeth. Seething, he slammed on the brakes so the kids would slam into the back of the truck. They never did. They jeered in their white uniforms.

"They eat, they drink, they fuck and die. And they leave their children in the street like a bag of bones."

It had been a long morning at work, he said—at the unsurprisingly vague-sounding Transoceanic Projects & Development—and I summoned the nerve to ask, cautiously, what he did. "Logistics," he said. The boat sticking out bottom up in the harbor—that had been captained by his drinking buddy, along with two other dhows that had sunk in the past year. He was a man in Joseph's debt.

We found the boat captain at a famous spot past the Catholic cemetery at the edge of the tunnel out of town toward the Sheraton, where bottles are handed through the sliding grate of a metal shed a few yards off the road. A Heineken was five dollars.

Together, with another quiet man Joseph seemed to know and picked up along the way, we tried to relax, squinting at the sea from cliffs baking in the afternoon. Too hot, we drove lazily back through the tunnel, Joseph singing every word along to "No Woman, No Cry." *Everything's gonna be alright . . . everything's gonna be alright, now.* I felt a little calmer, if only for escaping into a moment of the familiar.

He pointed out the repulsive cement President Dick obelisk. "We call it a very bad name in Arabic," he said, smiling broadly. Joseph roared with laughter: "He wants to remind the South people that this is my dick, I'm fucking all of you!"

And then my phone rang with Bamadhaf's number. Salma called me to return to the office: Imad had settled things—$100 for the ticket, $120 for the bribes, bargained quickly down as if we had returned again to legitimate dealings. Racing back with windows open under the reverberating call to prayer, Joseph took me back to be Bamadhaf's first dead-weight customer, and Naima wrote out a ticket like she had done it many times before.

The ship was to sail after *salat al-'asr*, the afternoon prayer. They were happy, too, as if we had overcome a great challenge together. Grabbing my bags, I promised I would e-mail if I could, unless, as their worst fears flashed, I drowned *en voyage* in a sea of warm chocolates.

Imad whisked me off to scarf chicken and rice; I spent my last rials on candy; I shook hands with the logistics man. Joseph played no direct role in this new plan, but he loaned me hope when I was running on empty. "To my American business partners, I never say inshallah," he said. "I say, 'I'll do or die.'"

I STOOD VICTORIOUS on the cement patterns of the Port of Aden. In a flourishing series of fortunate events, my plans to find a boat to Somalia were paying off, and after a month of daydreaming, a week of coordination and a considerable dollop of palm grease I was closer than I had ever been.

Brown and sun baked with curly black hair, Imad was short and sinewy in jeans and a worn T-shirt. Twenty-one years old, he had accepted me into his care like a brother. It was his ninth year working for Bamadhaf. His cousin Muhammad was always with us, riding in the passenger seat and disembarking often to fetch something or copy something else or handle unnamed problems.

I cashed a crisp hundred-dollar bill into small Yemeni notes. Every single person from the entrance of the port to the ship's rigging would get a cut. At the entrance, Imad presented a creased copy of my passport to a man out of uniform who made the universal gesture for *What the fuck is this? An American?* Imad leaned over his shoulder and placed one thousand rial (about $4.50) into the fold and pushed the paper closed with a rigid index finger: *What American?*

Everything ran smoothly from then on with Imad fielding every question and speaking so I wouldn't have to. In the immigration shed, a burly man retrieved a new date stamp from a closet, marked my exit from Yemen, and added my passport to the pile entrusted to the captain. I followed Imad onto the pier and around to the benches where the crew of *Al Medina* were sitting on the ground, chewing gat, waiting for her to pull around the corner from the docks.

And then, with an impossibly gat-puffed cheek, he answered his cellphone for the thousandth time that afternoon and disappeared to check on the boat. "Maybe fifteen minutes late," he said. "Mechanical problem," he smiled.

A fat orange sun was sinking into the jagged mountaintops along the coast. I snapped a few pictures from a perch on the pier where boys were diving or making their friends dive, or giving me intimate compliments: "What a beautiful hat. And a beautiful scarf. And a beautiful coat." Eccentricity, in a place where simply being foreign is enough to be eccentric, is excused by being foreign. It's a delightfully logical double negative: foreigners who act normal, whispers say, are probably spies.

So when they inevitably took to the game of volunteering others for photos, giggling and stabbing at the others with a finger—*Get him! Get him!*—I was happy enough to oblige. Where taking pictures is suspect, where people hear a camera snap and cringe, clicking away is a little like pulling hair or pinching cheeks. They bubbled with the kind of excitement that makes one kid push another kid into water with all his clothes on. And pretty soon, the divers were mugging for my camcorder and braving backflips, thrilled to watch themselves on video over and over and over until the sun boiled away into the sea and they shivered too much to go on.

Many of the boys—ages in the teens-ish, thirteen-looking-ten, eleven-claiming-fifteen, seven, or unplaceable—asked me if I had Face-book. What had seemed like a unified group revealed itself as a collection of mostly curious strangers proving their status in a new system by virtue of their interaction, it seemed, with me. A small boy with black skin and African hair sang and danced and hugged me and climbed on the others. "He will steal from you," said another, deadly serious in a gray dress shirt, greasily ingratiating himself as an advisor and confidant. There was Ahmed, the nephew of one *Al Medina* crewman, in a red sweatshirt with light peach fuzz on his upper lip, who became a quiet mediator. And there was a jester in a blue shirt who hovered near me and made jokes loud enough for the older boys and the divers' friends to hear.

"Give us seven million dollars!" The kid in blue was all smiles. "Okay, give a million!" Suddenly, his whole face and spirit changed. He kissed my shoulder, a gesture typical of panhandlers in Middle Eastern cities, then my hand. He wasn't smiling anymore. *Give me something.*

I told him I had spent all of my rials, which was true, as I was expecting to leave the country, which technically, with my passport stamped, I already had. He tapped the wallet in my pocket and made an eating gesture with his hand. "Check."

Ahmed explained in pieces: the kid in the blue shirt was one of Yemen's many neglected, known as the *bidun*—the "without"—those born and raised in Yemen but lacking passports or official identification and, therefore, denied access to any benefits of citizenship. The *bidun* live off the unfriendly land, in the backcountry of the UAE's poorer emirates, on Hangam Island in Iran, in shantytowns or no towns at all. The kid in the blue shirt had relocated from the north when he was younger, and his passport was lost in the move. His father was dead. His mother, Ahmed explained, was an amnesiac who could no longer read or write. Without money or identification, her children had no access to school.

Ahmed delivered this passively. I held out a couple candy bars I had in a backpack pocket. Ahmed and the boy sat with me a little longer, looking out at the ships' lights in port, waiting for the boat to come.

BUT AFTER THE DIVERS had gone home and the boy in the blue shirt left, *Al Medina* had yet to appear. There was an issue with the gearbox, someone reported, and it started to seem less and less likely that it could be fixed. Those first fifteen minutes, after fifteen minutes, grew into half an hour. *After half an hour* became an hour's wait, then an hour and a half, then two. The longer we waited, the longer we had to wait. After six hours, Imad called to say the ETD was a "morning" that almost instantly became an afternoon. He and his cousin Muhammad came to fetch me from the port outcropping. I had no visa, no Yemeni currency, no way to change dollars and no way to get more. I had no phone credit. I was thinking about getting hungry. And with every inshallah, doubt grew and grew and howled.

I was without. Legally I had no right to be where I was, but I had even less right to go anywhere else. But I was not *bidun*—I was not without friends or without help. I was not abandoned: there were people willing to do more for me than I did for the boy in the blue shirt. The night immigration officer handed me a small, laminated orange card to issue me shore leave—CREW #75—and Imad collected my things and piled me back into the car, laughing a little and telling me not to worry. He pulled the brake up in a parking space in Mualla mostly free from bottles and flattened containers and gravel and Muhammad jumped out to bring me egg sandwiches and mango juice from a late-night cafeteria.

I begged them not to; I asked for boat updates and nothing else, but for Imad, this hospitality was automatic. He would sleep on the floor of the office tonight instead of returning home to his wife and baby daughter outside the city. He would buy us gat to chew in the double room of the hotel he paid for, just for me. "You're a human being, I'm a human being. Correct?" he said. That was all. And, "Maybe one day I'll be in America."

On the top floor of the hotel, Imad and Muhammad sat quietly on one of the two queen beds pushing leaves into their mouths. We watched TV. The room was clean, white, with beds so hard it seemed like they had never been used, and it looked from the cousins' eyes like they had never been in a room so proper in their lives. I sipped the thick mango juice from its Styrofoam cup.

Imad flicked through photos on my phone asking questions. "That's my cousin in Israel," I blurted. Soon, they left, and caffeinated out of my mind by our midnight gat chew, I would stay awake all night with my doubts. The mosque loudspeaker pointed upward from three floors below, and my window took the blunt force of the screaming *azan* at three o'clock and five-thirty. For a few minutes it was too loud to worry. Soon after it was light out, I called Imad. "Go back to sleep," he said.

Past the time when he said he'd call, past the time the boat was scheduled to leave, there was no news. Calls and reluctance to call— was Imad mad about Israel? I let my anxieties coil themselves into a monster that reeled when I looked at it—*Yes!* it said when I asked if something was wrong. *The gearbox can't be fixed! Their magnanimity ends in Jerusalem! You've failed!* I couldn't stop chewing at air, an aftereffect of the gat, compounded by the fidgetiness of waiting.

All I wanted was that one meaningless hello to know I was still unforgotten. I just wanted to call Imad again and let him know I was still there, still waiting. I wanted to express my excitement and ask how he was feeling at the same time. I wanted to call just to say *Waaaa-owwww!*

I walked the mile or two to the Bamadhaf building and said a sad good morning to Naima and Salma. The boat would leave, they said. It had to—its permit was going to expire, and every day of delay was losing them money. We ate beans and drank tea.

Even when Imad came back for me, I couldn't feel optimistic. I quivered when I overheard the words *problem* or *tomorrow* in phone conversations I mostly didn't understand. "It's going to leave. Three o'clock," Imad said. "Inshallah." But it was Groundhog Day as we circled Main Street, gathered photocopies, ate chicken and rice. His brother Sameer had returned that day from Bosaso on a boat carrying 645 cows and sat down to eat with us carrying with him in his thin sweatshirt the smells of every one.

We sat in the car together, moved it, moved it again, and parked it somewhere else. At three, we were still nowhere. Three guys in the backseat looked amused at how tense I was, how obsessed with time I was, how un-Yemeni. I asked to be deposited at the port where at least I could wish again to see the boat pulling in—something about that seemed like a place for a more tangible possibility. It was like squinting in prayer for a seven on a craps table and having that moment of calm, of suspended hope in opening your eyes, and by opening them forcing the Fates to deal their cards. *Enough sitting*, I thought, as more unoccupied brain cells twirled off to help dramatize and mix metaphors. *I'm going crazy.*

WHEN I WAS A KID, I learned a cool game.

Not a game, really, just: I'd stand on the threshold between rooms and hold my arms at my sides. Then, keeping them straight, I'd press them against the door frame. I'd push hard for a minute or two, or longer. The longer I held and the harder I pushed, the better the reward: when I stepped away my arms would rise, weightless. My whole body felt lighter. It was fun to invent new pressures just to feel the relief in lifting them.

If I could have held it for longer, I was sure, I would have been flying.

———

IT FELT SO URGENT NOW. *This was what I needed to feel relieved and satisfied*, I told myself, as I did before every visa application, every booked flight, every hassle made doubly desperate. This corner of Somalia was the next fix. *I'll feel fulfilled*, I told myself, all the while knowing it wasn't true, knowing I was feeding a lazy addiction and calling it bold. *Just one more step higher on the ladder of Mother-Frightening Nations. . . .*

In the port, I slumped onto the floor of an office to chew gat with the entirety of the port staff—clerks of some sort, immigrations officers, coordinators of something or other. And I hardly registered the fizzle of a radio and Imad's bulletin that *Al Medina* was on the move. I chased my legs as they followed him back to the immigration shed to exit Yemen a second time.

There were no divers that day. And with the fat sun setting again, I dropped into the motorboat to taxi out to *Al Medina*. She was a Somali-made dhow, deep brown wood with a white stripe along the hull as if she wanted to race, not much longer than a hundred feet of mostly boxes covered with tarp. From the tiny deck painted robin's-egg blue, the crew peered over the railing and I climbed the ladder up the side. A young Somali bowed and sang the *azan* out into the Gulf of Aden. Waving good-bye to Imad and the city, we chugged slowly through the harbor, passing the rusty carcass of something larger that had sunk, until, as the last light faded, we stopped. We were a few hundred yards from shore.

The engine wasn't running properly—some gear or clamp was stripping a crankshaft. "We might be going back," said the Kenyan engineer. I dangled my legs over the side. *I'm not getting off this boat.* If she did leave, I knew, it wouldn't be because she was entirely seaworthy, it would be because the permit was going to expire and it was time to roll the dice and throw them into the sea. That was the captain's choice, too.

We set sail at the end of a gray day, the wind dead, leaving bureaucratic and existential stresses under the piles of garbage on Mualla Main

Street. *Twenty-three*, I thought, as if it were the biggest number I'd ever heard. It was my birthday. An Aquarius taking to the waveless alley. The ship yielded to the wine-dark sea, and we moved into that part of the Gulf where contemporary pirates were all too well-known. Yo ho.

ONBOARD, THERE WERE phone chargers and outlets for iPod speakers; a four-foot-tall kitchen where Atham the cook steamed the spiciest curry and taught me to roll roti; cushions and a flat spot between the cookie boxes on top of the cabin for the ten sailors to sleep in shifts. Late January in the Gulf of Aden, the night air is luxurious and perfect with one blanket.

Digestive responses to the curry were delivered from a man-sized plastic bucket with the bottom cut out that hung from the side of the boat. It was terrifying stepping in at first, what with the sea frothing past below and tales of sharks, but it got easier.

I knew what was coming: as per my seafaring traditions, I puked violently over the side of the boat after three hours. I closed my eyes and thought of whale-watching trips I went on as a boy, vomiting and trying to spot whale flukes and vomiting. Somehow, no one on *Al Medina* made fun of me, and as watchman shifts were rotating in the dark, someone unrolled a mattress on a bench and told me to go sleep. I obeyed without protest, having hurled myself to exhaustion. Just before dawn, we floated out of Asia and into Africa.

LATER, I'D UNDERSTAND that there was almost no risk of attacks on Somali dhows like the injured *Al Medina*, and that increased presence of naval warships in the Gulf had helped create a safe channel. Pirates make more frequent attempts on tankers in the narrow strait between Yemen and Djibouti, and on dhows sailing through the Gulf farther east. As reported to the International Maritime Bureau Piracy Reporting Centre, 113 attempted attacks in the Gulf of Aden in 2009 fell to 13 by 2012. The year we sailed, the only three successful hijackings in those waters were on the route between Mukalla in Yemen and Bosaso in Somalia, more than two hundred miles off our course. I'm not sure I would've cared how close they came. I knew these men would sail anyway—they had to, and I wanted to be with them.

I was unusually at peace. This was my sweet spot in the place between places. Everything I was seeking was ahead of me, and it was approaching, and restlessness abated in the way that hunger does when dinner is in the oven.

Before daybreak, while the Somali watchman sailed without radar, someone had lowered the Yemeni flag and raised the Somalilanders': red, white and green and bearing a black star and the Islamic credo, *There is no god but God and Muhammad is his prophet.*

For the crew, a turn at the wheel is a chore, and Jirani was more than happy to trade me for it. Just like that, I was in charge of all the ship's load: as it turned out, all we were carrying was a quarter-million pounds of chalky Abu Walad Sandwich Biscuits. I felt like I'd never been seasick in my whole life. No one looked nervous. The two officers and the cook were from India, and the remainder of the ten-man crew hailed from Kenya, Tanzania and Somalia. Abdulfaqih, a twenty-two-year-old from Hargeisa, had been working the job for eleven years on a $150 monthly wage, plus fifty or a hundred for full shipments.

A friendly bunch gathered to hang out and watch me try and aim south. It was harder than I thought; an inch clockwise on the wheel could have a huge effect, or none at all, and the waves pushed us gently, irregularly, toward Djibouti.

I plugged in portable speakers and put on bubbly soukous music from the D. R. Congo—it seemed like the closest thing I had to "local." Soukous gained popularity as the African rumba in the 1960s. The style is still incredibly popular and influential across Africa, but I started to feel like I was trying too hard.

Outside the cabin, the Tanzanian was playing Tupac's "Po Nigga Blues" from his phone. He gave a big laugh. "I do not understand!" The beat lifted his shoulders and dropped them. "This is power," he said.

I changed my iPod to Tupac.

Soon, the others let their preferences show. "Have any Michael

Jackson?" Jirani asked. For the rest of my captainship, we jammed to MJ's number ones and, on Hari's urging, a solid hour of Bob Marley. It couldn't be too loud, though, since one shift was always sleeping.

But after winding myself so tight in Yemeni offices, I was barely able to sit and chill. I wanted to move. Sitting on the key-lime-green captain's bench with my feet on the steering wheel, I felt the urge to nudge the throttle with the butt of my palm. We were only going seven knots. *I can jog that fast.*

I nudged.

Passing back through the wheelhouse, Hari noticed the gentle increase and tapped the throttle back. I shrugged innocently. The sea wasn't glassy, he said. If we went any faster, the boat might pitch against the waves and crack apart at the seams.

After all that could have been, that moment was the trip's most perilous. Crossing Pirate Alley, the closest I came to real danger—and to killing everyone onboard—was at my own hands. I knew that to be a powerful lesson . . . about . . . not to . . . of . . .

Who's bad? MJ said from the speakers.

"Who *is* bad? Who is *nice*?" answered the Tanzanian. He bubbled over with laughter. Berbera emerged just visible on the horizon.

It is 140 nautical miles (160 miles) due south from Aden to the shores of Somaliland, and sailing gingerly, we made it in twenty-two hours. The Ogo highlands sloped back from the coast, lion's yellow under a winter's haze. Farther away it was green. At the eastern end of the port of Berbera, hulking shipwrecks and rusting half-sunken ships clumped together like car parts in Camden.

"Welcome!" Hari beamed.

CHAPTER 13 | SOMALIA

IS THERE PEACE?

"*War ! mel 'absileh ina gei,*
take us to a dangerous place."

—EXAMPLE FROM A SOMALI-ENGLISH DICTIONARY, 1897

THE CONTINENT GREETED ME easily. For a fee, the Oriental Hotel in Hargeisa had sent a driver to meet me two hours away at the sea, and he was waving before the boatmen had secured the moorings. We followed foot traffic between the stacks of containers marked with Asian script until we found the two-room immigration building. My papers were cross-checked by a man in a beret who seemed only mildly caught off guard.

While I waited, I leaned against the threshold of the outer room where a group of kids pored over Jason Statham on Dubai's MBC Action channel on satellite TV. They saw the American watching over their shoulders. "Isn't it dangerous?" they asked about my home. All they saw was Jason Statham and his explosions and the bank robberies and the drive-by shootings on sunny American city streets.

My questing stresses had faded, replaced with a heavy solidity like the lull after Thanksgiving dinner. So much of my motivation for getting to Somaliland had been, in my gut, to get to Somaliland. The beret cashed my visa receipt for an inky blue passport stamp.

I saw Berbera only from the backseat of an old car. A heavy tinting sticker was peeling from the window, and through it I could glimpse the crescent beaches between low-slung houses and the shops on the way out of town.

The road from Berbera to the capital is exactly one hundred miles southwest and tilted upward. Hargeisa is forty-four hundred feet above sea level on the Ogo plateau. When the long road was empty, the driver often preferred spending long stretches in the oncoming traffic lane. This was a common trait I'd noticed in other places, too—perhaps it kept the drivers alert. They always had simple justifications, like *The road is smoother.* And yet, driving in the other direction, it isn't. But I didn't need Bataille or a twelve-year-old to explain that draw of the forbidden and the excitement of fear.

I bought a SIM card for two dollars and charged it for one while the man in the passenger seat, gray haired and skinny in camouflage fatigues, got out to buy soda. He was the soldier escort required by law to accompany tourists traveling between cities. He pushed his rifle down between his knees like it was bothering him.

My eagerness grew as east Africa blurred into orange and purple. Perfectly flat scrubland stretched out to rough mountains.

Just north of the highway outside Hargeisa, there are two small conical hills named Naasa Hablood: "Girl's Breasts." But the country revealed itself to me modestly—the hills were hidden in the dark as we rumbled into town.

I WIPED SLEEPY DROOL from the corners of my mouth with the back of my hand and rubbed my eyes with the front of it. Then I stepped out for the first time in the big city.

"Beautiful *man!*"

A woman was glaring into my eyes with such intensity that I almost got back in the car. She, in flowing black cloth; me, in something dirty.

It was the most aggressively nice thing I had ever experienced, there in the middle of a lumpy dirt road outside the Oriental Hotel.

I smiled back, and she disappeared.

My light skin was a rare coloring in Hargeisa. I had let my hair grow over the thirteen months since my cousin had buzzed it in Jerusalem, and it was curly and sea swept.

I entered the Oriental Hotel emboldened, feeling welcome in my differences, but knowing I would never be able to hide my foreignness here, or delay its discovery, as I had been able to do almost everywhere else. This for me was the first feature of Somaliland.

HARGEISA HAS ALWAYS BEEN a market town. According to one popular etymology, the name means "the place where you take animal skins." For centuries, pelt merchants from Africa bartered with traders from the Arabian Gulf for sugar and dates.

Since 1953, the two-story Oriental Hotel has been hosting travelers in the very heart of the city. Outside, the facade is a flat, white box sticking out over the goldsmiths' shops and the travel agency below. Inside, rooms open out onto a wide atrium and plants cascade lobbyward from the mezzanine. There is wifi from the comfy chairs under umbrellas where breakfast is served with a pot of Somali tea. All of this for fifteen dollars per night.

But even that was too much, said the earlier generations. An older Somalilander told me that locals critiqued the idea of monetizing hospitality. "They were saying, 'You shouldn't rent a space to a guest! You should give him a space. Free! You know, in your house or something, *haa*.'"

That word—*haa*, "yes"—functions even more in Somali like a capital on a column, like "indeed" or "exactly" at the end of a sentence or as a weighty reaction. It was the opposite in my America-bound text messages—*haa* was a clue to read more lightly—but here, the old man was extra adamant: this was why the hotel was called *oriental*, because it was built on such faraway concepts. (Maybe he knew about the $189 the port pickup had added to the hotel bill, as if that wasn't most of the nation's GDP per capita.)

I made my way back outside to the corner. At ten o'clock, vendors were still out on the street, selling things from behind a grooved, knee-high barrier. When I got closer, I realized that there was no barrier at all—only the goods to be traded. On pallets piled five bricks high and five bricks deep, blue Somaliland shillings took in the night air.

The price was simple and non-negotiable: six thousand shillings for one U.S. dollar, and only in that direction. But the most common note in circulation was the five hundred, and so, for twenty dollars, I returned to the hotel with two rubber-banded stacks that bulged in my pockets like contraband. There are pink thousand-shilling notes and green five thousands, too, convenient but harder to come by. They are clean and crisp and unhandled, unlike the faded one hundreds, and papery fifties worth less than a penny, promising to dissolve in your pocket.

This was the second feature of Somaliland, the money bought practically by volume as if we were again trading skins for sugar.

In Hargeisa, the money sits on the street, unafraid—there are no armed robberies or drive-bys: these ramparts built of banknotes are safe. This was what made the boys who watched MBC Action ask, Isn't America dangerous, when bags of money are snatched at gunpoint in broad daylight?

FLUSH WITH SHILLINGS, I found a restaurant still open and learned to eat pasta with my hands. I went back every day. An olive-skinned man rushed to bring me *baasto* tossed in sauce and vegetables, and orange juice watered down and sweetened to the point of addiction.

By my second plate, I was learning to flip spaghetti back and forth over my hand—as everyone else did at the long tables—until the strands were folded enough to handle as a ball, which, with practice, could be rolled over the finger tips and popped into the mouth.

"I'm Hussein. My mother is Layla. My father, Mahdi," said the olive-skinned man. Hussein brought me a pink juice, too, called *cano Vimto*, a mixture of the fruity, purple British soft drink Vimto and milk. It made me feel like a baby discovering ice cream.

We spoke in Arabic, his like the French spoken in West Africa—clear, light. At the end of every month he sent his wife and mother in Mogadishu fractions of his pittance through the omnipresent funds transfer service Dahabshiil. Other forms of communication were more difficult. "I don't have a telephone," he said. He had his eye on a 150-dollar plane ticket home to the Somali capital. "God, I'm sad. God, I want to travel."

How could I respond, standing there, traveling right in his face? His young man's wrinkles and wide eyes were fixed in a permanent smile, but transparently lacquered that way. He asked how long I would stay in Somaliland. "How many years? How many months?" For a week, I said, after visiting Yemen. "How many years, how many months?" he asked again.

"Dubai, did you see it? How many years?"

A period better measured in months than in years, I didn't say—I flit through these places like subway stops. Hussein thought in longer units.

Hussein didn't have protection in the north, or connections—what the Arab world called *wasta*. His skin color was perhaps the only thing he liked about himself, and even that caused trouble. "I'm not well here," he said. "Every night I don't sleep. I have too many thoughts, *haa*." Mostly, they were about going home to Mogadishu.

"In Hargeisa they say '*iska warran*,'" literally, *give news of yourself*. "In Mogadishu: '*nabad miyaa*.'" In the south, the greeting addresses the environment, not the individual. *Nabad miyaa* means "Is there peace?"

He said he'd call when he left. Or when I did. He mimed the entire conversation: "I'll call you when you leave, *Hey, my friend, how's it going? How's your mother, how's your father?*" The idea made him happy.

The bill: fourteen thousand shillings (two dollars). I unfolded dozens of blue notes from my stack.

I COULD NEVER FORGET who I was in Hargeisa. I wandered the streets in the morning, noticing how the city colorized the higher I looked—

beige at my feet, faded red in the throng of roadside umbrellas at the mouth of the market, always blue overhead. Stores were often painted with bright murals depicting glamorized versions of the items sold inside—cellphones, CDs, sandwiches. At first, I did my best to be unremarkable.

"Hey, Irishman!"

This was the city's way of telling me "Good morning."

"White man! Your name? Hey, Italian man!" In my first days, I smiled back. That was the extent of most conversations.

Sometimes when I was walking, I slowed near a shop called Adam Electronics. That way, if anyone happened to shout *Hey Irishman! Your name!* I could just point behind me. Sometimes I said it was my shop.

It was a lesson quickly learned that eyes would follow me through Somaliland. Not all of them—not even most—but enough to feel the heat on my back. Once, when I sat on a stoop near the market and the shack titled "Business Royals," and the red building painted with the Coca-Cola logo, a young Somalilander offered explanation. In a perfectly white thobe, he looked down from under a brimless white cap, often known as a *kufi* in Africa, or as the Islamic *taqiyah*.

"They think you're a spy," he said. "When you take pictures, small pictures, they think you are collecting data."

It didn't seem unfair, in a region freshly familiar with colonization and suppression by foreigners and by their own government, that the alien would be suspicious. I was upset that my presence alone could be the source of stress for women on their way home from the butcher's, but I couldn't help smiling at the image of my sinister spreadsheet—the one with cells for the pattern of the flowing *garbasaar* that framed their faces and extended below the knee, for the style of their gait, for the color of the long *khimar* headscarf if they were styling something more tradition-ally Islamic. Every molecule of Hargeisa was a potential data point.

The young man might have caught me smiling. "If they don't under-stand, they think there is some secret."

Yet for every chary reservation, there is another curiosity unre-served. Over pasta the night before, I had met a high-schooler named Ahmed who delighted in practicing his English with me. As a former

British colony, Somaliland does a fair job of teaching English in high schools, at least in the regions where there are high schools. I practiced my Somali.

Ahmed rushed me into shops at random.

"Tell them!"

"*Habeen wanaagsan*," I'd try. *Good evening.* The men in the restaurant or working around the sewing machine would explode laughing. *Where'd you find this guy?*

There, my secret was assumed less suspicious and more absurd. I was just a guy, galumphing in the evening, telling people to have a nice one. Another Hargeisan appeared to have vetted me for them, and this was almost always enough.

THERE WAS ALWAYS a light on in the back of my mind: I had books to deliver for Yusuf Gabobe at Haatuf News. This was the objective I used to justify my footfalls. I was tricking myself, and I knew it, but still it worked. The next morning, though, I traded this goal for one so concrete it didn't need tricks: the Neolithic cave paintings in Laas Geel, dated to seven thousand years old or so, give or take a couple millennia.

I bought a second SIM card from another of Somaliland's major communications companies—Somtel and Telesom numbers do not connect to each other—and called Ahmed as he'd asked from the noisy taxi yard. No answer.

I negotiated for the drive northwest into the plains with a hoard of drivers who had fenced me inside a firm semicircle. I called Ahmed again. "Stay there," he said.

Ahmed's somewhat older friend had cars, he said, and we could go with him. The Oriental offered its own morning sightseeing package for the price of 120 plates of pasta but this way I could rely on the kindness of new friends. Soon, we were navigating through potholed streets in the cab of the friend's enormous flatbed truck, looking to find something more appropriate at one of his family's stores. But as we continued to make large figure eights through the capital, I began to lose my fragile faith.

"Do you care if it's a big car or a small car?" he asked.

"What? No. No, anything."

"Don't worry okay?" said Ahmed. "Why are you worried? Don't worry." I felt like a bad traveler when I didn't trust him—it seemed like a good MO to put trust in strangers in strange places—but I didn't trust him. That is, I didn't trust he would help do the thing I wanted to do. I started to miss the taxi drivers.

Eventually, Ahmed accepted that all of the friend's cars were unavailable, and that the seventy-foot truck wouldn't be ideal for the drive, and the friend went to rent something at twenty dollars per day. Cash is particularly necessary in a country without ATMs. I had hoped to have enough leftover from Yemen. I wouldn't—not even close—when the bill came for the Oriental. Larger transactions are almost always handled in American currency, of which I had only a few big bills left from the emergency stash. I handed Ahmed's friend a fifty, expecting thirty dollars or the equivalent bale of shillings in return.

He returned minutes later with no change. It was a two-day minimum, he said, and we needed to buy gas. Trust faltered, but there was no recourse except to whine and ruin everything. I let my displeasure show faintly. I think this put even more pressure on Ahmed. Tourist guides officially required a soldier and government approval, and maybe he started to realize that he couldn't come through.

Twenty-five minutes outside the city on empty roads, the friend looked worried. He didn't think we'd have enough gas to make it to the caves. So we doubled back almost all the way to the city, added fuel, and left again, everyone loathing one another more and more.

We approached the checkpoint. "Are you sure we don't need . . ." I began.

"Don't worry."

And when we halted at the metal barrier, the officer took one look in the backseat, at my face and at the papers that didn't exist, and—I translated on my own by the tone of his voice—told us to have ourselves fucked.

No one really spoke after that. I stewed in the back as we drove solemnly back to Hargeisa, thinking, *The only way to travel is to lose your-*

self in the moment, and that *this was the long moment of a beautiful day squandered*. As always when I saw that I had drifted out of the present, I berated myself. I wanted so desperately to see things from my eyes and not from far behind them.

Outside the car in an unfamiliar part of town, I asked the friend for the thirty dollars in car rental change. I'd forgotten entirely the math that had gotten us here. At first he was apologetic, shockingly so, and then, as if a switch had flipped, he turned angry. A small crowd surrounded us, gathering information like a lawyers' barbershop. Ahmed was overwhelmed. Minutes of argument later when I looked back to the car, he was gone.

His friend dropped the car keys in the sand and walked away.

The casus belli was my confusion alone. But no matter how many people I offended, I was still a visitor in their city. A thin and soft-spoken member of the gaggle joined me, and together, as is doable in Hargeisa, we tracked down Ahmed's friend's father.

We found him issuing orders in his auto repair shop. "I'm going to solve this. Because one of those kids is my son."

I talked softly, explaining that his son had spent thirty dollars that wasn't his.

"What do you want me to do? Where's my son?" the father began to say, in that part of the day when most men were chewing gat in the shade. He repeated this several times with varying inflection. "Where's my son?"

"I don't know. But you can fix this, and maybe you'll find him one day." I couldn't filter all my snideness in the heat, and I hoped it would go unpunished.

"What do you want me to do," he bit.

It wasn't a question anymore, and so we left. Reflecting my anxiety in the wrinkles of his own forehead, my new advocate found the owner of the car rental on the street. Because we'd only kept the car for four hours, he gave me ten dollars.

But that wasn't the issue then. I had let my frustrations—a day poorly spent—turn me sour.

And then I got a call that would fix everything but hurt feelings. The voice on the other end of the line was a friend of Joseph George, the man who always came through.

THE DOORS of the Oriental boxed out memories of the day, the last heat of January replaced by a dark, cozy evening. In the hotel's leafy atrium I met with Joseph's friend Omar, a director in the Somaliland Ministry of Youth and Sports. He paid close attention to his phone while we drank spiced tea, *oh!*—how restorative was the manna from Somali teapots, *shaah hawash*. The name hints at its relations—to *hawayij*, that Yemeni spice mix for coffee and a hundred other things—and its role. In Arabic, *hawayij* means "necessities."

I hadn't fully finished a sentence about what I was doing in town before Omar began solving problems. *I'll take you to get the permit*, he said. *I'll take you to get your flight tickets tomorrow. Then we'll get a soldier and I'll drive you to the caves in my Land Cruiser.*

Again, I let myself lean on the goodness of new friends. I wondered if he was one. He was tall, middle-aged bordering on three-quarters, and moved the way a man does when he grew quickly as a boy. While we sat, he looked away often, his face set and distracted. I wondered if he felt an obligation to babysit.

True to his word, Omar whisked me in the morning to the Ministry of Tourism and Culture to reserve a twenty-five-dollar ticket to see the caves and sped through town to the station where soldiers are rented. My eyes unfocused and took in mostly colors. And then: a billboard for Haatuf News, where Brittany's friend Yusuf worked. I scribbled down the large-lettered Hotmail contact as we tore past.

LAAS GEEL WAS "DISCOVERED" in much the same way America was, as a work of publicity far more than actual unearthing. In 2002, a French archeological team learned of the site's existence, about five kilometers off the main road. As far as outsiders were concerned, Somaliland put its first treasure on the map. Since then, tourists have learned to ask for directions here, generally making a side trip from Ethiopia. Marked with the previous month's dates, there were about fifty names in the Laas Geel Visitors Register.

The pre-Islamic shelters are largely unexplored. Some pastoral communities might be aware of the artwork in their area. Some nomads use them as temporary refuge. Some imbue the pre-Islamic art with mystical properties, or avoid the caves for fear of evil energy. To others, the large slabs of rock are good material for toilets.

The Holocene legacy does not filter into Somali or Somalilander identity like the Pharaonic does in Egypt—there aren't five hundred-foot pyramids staring anyone in the face. The caves haven't had thousands of years to find their place in the consciousness of any particular collective. The State hasn't built a national myth here. Celebration of pre-Islamic history can incite a cognitive dissonance in religious circles, as in Saudi Arabia, where the first-century Mada'in Saleh complex carved by the Nabateans (of Petra fame) has suffered the legend of a Quranic curse. In Laas Geel, the major obstacle toward embracing history was the confounding effect it has on modern tribal demarcations. *I am proud of this, our shared history; however, we do not share this history.* Or, *Behold! Something older than I can accept!* The cave paintings are a shared ancestor. Preserving this heritage, says Somaliland's ten-year-old Department of Archaeology, is a major key to peace. It was easy for me to love it all, because I came from the outside.

OMAR'S LAND CRUISER found a little red-roofed house in the shade of a desert tree. A sleepy guard emerged to walk us up the stairs—there are stairs now—to the first of the twenty shelters so pristine I thought they might have been painted within the week.

For the first few seconds I saw only bloodred contours as my eyes rebounded off shapes only man could have made. There are 350 images on the surfaces of Shelter One alone.

My favorite among the cows was not one with strings across its harp-shaped neck, or alternating bars of red ochre and white, but a rare one that filled the space of the lyre with pure abstraction. There were red strings, yes, but then there were the teeth of a comb, and squiggling blobs, wild but contained. They reached the border of the neck, where wide horns appeared in smooth arches, and stopped. I started to see these cow wattles like signatures. Maybe this was an assertion of the artist—in each of these empty necks, there is squiggle room for the individual to take shape.

On the rocks down below, there were real goats, a real camel bravely suckling on the pads of a cactus, an iguanid lizard with perfect camouflage, and an antelope so unflinchingly adorable that our soldier gazed at her with soft eyes. I caught him. The space is spectacular. These are not the electric torch-lit grottos of western Europe, where humans hid from the cold in the bowels of deep caves. Laas Geel, "the camel's watering hole," covers a high outcropping where the region's early settlers could oversee the sloping scrubland below with granite at their backs.

Beholden to few hard facts, we could interpret these discoveries as we wanted. I saw the painted people standing underneath their cows, arms raised high, and wondered who they might have been. The solid white figure with red legs had just bought new pants. Another shape was proud of his coat.

The guard-guide was getting excited, and Omar was, too, as if he hadn't expected to be. The guide leaned through a tight aperture in a cave wall, narrowing his eyes along the barrel of his index finger and following the sight down into the valley. "When enemies come, they could look out from here."

"Sure," I said. "Cool."

Another natural ledge was the throne room. On the ceilings there were drawings too high for us to reach. "Back then they were five meters tall," said Omar.

AS WE DROVE HOME, I realized the steering wheel was on the right even though traffic kept to the right. This was a rare combo, shared by some taxis in Afghanistan, like a British string around the new country's finger. The lettering on the dashboard was all in Japanese. The air-freshening spray was all Omar's own: "Pure Cigar."

This might have been where he asked for sixty or eighty dollars. These one hundred kilometers were not a gift—I had mistaken an extra day's work for charity. Even a director of the Ministry of Youth and Sports could use gas money. ("I have twenty-two children," he said.)

It is embarrassing to assume extraordinary goodwill in the place of mere politeness. I panicked at the thought that I had been doing this across the Middle East, recognizing an offer but mistaking its kind, making assumptions at lunches proffered, and then leaving local couples shrugging at each other: *I guess that's just what the Americans expect.* I'd figured out that the Somali letter *X* was the same as the hard *H* in Arabic, the one I once couldn't distinguish or pronounce without choking a little—and it felt so good to recognize something in a place I couldn't otherwise read. But the Semitic grammar I'd studied in school, the few Cushtic phrases I'd absorbed here, did not make me part of the family. Recognition is not awareness.

Omar and I began to bargain, factoring in gas and our moods and the soldier-for-hire, to land somewhere a little under the hotel's package price. And then, somewhere on an empty stretch the car gave up and sputtered to a stop, steaming. We looked inside the hood, and then milled about. The soldier stood at the edge of the pavement, his shadow reaching nearly across the road. A woman in a floral robe and a green shawl strode by, a toddler jouncing on her back. A man passed in mismatched shoes. We looked to be miles away from any shade we didn't cast ourselves.

When a van came with space for one, Omar ushered me inside, out of hospitality, or automatic custom, or to get rid of me.

THE NEWS ISSUED LOUDLY from the van speakers in a northern accent. In the back, Mogadishu-born Abdirazak and I talked over the radio. His hometown was safe now, he said, but Hargeisa offered more opportunity. And he argued the southerner's call for unity, appealing to my United States for support.

"Which is better, fifty states or one government?"

"Both," I suggested. "The states can focus on local services while the federal government can have more power."

He picked up only on the five-dollar word. "More power," he repeated. "Somalia is one state. Same language, same religion, same culture."

IN THE END, the cave paintings told me about as much about Somaliland as a woolly mammoth would tell me about Alaskan politics. But now Yusuf, Brittany's friend, who had answered the e-mail I sent to the address I'd spotted on the billboard, was coming for tea in the Oriental.

He had the kind of voice Goldilocks would have followed, in English, neither high nor deep. His glasses, with the simplest of frames, were the kind I stopped noticing. A small space between his front teeth, and body language that was never loud. When he laughed, not too often, I felt fully understood.

Just after New Year's in 2007, Yusuf was arrested with two other colleagues for "defaming" Somaliland's third president, Dahir Riyale Kahin, and his wife. (In fact, he was charged with obstructing the police work of arresting *others* in the newsroom for defamation, but he hardly remembers.) As the chairman of Haatuf Media Network, he had published a series of articles outlining the depth of the president's nepotism and corruption. He waited three months in prison for the trial. By the time of his conviction, the reaction to his cause célèbre forced the government to let him go, a free man with a guilty record.

At our table in the leafy lobby, I delivered my cargo from the Emirates, and Yusuf spoke to me about where I was. "Hargeisa was the bastion of the 'Greater Somalia' concept," he told me. "Hargeisa was spearheading this Somali idea of unifying the whole Somali-speaking territories on the Horn of Africa. 'Let's make sacrifices.' But this didn't materialize. The only two parts which united were Somaliland and Somalia out of the five—and their unification didn't work well.

"The armed struggle began in earnest at the end of '82. At the beginning of '83, I was expelled from Qatar because I was mobilizing people," Yusuf said. Despite sweeping achievements in road paving and irrigation and education and literacy—and the unifying power of the newly codified Somali language—Somali president and communist autocrat Major General Siad Barre had been assassinating his critics for more than a decade. With despotism lingering in the Somali government and the economy in shambles, the champions of unification were now fighting for separation. In 1988, guerilla campaigns converted to full-blooded war, attacking Somali Army troops in Somaliland. Siad Barre retaliated with carpet bombing and massacre. "This city was destroyed completely. Most urban centers in Somaliland were completely razed to the ground."

Other rebel groups contested in the south and by 1991, Siad Barre was ousted by the southern United Somali Congress, who became the factional new rulers of Somalia.

Four hundred meters from the Oriental in the center of Khayriyada Memorial Square, a MiG fighter plane that once bombed the city is immobilized on a painted pedestal. On one side of the mount: 26 JUNE, a reminder of Somalilanders' first taste of self-rule in modern times, in 1960, when British Somaliland was granted its independence. Five days later, they joined with Italian Somaliland to form the Somali Republic. On the other side of the fighter plane memorial: 18 MAY. In the wake of the gruesome civil war, on May 18, 1991, the Republic of Somaliland declared itself independent. It is recognized by no one.

"Has Hargeisa recovered?" I asked, pouring cream-colored tea into our cups.

"It recovered and expanded—it's larger than before. Of course, infrastructure and things like that are still bad, but Hargeisa is far better than it was before being razed to the ground."

With passports meaningless in every country but Ethiopia, though, Somalilanders are still trapped. Until now, the international community has rejected their plea for self-determination.

Whenever I wrote friends or spoke of Hargeisa to myself, I never knew what to call the country it was in. *Somalia*, maybe, when I wanted to invoke its relationship to the world. On the ground, I saw why the name was meaningless, or repressive. No matter what, when I gave the place a name I gave one argument power.

———

YUSUF WAS RESTING his hand on Brittany's book. "People take the same language, the same religion, and say it's okay, it's this homogenous society. But the peril is—there is the caste system in Somali culture."

Somalia's demographics are at the top of the homogeneous list in Africa: more than four-fifths of the country is ethnically Somali. A common language is a sign of pride, but it is also a mechanism for conde-scension. The four seminomadic clan families whose Northern Somali language was declared "official" are known as "noble" clans. About 15 percent of Somalia is non-Somali, speakers of Bantu languages and the Swahili of neighboring Kenya.

In 2000, the transitional federal government introduced the noto-rious 4.5 system, whereby each of the four noble clans is allotted one share of the power structure, and the remaining minorities are given a collective half.

Another autonomous region had sprouted in the center of the coun-try, and another still on the southern tip, supported by Kenya and Ethi-opia as a buffer against Al-Shabab insurgents. (Once, the newly elected president of this state had come to Abu Dhabi for a conference at the NYUAD Institute. Through cosmopolitan Gila, he had extended me an invitation to visit. I could never reach him. "*J'habite dans le brousse, moi*," he had said. *I live in the bush*. The president couldn't even live in his state, because, insofar as a state exists, it didn't.) The new names on maps hardly touched life on the ground. It seemed like the region was trying to fight terrorism with semantics.

Each subdivision created a new majority in a smaller place, appear-ing like cracks across a frozen river. New minorities found them-selves stranded and divided. In Somaliland, too, there are segments that decry the Ishaq clan's hegemony and seek adoption into Somalia proper. These contested districts have opted to create their own auton-omous state with a kind of aspirational branding. The Khatumo State, which endeavors to secede from the secessionists, takes its name from Arabic: *khatima* means "conclusion."

———

"A CLAN IS OF COURSE a kind of tribe, but it's more complicated: it has a system of lineage," said Yusuf. The obsession with this lineage is soil for the roots of all Somali conflict. Somewhere though, between the painting of Laas Geel and the cornerstoning of the Oriental, there is a shared root. All Somali clan families trace their lineage to the patriarch Soomaal, a descendant of the house of Muhammad. The clans break off at different points in the family tree, spidering into subclans and sub-sub-clans and blood-money-paying groups. Each element is a vital part of a Somali's identity.

"I have to know," said Yusuf, who was a part of the same sub-sub-clan as the owner of the Oriental. "Ishaq, Habr Awal, Sa'ad Muse, Gedi." Ishaq was the family, Habr Awal the clan, Sa'ad Muse the sub-clan, Gedi the sub-sub-clan. "Gedi—it's the common ancestor we have, my eight ancestral grandfather." Habar Awal, the clan eponym, he said, was twenty-four to twenty-five links of male lineage ago.

"I don't know some of my great-grandparents' names," I said.

"Good and bad," said Yusuf. "Many people would rather die if they don't know," he laughed.

The system is not without its benefits: names function like addresses. In a nomadic lifestyle, lineage systems have already mapped out potential bed-and-breakfasts, available watering holes, friends. This was why some Somalis said, "We are like the Jews of Africa!" ("With no paperwork you can just trust me," said a new Somali friend, about meeting new Somali friends.)

In times of trouble, compulsory donations also lift the burden on the individual. "It's a kind of insurance," said Yusuf. "So if somebody from the tribe inflicts injury or kills somebody, you have to pay dear. Blood money. It's collected."

"How much?"

"One hundred camels for a person. And then you have to change that—" his phone rang, and, with every politeness, he took his leave for some pressing business in Ethiopia.

He would have said that you have to tweak that figure—the Sharia rule for blood money in the school of Islamic jurisprudence honored by Somalis—according to the *heer*, the interclan contracts. *Heer* covered everything, and when it didn't, the clans inked more. Tribal treaties, a Somali scholar noted in 1959, became "a source of law" in the British Protectorate. (The repercussions are obvious: When the colonizers left, Somaliland did not fall into an anarchic vacuum the way their Italian-run cousins did to the south.) Based on Sharia but not beholden to it, the interclan contracts remain flexible. Killing a really good guy or disturbing a long-standing peace between trusting clans, for example— that could raise the hundred-per-man, fifty-per-woman minimums.

The money to be paid is called *mag*, or *diya*, in Arabic, and is generally paid in cash at the local market value of the camels—about three to four hundred dollars each in Somalia. (In Saudi Arabia, rising camel values induced legislation in 2011 that capped the penalty for murder at just over one hundred thousand dollars.) The weight falls on the *mag*-paying group: four to eight generations, totaling somewhere between a few hundred and a few thousand men. This group is perhaps the most important single category for a Somali man.

The woman's half-value is not as much sexist itself as it is an unsavory product of sexism: Women are not a part of the *mag*-paying groups. As they do not contribute, they do not collect equally. Women are swept up in these systems like an afterthought.

Marriages are most common within the clan between spouses of different subclans. Next most likely is interfamily marriages—that is, close is good, but *really* different is better than *just a bit* different. As a Philadelphian Pennsylvanian American, for example, I'd likely pair with a Pittsburger Pennsylvanian American. After that, I'd rather any Canadian over an Iowan or New Yorker or Dakotan. Mostly, exogamous marriage is alliance building, a diplomatic tool and an expansion of protective bonds.

The word for clan, *tol*, is also the word for "to sew, bind together." Weak clans very literally became unbound. When they were out of place, locals could call them *qaldan*: "wrong." The Somali refugees landing by the thousands every year in Yemen, the families I saw sleeping on cardboard in Aden alleyways—these were almost always escapees from weak clans, those who found themselves *qaldan* everywhere.

IN THE *BLACK HAWK DOWN* DAYS, America went to war against the dictator who had ousted the dictator who had marshalled young Somalia into bloody unity. The poorly planned objectives—to facilitate and protect humanitarian efforts in Somalia, and later to capture the dictator—were failures.

"The helicopter used to come at night. You can't sleep," I heard from a Somali friend who said he used to play on the Black Hawk wreckage on his way to market. "*Dooh dooh doooh dooh. BOOM!* Throwing things, bombs, firing from the sky."

Somalis were trapped between a militant dictator and foreigners infringing on their freedom. "The Americans have no clue," he said, as they patrolled and confiscated weapons blindly across tribal lines. "They tried to make a peace-making. You don't make a peace with people you don't even know."

For a moment, the subclans of Mogadishu united against the outsiders. And when the outsiders left, the boundaries reappeared like glow-in-the-dark ink.

IN THIS WAY, Somalis were not the Jews of Africa. Jews have all but forgotten the tribes of ancient Israel—ten of the twelve are accepted as "lost." The clan base is expanded, in part because there is a long tradition of troubles imposed from outside.

I could probably guess my tribe from my last name, but it would be useless. I don't, like the Ishaq or Dir or Darod or Hawiye, have pre-arranged grazing territory for my herd. And I don't have a hundred relatives to call when I'm in a bind. I have AAA. I have Blue Cross/Blue Shield.

The *mag* process, in its eye-for-an-eye formation, can cut both ways. I would know that there were a few hundred to a few thousand men who would vouch their eyes for mine. When I wandered in the desert,

I would know that I had the might of those thousands behind me. But . . . *the individual is no longer responsible for homicide.* My kin's relationships, their *grudges*, must become my own.

My objections to Somali communalism came from the *me-first* ego of the American Dream and my first-person destinies made manifest in the bank accounts I shared with no one. Tribes, clans, serious crime resolved by traditional law—this was not the structure of my childhood. The idea that my *worth* was not a fully individual accomplishment offended the aspirations of all American boys: I would never be a man entirely of my own making. And yet . . .

"Qolomaad tahay?" *What is your clan?*

A checkpoint.

Ishaq.

A passport flashed.

When I moved, I declared my clan again and again, too. Traveling to some countries, I'd paid 4.5 times the visa price of Chinese and Japanese tourists because their countries had stronger economic ties with our host. In Europe, my Americanness affords me ninety days of visitors' rights for free. In Yemen I had to watch my ass, but the government had an interest in keeping me safe. These are my *heer.* These are my contracts.

I saw the smaller elements (of people to trust without question) and said, "It's too big! Too unstable!" I saw the larger elements (the families bound by contract) and said, "It's too small! Too arbitrary!" as if the world's borders weren't silly enough. There's a reason that map in the classroom is called a *political* map. But nomadic Somali polities have never conformed perfectly to this system.

The Somali sultanates have gone; the most influential units today are subgroups of respected men. The upper house of the Somaliland parliament is called the House of Elders. But unless he's a hunchback, clan identity is probably the first known fact about a president and, unsurprisingly, his particular networks reap inegalitarian benefits.

Kahin, whose "defamation" put Yusuf in jail, had been in office for five years, the first minority clan president in Somaliland. Haatuf's reporting could have been a tribal issue—Yusuf and his Ishaq clan against the upstart—but it wasn't: the only difference between the new president and the former dictator Siad Barre, Yusuf told a reporter from prison, was that Barre "was a dictator whom we did not know, but Dahir Riyale is an enemy from within our community and we unknowingly trusted him thinking he is one of us." It was transcendent in its way: the ruler despised not for clan but for performance.

So long as the political clings to the ancestral in Somalia, it will seem an unprecedented loss of autonomy for those without footholds at the top. One Mogadishan told me what happens when a clan loses supremacy, in a Somali adage addressed to a piece of meat: *Ago ko'one a mako areyye.* "Either I eat you or I throw you in the sand." That's why, among other reasons, there are still Somalis saying, "We need another Siad Barre": only a totalitarian can override the system.

I LEFT THE ORIENTAL. I walked uptown past the bus station to the packed dirt street named after Abdirahman Ahmed Ali "Tuur," Somaliland's first president. His nickname means "hunchback." I ducked through the walk-in-refrigerator-style curtains and the inquiring glances at a restaurant I hadn't tried. I felt a little guilty every time I didn't visit my pasta place, but this one was bigger. They had dry, dense goat meat. They had rice.

I ordered a shared plate of rice and pasta. It's a dish that claims a certain status because it can be served only in restaurants—a family would never cook the two for the same meal, but a restaurant has both on hand. It is called, aptly, "Federation." Normally it is served with a banana.

It was cool and dark, and the glances faded. Inside, I was just a messy eater in the lunch crowd, but outside through the plastic curtains . . .

"White boy! Arab! Hey man! Where from! What's your name!"

"How are you fine! How are you!" The foreigner's salutations shouted like accusations, as if I hadn't forgotten how strange I looked.

"Man or woman!" jumpy men offered from storefronts. My hair was longer than theirs by all of it, blatantly frizzing in the sun. "Are you a man?" asked a fast walker as he passed. I answered in the affirmative. "If Allah says," he said. It was a slightly meaner refrain to the young Yemenis' "Boy or girl!" greeting. Maybe it was completely playful. Anyway, I had no allegiance to my lack of haircut either.

If I returned scowls with scowls, pressure built instantly. We'd steal fugitive glances and, if we caught the other staring, we'd raise and drop eyebrows until we were dizzy. If I smiled when they stared, they stopped scowling sometimes and smiled back. Or their brows shifted from a stare-at-something-suspicious to a stare-at-something-silly.

I never thought I was thin-skinned to teasing. I accept that I've got a nose that could sink a thousand ships. But teasing is certainly funniest when it's original, and this was getting old fast.

"Man or woman!" It came again from behind me. *Fuck it*, I thought. *What happens when I do this*. I put on my sternest face— *Whadjusaytome?!*—and whipped around. When I did, I saw a short, pudgy chunk of a man grinning odiously.

I had energy to burn, from the sugar with tea or the Federation or the too-short city blocks, and aggression seemed like the only kind of defense that wasn't passive.

He found my eyes, saw the macho posturing in them. His grin fell. He picked up a rock, and wound it back. We saw each other.

I could feel the street's attention click, the onlookers squeezing in on us. When push came to shove came to rock, I had no support system—I was clanless. That could have been why I was so easy to shout at: these jabs would see no retaliation from clan politics. I could be a release valve for man's natural urge to mock.

The division between clans can be great—they may not offer each other assistance, they could find each other on opposite sides of a severe dispute—but a foreigner has no place in this system at all. I was blank. I was a default human for those with history to respond to at will. In a world where ancestry is everything, we shared nothing. The shouts of "Irishman!" and "Italian man!" hoped to hit home—to make my presence explicable and to find a way to connect me to lineage—but when they didn't, I was purely a visitor again. Guests *do* have a place in the framework, though.

I turned back around, half-expecting to be knocked out anyway. I heard the rock fall into the sand.

THESE WERE THE WAYS the town got used to me, or I got used to it—sparring partners testing our distance with light jabs. Another day, I asked a man for directions to Somali fast food—small preprepared sandwiches of unidentifiable meat and lettuce on soft bread that is unfailingly delicious. He led me to a popular joint.

"Did you get your money back?" the man asked. He knew that I had sought compensation from the auto mechanic's son. Everyone knew everything. I'd recouped ten bucks, I told him, and he gave a satisfied nod.

For moments in the small town of a million plus, I felt I was part of it. And as soon as I did, I saw that I was *qaldan*. I walked through the street eating my mystery sandwiches.

"Don't you feel shame to eat outside?" A crinkled face appeared from nowhere. "There are some places where they will attack you just for that bit. You are eating when they have nothing to eat. You must feel shame!" I told him I didn't—but I did. I couldn't tell if he was angry, or forewarning me. I was starting to get defensive.

"My name is Willie. I speak Swedish also," he said. And then he was gone.

He left me in a moment riddled with guilt, feeling embarrassed and raw and so, so visible.

It was inescapable; with or without cameras or sandwiches or fat stacks of cash, the tribeless and foreign were lodestones for the curious and confrontational.

At the mouth of the market, a cluster of children—four girls and a tiny boy—hung about in bright robes that hardly covered unwashed shirts. They beamed when I lifted my camera, and relaxed even more when they saw that it didn't shoot lasers. The girl at the center, swathed in orange, embraced the boy's head and turned him toward me. She was radiant—and everyone hated her.

A small mob assembled to investigate the objects of my attention. It was exasperating to them, it seemed, that I could care even for a moment.

"These people, Oromo people. Not from Somaliland," a man said. "When you are writing your article, do not write that these people are from Somaliland. They are immigrants." I'd never said anything about writing, *but why else would I be there*, he thought. Or he had seen me before with a pen. Or someone had told him about me.

Oromo is generally translated to mean "The People." But while they make up the largest ethnic bloc in Ethiopia, the state continues to marginalize them with policy and shocking antiopposition violence. Emigrants to Somaliland (a territory that was largely Oromo a few hundred years ago) are even more starkly without a support structure, or clan connections, or opportunities. They are like the Somalis who flee to Yemen, leaving little behind and finding less.

I took pictures of them, as if the JPEGs would travel with me and take them away from this place.

Another man in Muslim garb put his face in mine. "I am Somaliland, you are Somaliland. They are not Somaliland."

"I am not Somaliland," I said.

"In your face, you don't like something," said the first man.

"They are not from here and neither am I," I said, getting ruffled. I became more indignant, less diplomatic in hiding my utter distaste with their attitudes, no longer playing along so they would take me further into their perspective.

If I read about places before visiting them, I might have quoted an old Somali poem:

> *Woman, the man who comes from next door,*
> *Is not your equal,*
> *He who travels through danger,*
> *And desolate country, like a lion,*
> *Is your equal!*

Instead, I seized the opportunity that I'd been waiting a lifetime of action movies for: "If you have a problem with them, you have a problem with me," I said, actually. I'd never imagined these would be the circumstances.

These children had traveled as much as I had, through countries far more desolate. Were they not our equals? Were they not *people*? But no one reacted, and the mob dissolved into the road's shady fringes. They gave me nothing more to fight, and I took heavy steps away on the packed dirt.

Later, one of the onlookers ran into me on the street. He was an old man, and he looked at me like I wasn't there. "I think you don't like yourself," he said.

What a crazy thing to say. I blinked to make sure he was real—that dehydration and anger hadn't put my own voice into his mouth. But he was there, and I could feel my eye sockets unclench from holding my squinting rage in place, and the anger drained into sadness.

Still I seethed. This was not an *all good* place. This was not an *all hospitable* place, and I let myself hate everything about everything for a moment before, sullen, I confessed that I didn't believe that either. I was tangled in an angry cycle: I didn't like that I didn't like these people for disliking other people. As I disliked them, I disliked me more, too.

The man was right, though. Shutting folks out is generally a bad response to prejudice. The anger faded some, taking with it some of the energy in my calves, and the old man disappeared into the twilight rabble.

IN THE LATE MORNING, I cast short shadows on the lobby of the Oriental. I asked Muhammad, the Djiboutian cook, if he might show me how to make local breakfast.

"No, no," he said. Why would the cook cook when he didn't have to cook? Wait, he said, and then we'll go chew qat, or *qaad*, as the stimulant leaf is known in Somaliland, or *chat*, as they call it in Ethiopia where the good stuff comes from.

While he finished his omelets, I flicked through e-mails from my parents. I had let my travel plans slip accidentally in a forwarded message. It was the first time they knew where I really was since I'd flown to Beirut. I would try to explain after I'd come home—*Afghanistan was lovely, mom, honest!* If there were a chairwoman for the unconvinced, it was my mother.

"Don't be stupid," she said, among other e-mailed prescriptions for Somalia. She was extremely worried. "You're *NOT* immortal or even invulnerable." No one in town would even call this Somalia, I said. I wasn't in danger. If anything, I was bored.

Bored because I didn't know how to spend time anymore. Bored because my head felt like an empty laboratory now that all the instruments I used to use had been cleared away. If I responded to boredom with my friends here, I might sidle into the *chat* rooms to chew until I felt like a god. And then there I'd be with all the power in the world and no idea where to spend it. I could think of no more audacious trips to take into the void, to insist to my friends and to myself that I had no fear.

The next plane to Dubai was in a few days. I still wanted to come home to Masha—I told her I would—but how could I so empty-handed? In the back of my mind, an infinite loop of destinations raced past like a split-flap display in a train station: Was there anywhere I could run where I wouldn't be stuck?

My mom was worried about the wrong thing. My trying-to-scare-myself addiction wasn't working, and I was feeling the onset of withdrawal. I didn't feel immortal, I felt I was dying.

Yes, I melodramatized in the soft chairs orbited by pots of *shaah hawash* that always seemed to hold more tea than I expected. I had to—mundanity was filling the space danger left. If *life* was traction on the planet, I saw lostness as a kind of death—and a bad one, like starvation or thirst or exposure.

I was still uncertain, still angry. Yes, the humanity and connections had been real, but what could I take home? What could I have faith in? I was more afraid than ever, with a fear that audacity could no longer mask.

MUHAMMAD THE COOK took me to pick half bundles of *chat* from the women at the painted stalls. The drawings made the bundles look like small trees or heads of bok choy. Above, the owner's name is often printed in bold letters. One stand said simply, TAWAKAL: "Trust in God."

These were the men, inside the dark room just off the main street, craving autonomy from the cares of the world—at least hiding from them—with their bare feet outstretched toward the pile of shoes and slippers collecting on the floor. While Yemeni gat-chewing rooms are often rooms with a view, in Hargeisa there are none, no windows. Instead, the cement housing is luxuriant in its coolness, shade from the equatorial sun.

We slouched back on woven mats against our stretch of wall. "The goats are eating this every day," said Muhammad. I imagined goats charging the border, wide-eyed and humping each other, gnashing their teeth and bleating bloody murder.

At first there were wide eyes trained on me, certainly the most goat-colored of the afternoon chewers, but they relaxed quickly.

"What are they saying?" I asked Muhammad, drinking his Mountain Dew.

"He say, 'He is chewing *chat*?' I say yes. He say, 'He like the *chat*?' I say, 'That's why he's chewing!' He say, 'Okaaay!' "

Despite my unusual arrival, I was joining the ranks of the chewers: Somaliland's 95 percent. And it was only as I prepared to leave, with one foot off the continent, that I could feel this kind of belonging, that I could feel we understood each other well enough. Maybe that was the only place I belonged: in constant flight with a warm perch for the afternoon.

We were chewing the *chibis* strand, fresh and powerful. The bushels were dry, more like eating paper and dust than Yemen, but consumed with a style more relaxed and elegant. You could hardly notice the bulges building in our cheeks. After this, my fourth session in two weeks, I stayed up all night feeling my thoughts swirling around at the top of my head. They whirled so fast I felt my crown might lift off at the ears like a toy helicopter. Sure, *chat* made me trust in God—but I thought the god was me.

If the pudgy man had threatened me again with a rock, I would have ordered him to throw it at me before tackling him to the ground and demanding he cook me dinner. I could have punched through walls.

I could have made Djiboutian breakfasts. I glared into mirrors and at the ceiling, raging at all the empty space.

AFTER THE KINDLY BANK AGENT e-mailed me in Yemen to say that I was deep in the red, I left Asia with what cash I had. Almost as soon as I saw Africa, I relied on my oldest connections. It took two infusions from friends and family to settle my accounts.

For better or worse, Somaliland is built for this. According to estimates by the United Nations Development Programme, Somaliland receives up to $700 million per year in remittances. This constitutes one-quarter of household income. I joined the throngs in the downtown Dahabshiil to sign for Neal's funds from Abu Dhabi.

My father transferred funds from the Western Union by the produce section of our local supermarket. Hargeisa's single branch is a few minutes outside of town, a ten-dollar round trip in a taxi running on empty. To claim cash, you answer a secret question.

"Question answer," said the man.

"What?"

"Question answer."

"Yes . . . ?"

"Question. Answer."

"What's the question?"

A moment. "Yes."

"What's the question?"

"This is."

"What is? I can't see your screen."

He bent forward ever so slightly to read. If this was the question—if it even was a question—it didn't sound like one my father would have composed. "Chocolate. Name."

A goat bleated just outside. I paused. He waited a moment, and then spoke. "Sunrise," he said.

We looked at each other for a moment. He gave me two hundred dollars. I questioned my assumptions about the universe.

I PAID LITTLE ATTENTION to a newscast on the TV in the back corner of the ceiling of my usual pasta place. A new tablemate joined me with a smile in the noodle-eating position: slightly hunched, left arm folded in front of the plate, right arm resting on the elbow and holding a supple wrist.

Flip, flip, flip, pop. I was amazed at how suited human hands could be for gripping slippery spaghetti, how one simple technique could make the difference between highchair etiquette and a business lunch. I didn't mind the saucy fingers. I knew the sink would be there when we'd finished, and I had nothing else to handle while I thought only of food.

A ball, popped into my mouth. Another. A swig of pink *cano Vimto* with the left hand, a brief scan of the lively cafeteria. I was grinning now. Another burst of perfect noodles: and then.

And then . . .

". . . ?" I thought.

And then it cracked. Maybe it was all the sugar from the soda milkshake. Maybe it was some rare vitamin in the pasta sauce, or the way the Question-Answer Man did away with a world that ran on logic. With my mouth full in that dusty corner of Somalia or Somaliland, at the intersection of the restaurant street and the *qaad* market in the shadow of the Oriental Hotel, something that had always been halfchewed erupted in my gut.

I didn't need more answers—not to satisfy the questions I had been asking. The questions had all been wrong: *Do you hate me? Will you kill me? Am I free* here *or* here *or* here? Are you "off-limits"?

The real fears—they were gone. Or—they were all unmasked as terrible decoys. The simple geographic prejudice against *this part of the world* had been like a pile of shit my half generation stepped in, and I had washed it quickly from my soles: it didn't take more than seven seconds in Afghanistan to see it was different than on TV, just like it didn't take more than a taste to realize that I was okay with early dinners of small Persian sharks. So why had my discomfort only deepened?

Discomfort came before its reasons did: finding something for it to stick to followed. I felt, *I am not okay*, and then thought, *maybe this is why*. I was unsettled for all the reasons any growing thing would be, but instead of recognizing my own teenage obsession with being understood, I convinced myself that I was anxious only because I did not understand the world. I needed to believe that—that there was always something else, something *out there* responsible for my unsteadiness. There was no seven-second answer that would have felt like justice.

The trouble was not so much that I didn't know my place in a changing world, but that I didn't know how to change in a world that was still spinning in ancient orbit.

And the way I looked for answers had made real understanding impossible. It was as if I'd set out on twenty-five thousand miles of blind dates, asking, "Are you awful?" at first blush. Even the answers that could have meant something sounded like total bullshit.

THIS CRESCENDOING DANGER, this quest to raise the bar higher and higher—to find my limits—this wasn't my quest at all. Plane flights into fear and back out, tickets booked with giddy pride: each "next trip" held within it the very preconceptions I'd been fighting all along. Syria embattled more than Lebanon, Afghanistan more tense than Syria—Pakistan, more terrorized. Then Iraq, Iran, Yemen, *Somalia*.

This was not the way to grade the world, along the axis of perceived terror.

If I survived the place, I thought, *it couldn't be considered off-limits—it might even be added to the tally of hospitable territory*. The greater the expected danger (according to my gut and to travel advisories and to the guts I heard rumbling on the news), the more I valued the discovery of safety. One fun Somalia was worth 17 fun Egypts, and 146 safe Kuwaits.

I charted dangers on a scale bounded by absolutes: absolute freedom on one end, absolute death on the other. Because I hoped for freedom, I assumed that it prevailed until threatened by guaranteed death or imprisonment. At rare moments, those guarantees were there: in earshot of Taliban checkpoints in Afghanistan, at the uncertain border crossing from Kurdistan into Iraq, at the shoreline of the Iranian mainland, on the new Al-Qaeda highways in southeastern Yemen. Every time I did strike one of those hard boundaries, it was an affront to my defense of the region, of humanity, of everything I believed in. Could it be true, that my freedoms really weren't limitless?

My tactics of avoidance were automatic: I could still be infinitely free, I said, even if a few boundaries were true. To continue without letting go of my absolutes, I reframed the limit as just one closed edge on an open space that expanded in infinite directions. *Sure I can't go there, but I can go countless other places.* I felt, in my every fiber as an American, as an adolescent, that I needed to prove it.

As it always is with binary frameworks, to be one thing is to be not another. Safe meant *not dangerous*, good meant *not bad*. To be truly free, I believed, must mean to live in a world with no walls.

I treated myself like an experiment, in a series of trials kept mostly random by deliberate ignorance, to test the hypothesis that had been worded for me on September 11: *you can't go there.*

All of this to preclude *Decision Making*. With thinking like this, there are no shoulds and maybes; there are no responsibilities of choice.

I had not accepted my responsibilities as a man, to choose, who to be, where to go—and then to protect that choice, to work for it— because I had not accepted my most basic responsibilities as a human. What more primal choice could there be than the choice to live?—to refuse to become a rolled die by a random hand?

I held on to the comfort of the absolute authority of fear by fighting it, and by calling the fight absolute freedom. I kept the fight alive in the teenage way, screaming, "You can't tell me *nothing!*" when I wanted more than anything to be told what to do.

If I took control of my own life—if I made choices to make them, and not to unmake their opposites—all of the absolutes would crumble. The gods of *Do* and *Don't* would be swallowed up in the kingdom of real men.

I could have looked at the spaghetti and seen an exhibit for my case against Somali inhumanity.

Instead, I tasted noodles.

For the first long moment in five hundred days of short moments, I saw this room only as a room full of men and food. *That* was simple enough to understand, and so, I felt understood. The feedback faded. In my head there was a photo album for these pictures that, for once, did not share pages with an eleven-year-old September Tuesday.

I looked happily at my one hand caked in the tiny skins of grilled vegetables. This was it: messy and full of life and possibility. *The full catastrophe.*

A weight lifted.

IN HARGEISA, without reservations or demands to be elsewhere, there was no part of me shouting *Do this! You can't leave without that!* I wasn't squeezing every moment for my benefit anymore, or feeling trapped by waiting. So often, time pressed for "efficiency" ends up worthless, like a pressed penny.

I teetered downstairs in the morning, had tea, walked-and-talked, ate Ethiopian food or something new, took a nap maybe, wandered more, drank more tea, returned to the Somaliland Restaurant and ate plate after plate of pasta or something else. *Try this*, Hussein would say.

It was amazing that in a place at first so unfamiliar—and it continued to be—that I would become so fast a regular. People still shouted "Man or woman?!" every so often, but I hardly heard it. It was all becoming regular to me, too. That was the amazing part: feeling fully me in a new place. I was connected, and I was outside of it all, and I was grounded, and I was unleashed.

I bought my ticket to Dubai. When I left the travel agency next to Khayriyada Square, I patted my pockets with a familiar anxiety. Every time my apartment door closed behind me, this same alarm rang: I imagined myself back behind the lock scanning for anything I might have forgotten. There never was perfect closure; only the feeling that I had remembered enough to go on.

To:

MRS. H. VALEN

71 RIVERSIDE DRIVE

APARTMENT 5F

NEW YORK, NEW YORK

From:

CPL. HERB VALEN 32997723

SIGNAL DIVISION, SHAEF

APO 757

Somewhere in England

12 September 1944

I WANT TO BROADEN OUT, SEE THE WHOLE SKY, NOT JUST
THE PART . . . ABOVE THE VALLEY . . . I DON'T KNOW IF I AM
ACTUALLY SAYING ANYTHING. MORE OR LESS JUST FEELING
MY WAY ALONG.

I FEEL, THOUGH, I HAVE A WONDERFUL START. A SOLID
FOUNDATION ON WHICH TO BUILD EVERYTHING ELSE.

—V-mail from my grandfather to my grandmother

OUTRO

—

THERE WAS NO DEPARTURES screen for the day's single flight. We waited for the long-necked African Express plane to come up and down from Kampala to Nairobi to Mogadishu to Berbera, before it would take us on to Mukalla and Dubai. By the time it would land in the Emirates, the Ugandan crowd had had their ears popped like bubble wrap in a day care.

Before I paid the thirty-three dollar fee to exit Somaliland, I waited with the baggage handlers in a circle of lawn chairs out front under a knobbly tree. One of them, Muhammad, offered a seat and translated from Somali.

"He said, 'He came by foot?' I said, 'He came by boat from Yemen.' 'It's incredible!'"

I felt a flash of guilt. I'd spent two hundred dollars on that boat for curiosity's sake, and through their eyes, I thought, I looked cavalier with the fragile history of the region. I defended myself first on more unobjectionable grounds.

"It's really expensive for flights," I said.

"It's too expensive!" said Muhammad. He smiled big and often. He sat back in his green chair, in a white shirt with slanting green stripes.

"And also . . ." I ventured, "the boat is an experience. It's nice."

"It's an experience," he affirmed, as though we had decided something momentous.

We spoke in French. Muhammad's mother was a Somalilander but he was from Djibouti, Somalia's forty-year-old neighbor formerly run from France. His wife and two children lived in Hargeisa, and every two weeks he took the African Express shuttle home to visit them. He spoke of his friends who had left Africa. He spoke excitedly about how to do it.

"Yes! They left here by foot, they took a car." Those who had made it from his circle were minor legends. "By telephone he told me, *haa*, 'I'm in Oslo now!'" Muhammad gave a hearty laugh. It was less a memory than a set of instructions, a fantasy that we could live out by hearing it aloud.

"You leave here to Ethiopia by car, from Ethiopia until the Sudan border. You go into Sudan. You go until Khartoum, the Sudanese capital. When you get there, you take a car. You go by the Sahara, the desert. You go until Libya, and from Libya you take a boat."

He told me this twice. The price: a thousand dollars for the grueling escape by land, and another similar sum for the ferry, sometimes merely an inflatable dinghy, unprotected and unstocked. On these boats, Ethiopians, Eritreans and Somalis joined the ranks of west African refugees and victims of political uprising.

"How long at sea?" I asked.

"They tell me less than sixteen hours." Indeed, successful trips often take exactly that long to the Italian island of Lampedusa, hardly halfway from Africa to the mainland. In 2011, when the Tunisian and Libyan rebellions forced many to flee, the UNHCR estimated, two thousand of fifty thousand escapees across the Mediterranean drowned. In 2014, when ISIS coalesced as a regional threat, the number of crossings quadrupled.

A few degrees off course and the boats could strike Malta, where detention can last as long as a year and half before a decision is made. From Lampedusa, the hope is, refugees are shuttled more swiftly to Sicily, or through the UNHCR (Muhammad pronounced these letters in English) to the Netherlands or Scandinavia.

Muhammad was aware of the dangers. He had heard a pregnant woman had recently died. But all this was simply part of the no-regrets Gospel of the Refugees, both history and prescription, both legends and lessons for action.

"Why don't they send you back?" I asked.

Muhammad was practiced. "We don't want to go back to Libya

because they're going to kill us. There are people who will kill me there. 'Go kill me.'" He said his lines to the imaginary immigration police. "'You're okay that they kill me?' *No no no, come on.* 'Okay, I'll go.' *No no no, stop, stop.*"

As a Djiboutian, Muhammad and his friends could not claim refugee status. Instead, they destroyed their passports before making landfall. In order to pass off as stateless refugees, they became them.

"They say *where did you come from.* 'I came from the sky.'" *Je suis venu du ciel.* He repeated this. *Ciel* can also mean "heaven."

In another fantasy, someone might make it to America. "Your passport, we tear it up. Your picture, I put my picture, I take your name— my name is Paul and I'm an American."

Then, when you speak with fellow Africans, Muhammed said, putting on a grand American accent and swaggering in his chair, you act the part you want to play. "'I am an American, hey yo, good morning, man, good morning, yes! I'm from America, you know.'"

If you're lucky, you can bluff your way onto a plane. "When they say *in five minutes we are going to descend to Louisiana,* or even New York, you go in the bathroom and you tear up the passport." He made the sound of an airplane toilet flushing.

"When you get to immigration, *you came from where?* 'I came from the sky, I'm a refugee.' *Refugee from where?* 'I'm a refugee.'"

Muhammad clapped the invisible dust lightly from his hands, and then again. That was it. That was where the plan stopped.

"And that works?" I said.

"Yes. Because humanity there, it's good. But in Africa there is not humanity here."

Muhammad himself was radiating with humanity, but in his homeland, there remained too many missing parts of too many lives. So he and others were willing to tear up their legal identities in the hopes of finding one more acceptable.

"There are Somalis who have American passports, English passports, Norwegian passports," Muhammad said. They, too, had to pay the exit fee. "Thirty-three dollars!" he cried. For those Somalilanders, the fee might have been like the bitter herbs at a Passover Seder—a reminder of suffering. Where once it was an anxious journey, now it is a small tariff, paid in remembrance of more uncertain times. The rest of us foreigners paid it, too. It is the price you pay to leave because you can pay, and because you can leave.

MUHAMMAD HAD AT LEAST made it to someplace where those most basic freedoms, if not guaranteed, were respected. In Somaliland, "You can drive a car at one in the morning. No one will ask you why. Not one."

This had been a theme in conversations with all Somalis: the ability to walk places, and to drive, especially late at night, without bullets or intervening laws or hassle. The ability to move.

I didn't want to go drive around Berbera at one in the morning. Neither did Muhammad. Sometimes I was too tired to really want to walk around New York or Aleppo or Kabul or Hargeisa. But it was always important to know it was possible.

I felt a kinship—like we were from the same clan of those taking the long route. We moved because we could, and when we couldn't, we talked about it. I recognized that urge to *go*, to dare the world to spin under your feet so that when it stops, *ah!* you're somewhere else. And I was jealous, in a way, of Muhammad's friends who succeeded in fleeing war-torn nations and death threats and hopeless economies—of the feeling of finality that comes in reaching a destination that justifies the journey absolutely, doubtlessly. Of the clarity of direction. While many have no choice but to take life-threatening journeys, I took life-threatening journeys just to avoid making choices.

Muhammad's friends had trekked through the desert for a better life—I'd taken a boat for a better *experience*. And, three days later, my former employer had me booked on a business class flight over the North Pole. It would take just over sixteen hours to make it from Dubai to Los Angeles, where my brother lived. Then a half day on to Michigan, where Masha was waiting. In another life, I might have spent those exact same hours crossing my fingers against capsizing on the Tripoli-Lampedusa express.

Destination is a word that has been in the English language for a long time, its roots in Latin: "make firm, establish." It doesn't take a wanderer's desperation to see that few journeys' termini ever achieve that status. In our efforts to reach a destination, though, we are made to face something outside ourselves. For me, running toward gatherings may have been running away from solitude. Running toward the fears of danger might have been running away from the fears of peace. At the end, there was only the choice: Where would I run?

It took me twenty-three years to even begin to accept that someone who existed in a truly different way was not an existential threat. Muhammad's difference was no danger to my way of life, it was only ever an opportunity to question it.

There was a flash of high noon sun on the sea a mile away. I felt crisped like a hot cookie.

"*Tu rentres dedans, tu passes l'immigration—quand tu termines, tu reviens ici,*" Muhammad said. Birds were chatting in the trees. He gave me the instructions again. "You go inside, finish with your passport and everything, when you finish, come and sit back here."

The one-room terminal was bustling. The plane came sooner than I'd expected, and I never made it back to the baggage handlers' tree. I like to think the offer still stands.

ACKNOWLEDGMENTS

—

I'VE HEARD PEOPLE SAY they flip to the acknowledgements first to hear the writer speak at his most genuine and unfiltered. Well . . . shit, then—you caught me.

But: I hope this doesn't sound too different from the first 340 pages, because I wanted you to catch me there, too, and because these thank yous are all too simple to filter: these kindnesses kept this book alive by the hairs of its fingertips, and meant so much more than even that.

First: I owe all of this to my agent Jane von Mehren, who had the faith/courage/recklessness to say *This might just be a thing*—and who made it so. And to Alane Mason, without whose incisive, sanity-saving hand edits there would be no *thing* at all, and without whom you and I would probably not have met, like this, even on the page.

To my grandmother, who showed me that being a writer was actually a thing, too, and to my grandfather, who lived a life that said, *Your town can want to kill you, but that doesn't make the world mean.* And to the trans-century love between them that said: you can build a big, solid snowball around the connection between two flakes.

People have also said (and I know—for straw men, they sure do a lot of talking) that we do so much of what we do to prove ourselves to the ones we knew in high school. My high school was a nice one; I wasn't strung up by my suspenders or called Two Eyes for not wearing glasses. But still, there was always a kind of rejection—the rejection of young love, which doesn't crush a spirit, and which leaves only an impulse: *I'll show you!* Or: *One day . . .*

So—because it might be that all this was a way of asking you to prom—this goes out to my high school crush(es), too.

And: to the scholars who walked me through historical and conceptual and terminological intricacies throughout the writing process. And to my enlightening Arabic teachers Youssef Nouhi and Taoufik Ben Amor—because, if those classes hadn't been great, this'd be a book about the mid-Atlantic states.

To Rita, who read *East of Eden* with me. To Rebecca, who clarity-checked problem passages and kept me from going in infinite circles. To Kunaal, Billy, Maximo, and Yegor, for looking ahead. To Jonathan Green, for all the advice I needed (in the accent I wanted). To Masha. To Neal and Jake, among the other spot readers for the book, and travel partners whose perspectives—and field notes, and years of frantic texting—helped keep my memory 3-D, and alive.

And: to Justin Moyer, whose brilliant use of colons hit me once like a revelation (and like permission).

For everyone whose names were mentioned (or changed), whether we have remained in touch or not, whether I have asked you what color your couch cushions were again or not: getting to know you was what made this worth it.

And, because mood and smells and the colors outside the window all have a way of trickling into any open document, thank you to the towns where the bulk of this book was written and pulled apart and put back together: Abu Dhabi, Ann Arbor, Anchorage, New York, Geneva, Shanghai, Los Angeles, New Haven, El Bruc.

They say there's an incredible feeling to do something all on your own. But: all of this is a cocktail of borrowed benevolence, and the recipe is more complicated than I understand. If I could trace this gratitude as far as it would need to go to be fully honest, on the next page I'd probably be thanking Kevin Bacon and half the port district of Kiev.

They say *write* is a relative of German *reissen*, "to crack/rip/ wrench"—and though I have little trouble cracking myself open, I think I have only ever had the nerve to do so because of the glue I knew was close by. For my friends (who are always the first faces of a hoped-for audience): thank you for being glue.

(My cousin Yotam is handing me a beer now—I understand that this Selfless Act is not the most important part of making this thing, but it still feels crucial.)

Writing is always a kind of *lowering*, too, into a well wide enough just for one—and while good company gave me the charge for solo missions down deep, it was those familiar faces peering over the lip of the well that really pulled me back up.

To Ashley Patrick and Kyle Radler, and to everyone at Norton who have helped make this a reality: thank you. I think of your offices on the park the way I think about my first apartment, or about driving school if I'd ever gone—the site of a big change worth making. Thank you for guiding me through it.

To Richard Todd and Suzannah Lessard and the faculty and students at Goucher, who read many things in many stages—and especially to Jacob Levenson, without whom I would have melted, and with whom I cut the manuscript in half with a kind of confidence I did not have in myself alone. It feels very rare to find someone whose suggestions resonate as if they were your own decisions, all grown up. With Jacob, and with Alane, I feel I was handed the belle's dance card.

Thank you to Signor Pietro del Pizzo, the legendary tailor of Haverford, Pennsylvania, for fixing my six-pound jacket.

Thank *you* for reading.

A NOTE ON TRANSLITERATION

———

"THERE IS NO UNIVERSALLY ACCEPTED FORM for transliterating Arabic," as the *Chicago Manual of Style* puts it. There are many standards, like dialects along a spectrum of academicness—some importing useful symbols, some using only the letters you'd find in English—but there's no one way, and there are puzzles in every choice.

Luckily, English is surprisingly well-stocked with the phonemes for the 28 letters of the Arabic abjad (so called because it begins a-b-j-d). Choices here have been made, while staying true to proper spelling, with an underlying goal: that a non–Arabic-speaking friend could read straight off the page and have the best shot at being understood.

Even though there are two kinds of *t*, *s*, and *d*—one just like English, and one called "emphatic" because it should affect surrounding vowels as if the speaker has just gained a hundred pounds in his face alone—these are spelled out here with the same Latin letter. (The unemphatic letters are far more common.)

There are two Arabic letters for the English digraph *th*—voiced ("*th*is") and voiceless ("fif*th*")—and an emphatic third, too. These are all *th* here.

There are two kinds of *h*: the kind you know, and a squeezed kind that puts more air through less space. Both are simply *h* here—and people will probably understand if you misspeak on the softer side. There is a *kh*, the sound cats' claws make or the sound Russians make when they laugh, and a *gh*, like a quick gargle. (*Sh* also comes from a single letter. There is no *p*.)

Occasionally, there are unavoidable troubles for the simple approach. The name for literary Arabic, transliterated *Fusha*, is spoken "FuS-Ha." The *u* is pronounced like the "oo" in "foot" (and not like the "u" in "flute"), because the *s* is that emphatic kind that fattens up the neigh-boring vowels.

Mistaking *k* for *q* is more common: this is the difference between your neighborhood voiceless velar plosive and a voiceless *uvular* plosive. That is to say: the difference between the unspecial *kaf*, and the *qaf*, the consonant made by clicking the place deep in your throat where smoke rings come from. That is to say: the difference in where your tongue hits your throat makes the difference between *kalbi!* and *qalbi!*—"my dog!" and "my heart!"

Occasionally, transliterations shift to match pronunciation: *janbiya* becomes *jambiya* (mostly), because that's how it (mostly) comes out. The stimulant leaf *qat* (sometimes spelled *khat* in English, but always spelled *q-a-t* in Arabic) becomes *gat*, then *chat* to match the-way-you'd-say-it in Yemen, then Somaliland.

The most technical distinction retained in this book's transliterations is between two letters that, without using special markings, are both written as an apostrophe: one forward and one backward. The ' stands in for the Arabic *hamza*, a glottal stop that sounds exactly like the hyphen in the word "uh-oh." The ' is the ubiquitous *ayn*, a vowel during which you choke briefly, and then set yourself free. (Because it makes noise, and isn't over in an instant, it is written in the book—almost always—as '*a*.)

Proper nouns are written, however, in the simplest twenty-six-letters-only way in which they are already known in English: Sanaa, Baath Party, Shia. (Keeping all its letters intact, the Yemeni capital, often written Sana'a, could by more precise rules come out as *Sana'aa'*—or even *San'aaa'*.)

Mada'in (ma-*da*-in) Salch, as a small exception, has kept its apostrophe because it's already hard enough to find without asking the Saudis for directions to *Madane* Saleh—but maybe also because, as with Jonathan Raban in the 1970s, Saudi denied me visas to visit (because there were no visas to *visit*), and so remains just that much more foreign to me, known only by its little markings.

With no intention of erasing a word's history, the general choice to pluck apostrophes from place names may commit the cardinal sin Junot Díaz warned against: "I'd rather have us start out as fractured so we don't commit the bullshit and erasures that trying to live under the banner of sameness entails." My hope is that we can marinate in the differences—the foreign sounds we absorb without thinking, and the markings of all that uvular action—and then come to rest in a place where we remember that most of our history is never on the surface anyway. Otherwise, relentlessly maintaining apostrophes is a bit like asking a professional skydiver to wear a parachute to a dinner party.

Aspiring to an understanding a bit deeper than a glottal stop, and in accordance with the Eleventh Commandment—that saying "Fronce" instead of "France" does not make you cool—there is only one prerequisite: recognizing that any Arabic word in English context will always be different than an Arabic word in Arabic. Eventually, after a successful import, words lose their italics and become permanent residents or full citizens of the English language. *Hawai'i* becomes Hawaii.

And possibly because the iPhone suggests "Ba'ath," and the *New York Times* writes "Baath," and because both are technically fair—I think I might also be taking the side of humanity over the machine—if only because *algorithm* (from *al-Khwarizmi*) is a word that went through just that kind of human process.

The Full Catastrophe.

SELECTED SOURCES

———

Adams, Douglas. *The Hitchhiker's Guide to the Galaxy*. New York: Del Rey, 1995.

Adler, Cyrus, et al., eds. *The Jewish Encyclopedia: A Descriptive Record of the History, Religion, Literature, and Customs of the Jewish People From the Earliest Times to the Present Day*. Cornell University Library, 1901. http://www.jewishencyclopedia.com/contribs/481.

[Al-Sabʿ Al-Muʿallaqāt]: The Seven Poems Suspended in the Temple at Mecca. Trans. Frank Johnson. 1893. Reprint, New York: AMS Press, 1973. https://archive.org/details/alsabalmuallaqat00johnrich.

Arberry, A. J., ed. *The Koran Interpreted: A Translation*. New York: Touchstone, 1996.

Badger, George Percy. *The Nestorians and Their Rituals with the Narrative of a Mission to Mesopotamia and Coordistan in 1842–1844*. Vol. 1. London: Joseph Masters, 1852.

Bataille, Georges. *Eroticism: Death and Sensuality*. Trans. Mary Dalwood. San Francisco: City Lights Publishers, 1986. Originally published as *L'Érotisme* (Paris: Les Éditions de Minuit, 1957).

Bell, Gertrude Lowthian. *Amurath to Amurath*. London: W. Heinemann, 1911.

BibleGateway.com. https://www.biblegateway.com/.

The Book of Good Counsels: From the Sanskrit of the "Hitopadesha." Trans. Edwin Arnold. London: Smith, Elder and Co., 1861. http://www.columbia.edu/itc/mealac/pritchett/00litlinks/hitopadesha_arnold/.

Bulloch, John, and Harvey Morris. *No Friends But the Mountains: The Tragic History of the Kurds*. Oxford: Oxford University Press, 1992.

Bury, George Wyman. *Arabia Infelix; or, The Turks in Yamen*. London: Macmillan and Company Ltd., 1915.

Calvino, Italo. *Numbers in the Dark and Other Stories*. Trans. Tim Parks. New York: Pantheon Books, 1995. Originally published as *Prima che tu dica "Pronto"* (Milan: Arnoldo Mondadori Editore, 1993).

Camus, Albert. *Resistance, Rebellion, and Death: Essays*. Trans. Justin O'Brien. New York: Vintage, 1995.

——. *The Myth of Sisyphus and Other Essays*. Trans. Justin O'Brien. New York: Vintage, 1991.

——. *The Rebel: An Essay on Man in Revolt*. Trans. Anthony Bower. New York: Vintage, 1992. Originally published as *L'homme révolté* (Paris: Librairie Gallimard, 1951).

Central Intelligence Agency. "North and South Yemen: In Search of Unity." Jan. 19, 1990. https://www.cia.gov/library/readingroom/docs/DOC_0000244584.pdf.

Cole, Calvin Lax. *some of its parts*. New York: Compass Rose Publishing, 2015. https://www.calvinlaxcole.com/some/.

Doi, Takeo. *The Anatomy of Dependence*. Trans. John Bester. New York: Kodansha USA, 1973. Originally published as 甘えの構造 (Tokyo: Kōbundō Ltd., 1971).

Douglas, Mary. *Implicit Meanings: Selected Essays in Anthropology*. London: Routledge, 1978.

——. *Purity and Danger: An Analysis of the Concepts of Pollution and Taboo*. London: Routledge & Kegan Paul, 1978.

Fanon, Frantz. *Black Skin, White Masks*. Trans. Charles Lam Markmann. London: Pluto Press, 2008. Originally published as *Peau noire, masques blancs* (Paris: Éditions du Seuil, 1952).

"FDR's First Inaugural Address Declaring 'War' on the Great Depression." *National Archives*. https://www.archives.gov/education/lessons/fdr-inaugural.

"Hadith Books." SearchTruth.com. http://www.searchtruth.com/hadith_books.php.

Hoffman, Valerie. *The Essentials of Ibadi Islam*. Syracuse, N.Y.: Syracuse University Press, 2012.

Hogarth, D. G. *Arabia*. Oxford: Oxford University Press, 1922. https://www.archive.org/details/arabiaho00hoga.

Ingrams, W. H. *Zanzibar: Its History and Its People*. 1931. New York: Psychology Press, 1967.

Kennedy, J. G. *The Flower of Paradise: The Institutionalized Use of the Drug Qat in North Yemen*. Dordrecht, Netherlands: D. Reidel, 1987.

Kerouac, Jack. *On the Road*. London: Penguin Group, 2002. First published in 1957 by Viking Press.

Kierkegaard, Søren. *The Concept of Anxiety: A Simple Psychologically Orienting Deliberation on the Dogmatic Issue of Hereditary Sin*. Ed. and trans. Reidar Thomte. Princeton, N.J.: Princeton University Press, 1981. Originally published as *Begrebet Angest*, 1844.

Kreyenbroek, Philip G., and Khalīl Jindī Rashow. *God and Sheikh Adi Are Perfect: Sacred Poems and Religious Narratives from the Yezidi Tradition*. Vol. 9. Wiesbaden, Germany: Otto Harrassowitz Verlag, 2005.

Larajasse, Evangeliste de. *Somali-English and English-Somali Dictionary*. Cornell University Library, 1897. https://archive.org/details/cu31924026888820.

Layard, Austen Henry. *Nineveh and Its Remains with an Account of a Visit to the Chaldean Christians of Kurdistan, and the Yesidis, Or Devil-Worshippers; and an Enquiry Into the Manners and Arts of the Ancient Assyrians*. London: John Murray, 1849.

Lewis, I. M. *Blood and Bone: The Call of Kinship in Somali Society*. Lawrenceville, N.J.: Red Sea Press, 1994.

Parfitt, Tudor V. *The Road to Redemption: The Jews of the Yemen, 1900–1950*. Leiden, Netherlands: Brill Academic Publishers, 1996.

Quran.com. https://www.quran.com/.

Raban, Jonathan. *Arabia Through the Looking Glass*. London: William Collins, 1979.

Rumi, Jelaluddin. *The Rumi Collection*. Ed. Kabir Helminski. Boston: Shambhala Publications, 2005.

Sommer, Doris. *Bilingual Games: Some Literary Investigations*. New York: Palgrave Macmillan, 2003.

Steinbeck, John. *East of Eden*. Steinbeck centennial ed. New York: Penguin Books, 2002. First published in 1952 by Viking Press.

Wehr, Hans. *Arabic-English Dictionary: The Hans Wehr Dictionary of Modern Written Arabic*. Ed. J. Milton Cowan. 4th edition. Urbana, IL: Spoken Language Services, 1993.

Wiles, Peter John de la Fosse. *The New Communist Third World: An Essay in Political Economy*. Kent, U.K.: Croom Helm Ltd., 1982.

Wilkinson, John C. *Ibadism: Origins and Early Development in Oman*. Oxford: Oxford University Press, 2010.

The World Factbook. Central Intelligence Agency. https://www.cia.gov/library/publications/the-world-factbook/.

Yergin, Daniel. *The Prize: The Epic Quest for Oil, Money, and Power*. New York: Free Press, 1993. First published 1990.